Internationalizing Curriculum Studies

Cristyne Hébert · Nicholas Ng-A-Fook
Awad Ibrahim · Bryan Smith
Editors

Internationalizing Curriculum Studies

Histories, Environments, and Critiques

Editors
Cristyne Hébert
Faculty of Education
University of Regina
Regina, SK, Canada

Awad Ibrahim
Faculty of Education
University of Ottawa
Ottawa, ON, Canada

Nicholas Ng-A-Fook
Faculty of Education
University of Ottawa
Ottawa, ON, Canada

Bryan Smith
College of Arts, Society and Education
James Cook University
Townsville, QLD, Australia

ISBN 978-3-030-01351-6   ISBN 978-3-030-01352-3   (eBook)
https://doi.org/10.1007/978-3-030-01352-3

Library of Congress Control Number: 2018956821

© The Editor(s) (if applicable) and The Author(s) 2019
This work is subject to copyright. All rights are solely and exclusively licensed by the Publisher, whether the whole or part of the material is concerned, specifically the rights of translation, reprinting, reuse of illustrations, recitation, broadcasting, reproduction on microfilms or in any other physical way, and transmission or information storage and retrieval, electronic adaptation, computer software, or by similar or dissimilar methodology now known or hereafter developed.
The use of general descriptive names, registered names, trademarks, service marks, etc. in this publication does not imply, even in the absence of a specific statement, that such names are exempt from the relevant protective laws and regulations and therefore free for general use.
The publisher, the authors and the editors are safe to assume that the advice and information in this book are believed to be true and accurate at the date of publication. Neither the publisher nor the authors or the editors give a warranty, express or implied, with respect to the material contained herein or for any errors or omissions that may have been made. The publisher remains neutral with regard to jurisdictional claims in published maps and institutional affiliations.

Cover illustration: © Qvasimodo/iStock/gettyimages
Cover design by Fatima Jamadar

This Palgrave Macmillan imprint is published by the registered company Springer Nature Switzerland AG
The registered company address is: Gewerbestrasse 11, 6330 Cham, Switzerland

ACKNOWLEDGEMENTS

The editors would like to begin by acknowledging the International Association of the Advancement of Curriculum Studies, the University of Ottawa, and the Canadian Society for the Study of Education for all of their support. We would also like to thank the University of Ottawa and the Canadian Society for the Study of Education for their generous sponsorship.

We are grateful to all the amazing contributing authors. Your ongoing breakthroughs in curriculum theorizing make such thought-provoking collections possible. Our thanks also to Jesse Butler, Tylor Burrows, and Jonathan Weber who all helped to ensure the success of the 5th IAACS conference at the University of Ottawa and supported the ensuing copy-editing of the collection. We would like to give a special shout-out to Karina Czechowski who worked tirelessly over the past few months to help our editorial team bring the project home. All of you are role models for future graduate students committed toward enhancing their respective research communities.

I, Cristyne Hébert, want to thank Nicholas, Bryan, and Awad for all of their tireless work in making both the IAACs conference at the University of Ottawa and this collection possible. Much love also to Nicholas for your 10+ years of mentorship and to Celia Haig-Brown and Jennifer Jenson for your support, guidance, and hospitality.

I, Nicholas Ng-A-Fook, would also like to acknowledge the commitment of my fellow editorial team to the vision and academic rigor that brought this collection to fruition. No doubt, this collection promises to make a significant contribution toward the international advancement of curriculum studies. I would like to offer my deepest thank you and gratitude to my mentors who once were (like Bill Doll, Bill Pinar, Denise Egéa-Kuehne) or are still at the Curriculum Theory Project at Louisiana State University (like Petra Munro Hendry). Their life works continue to inspire my thinking and writing as a form of "internationalizing" curriculum studies.

I, Bryan Smith, would like to thank my co-editors Cristyne, Nicholas, and Awad who have each pushed me to think differently about curriculum and education more broadly. I'd also like to thank Tim Stanley who has been (and remains) a great mentor to me, both before and during the putting together of this book. Finally, I'd like to thank my family who have always been there and who continue to encourage me in my work and academic pursuits.

I, Awad Ibrahim, feel so blessed working with such a great and committed team of editors. Nicholas, you have shown how a humanizing friendship might look like. Cristyne and Bryan, you have shown how brilliance might look like. Thank you for working so hard in making this project possible, especially in a Trumpian post-truth time. SNAP, team! Of course, family and friends have always been the support anyone could ask for. From Australia (Alastair) to Cali (Alim), to Saudi (Osman) to Sudan (big up fam) to Canada (partner, mother-in-law, and all the fam): thank you! This is the internationalization of curriculum in practice. WORD!

Contents

1 Internationalizing Curriculum Studies: Histories, Environments, and Critiques   1
Cristyne Hébert, Awad Ibrahim, Nicholas Ng-A-Fook and Bryan Smith

Part I   Grounding Curricular Histories

2 Toward a Complex Coherence in the Field of Curriculum Studies   15
Theodore M. Christou and Christopher DeLuca

3 Making Manifestos in Absentia: Of a World Without Curriculum Theory   35
Molly Quinn and Niki Christodoulou

4 Curriculum Theory in Brazil: A Path in the Mists of the Twenty-First Century   53
Antonio Flávio Barbosa Moreira and Rosane Karl Ramos

viii CONTENTS

5   Talking Back to Second Language Education
Curriculum Control   69
Douglas Fleming

6   A Phenomenography of Educators' Conceptions
of Curriculum: Implications for Next Generation
Curriculum Theorists' Contemplation and Action   83
Jazlin Ebenezer, Susan Harden, Nicholas Sseggobe-Kiruma,
Russell Pickell and Suha Mohammed Hamdan

7   Crossing Borders: A Story of Refugee Education   107
Karen Meyer, Cynthia Nicol, Siyad Maalim, Mohamud
Olow, Abdikhafar Ali, Samson Nashon, Mohamed Bulle,
Ahmed Hussein, Ali Hussein and Muhammad Hassan Said

Part II   Grounding Educational Environments

8   Curriculum Theorists in the Classroom: Subjectivity,
Crises, and Socio-environmental Equity   125
Avril Aitken and Linda Radford

9   Curriculum for Identity: Narrative Negotiations
in Autobiography, Learning and Education   139
Eero Ropo

10   High Passions: Affect and Curriculum Theorizing
in the Present   157
Alyssa D. Niccolini, Bessie Dernikos, Nancy Lesko
and Stephanie D. McCall

11   The Power of Curriculum as Autobiographical Text:
Insights from Utilizing Narrative Inquiry Self-Study
in Research, Teaching, and Living   177
Carmen Shields

CONTENTS ix

Part III   Grounding Curricular Critique

**12 Nonviolence as a Daily Practice in Education:
A Curriculum Vision**   193
Hongyu Wang

13 *Currere's* Active Force and the Concept of *Ubuntu*   207
Lesley Le Grange

**14 For Us, Today: Understanding Curriculum as
Theological Text in the Twenty-First Century**   227
Reta Ugena Whitlock

Index   245

NOTES ON CONTRIBUTORS

Avril Aitken is a Full Professor at the School of Education of Bishop's University, in Sherbrooke, Quebec. She inquires into the implications of teachers' beliefs and desires, particularly how these influence perceptions of self and others, and the possibility of educating for a more democratic, diverse, and socio-environmentally just world.

Abdikhafar Ali is a recent graduate from Sauder School of Business at the University of British Columbia who has completed a Bachelor of Commerce with major in Accounting.

Mohamed Bulle is currently a third-year undergraduate student in the Faculty of Science at the University of British Columbia studying statistics.

Niki Christodoulou is Associate Professor of Curriculum and Instruction in the Department of Advanced Studies and Innovation, College of Education, Augusta University in Georgia, USA. She was the Coordinator of the Cyprus Oral History and Living Memory Project and she worked with teachers for the implementation of oral histories in schools. Currently, she is the Coordinator of the Central Savannah River Area Education Oral History Project. Her academic interests include curriculum studies, curriculum theory, democratic teaching and learning, teacher education and pedagogy, narrative inquiry, learning experiences of teachers and students, politics of education, equity and social justice, and oral history education.

xii NOTES ON CONTRIBUTORS

Theodore Michael Christou is an Associate Professor of History Education and co-editor of the *Canadian Journal of Education*. Theodore authored *The Problem of Progressive* Education (University of Toronto Press, 2012), awarded the Canadian History of Education Association's Founders Prize for best book in the *History of Education*, and *An Overbearing Eye* (Hidden Brook Press, 2013), a book of verse and short fiction. He co-edited *Foundations of Education: A Canadian Perspective* (Canadian Association of Teacher Education, 2013). *The Curriculum History of Canadian Teacher Education* (Routledge), an edited collection, and *Byzantium*, a book of poetry (Hidden Brook Press) are forthcoming. See: http://educ.queensu.ca/faculty/profiles/christou. Theodore is the Past President of the Canadian Association for the Foundations of Education and brings historical and philosophical perspectives to bear on curriculum studies.

Christopher DeLuca is an Associate Professor and Graduate Faculty member in Curriculum Studies and Assessment at the Faculty of Education, Queen's University. Previously, Dr. DeLuca was an Assistant Professor at the University of South Florida (Tampa, USA) and has worked in the area of policy research in London, England. Dr. DeLuca's research examines the complex intersection of curriculum and pedagogy as operating within frameworks of educational assessment and accountability. In particular, Dr. DeLuca's research centers on how pre-service and in-service teachers learn to engage the complexities of assessing student learning in relation to the evolving accountability culture in today's classrooms. Dr. DeLuca's work has been published in national and international journals with continuous funding by the Social Sciences and Humanities Research Council of Canada. Dr. DeLuca is Past President of the *Canadian Educational Researchers' Association* and co-editor of the *Canadian Journal of Education*.

Bessie Dernikos is an Assistant Professor of Reading and Language Arts at Florida Atlantic University. Her research interests connect to two interrelated projects: examining the literacy processes of young children in urban contexts, with a focus on the material, discursive, and affective forces that impact language and literacy learning; and rethinking normative literacy practices in order to foster cultural, linguistic, and gender diversity. She has authored publications in peer-reviewed journals, including the *Journal of Early Childhood Research* and *M/C Journal ~ Media/Culture*.

NOTES ON CONTRIBUTORS xiii

Jazlin Ebenezer is a Professor of Science Education and Chair of Curriculum and Instruction Doctoral Studies, College of Education, Wayne State University. She has established reputation through her numerous refereed publications and worldwide invited presentations on science learning and teaching. Her books *Learning to Teach Science* for elementary teachers and *Becoming Secondary Teachers* and publications in science education journals reflect a close weave of her more theory-based research with sound practical contributions to the field of science teacher education. She specializes in diverse learners and multicultural populations, both in her university teaching and in preparing science teachers and school leaders for public schools.

Douglas Fleming is an Assistant Professor in the Faculty of Education at the University of Ottawa. He completed his Ph.D. in Education at the University of British Columbia. Doug's research and teaching interests are primarily focused on English as a second language methodology, second language policy development, citizenship, and equity. Before becoming an academic, Doug taught ESL and Literacy for over 20 years in public school districts, community colleges, and immigrant serving agencies. He has also supervised immigrant ESL programs and worked on numerous curriculum and professional development projects at the local, national, and international levels. For more information, go to http://www.education.uottawa.ca/profs/fleming.html.

Suha Mohammed Hamdan is a Ph.D. candidate in Education, Curriculum and Instructions Department, Wayne State University. She also holds a master's degree in Bilingual/Bicultural Education from Wayne State University, and a bachelor's of English Language and Literature from Riyadh Literature College, Saudi Arabia.

Susan Harden is a Ph.D. candidate in the Educational Evaluation and Research program at Wayne State University in Detroit, Michigan. She also holds a master's degree in Reading and Language Arts from Oakland University in Rochester, Michigan, and a bachelor's of science degree in Elementary Education with a major in mathematics, also from Oakland University. Professionally, she has taught at in K-5 classrooms since 1996 and enjoys staying current with research in the education field. Currently, she is working on her Ph.D. dissertation.

xiv   NOTES ON CONTRIBUTORS

Cristyne Hébert is an Assistant Professor in the Faculty of Education at the University of Regina. Her work appears in *Media and Communication*, *The Educational Forum*, the *Journal of Curriculum Theorizing*, the *Journal of the Canadian Association of Curriculum Studies*, and *Reflective Practice: International and Multidisciplinary Perspectives*.

Ahmed Hussein is currently a fourth-year student in the University of British Columbia, majoring in Geography with specialization in Environment and Sustainability.

Ali Hussein is a recent graduate from the University of British Columbia with a B.A. in Political Science and International Relations.

Awad Ibrahim is a Professor in the Faculty of Education, University of Ottawa. He is a curriculum and cultural theorist with special interest in cultural studies, Hip-Hop, youth and Black popular culture, social justice, diasporic and continental African identities, ethnography and applied linguistics. Among his books, *Provoking Curriculum Studies: Strong Poetry and the Arts of the Possible in Education* (with N. Ng-A-Fook & G. Reis); *Critically Researching Youth* (with S. Steinberg, 2016); *The Education of African Canadian Children: Critical Perspectives* (with A. Abdi, 2016); *Critical Youth Studies Reader* (with S. Steinberg, 2014); *The Rhizome of Blackness: A Critical Ethnography of Hip-Hop Culture, Language, Identity, and the Politics of Becoming* (2014); and *Global Linguistic Flows: Hip-Hop Cultures, Youth Identities and the Politics of Language* (with S. Alim & A. Pennycook, 2009).

Lesley Le Grange is Distinguished Professor in the Department of Curriculum Studies at Stellenbosch University, South Africa. He is a former Chair of the Department of Curriculum Studies and former Vice-Dean (Research) of the Faculty of Education. Lesley teaches and researches in the fields of environmental education, research methodology, science education, curriculum studies, and assessment. He has 203 publications to his credit and serves on editorial boards of eight peer-reviewed journals. Leading international journals that he has published in include: *Educational Philosophy and Theory*, *International Review of Education*, *Journal of Curriculum Studies*, *Journal of Moral Education*. Lesley serves on the International Editorial Advisory Board of the book series *Curriculum Studies Worldwide*. He has contributed to several international handbooks on/in education, including *Encyclopedia* *of Curriculum Studies* (2010), *International Handbook of Research on Environmental Education* (2013), *International Handbook of Curriculum Research* (2014), *International Handbook of Interpretation in Educational Research Methods* (2015), *International Handbook of Philosophy of Education* (2018). He is a chairperson of the Accreditation Committee of the Council on Higher Education (CHE) and member of the Higher Education Quality Committee of the CHE in South Africa, and Vice-President of the International Association for the Advancement of Curriculum Studies (IAACS). In 2015, Lesley was elected Fellow of the Royal Society of Biology in the UK. He is a rated social scientist in South Africa and is recipient of several Stellenbosch University and national awards and prizes.

Nancy Lesko is Maxine Greene Professor at Teachers College, Columbia University. She teaches in the areas of curriculum, social theory, gender studies, and youth studies. Her research interests focus on affective approaches to curriculum studies, youth, and gender and sexualities in school. Recent publications historicize the affective dimensions of teaching, such as, "Historicizing affect in education" (co-authored with Alyssa Niccolini) in *Knowledge Cultures*. She is co-editing a forthcoming volume, *High Passions: Affect Studies in Education*.

Siyad Maalim is a recent graduate from the University of British Columbia with a major in Statistics.

Stephanie D. McCall is Assistant Professor at East Stroudsburg University in Pennsylvania. Her research interests engage a feminist post-structuralist analysis of gender and sexuality in education, curricular knowledge, the education of girls, and single-sex schooling. She teaches courses in curriculum theory, social foundations of education, and gender difference in schools. She is writing a forthcoming book, *Girls, Single-Sex Schools and Postfeminist Fantasies*.

Karen Meyer is Associate Professor in the Department of Curriculum and Pedagogy at the University of British Columbia.

Antonio Flávio Barbosa Moreira holds a Ph.D. in Education from the Institute of Education, at the University of London. He is currently an Emeritus Professor of Curriculum Studies at the Federal University of Rio de Janeiro and Professor of Curriculum Studies at the Catholic University of Petrópolis. He has written in the areas of education, curriculum studies, and teacher education. His publications include "Currículos e Programas no Brasil" (2009).

Samson Nashon is Professor and Head of the Department of Curriculum and Pedagogy at the University of British Columbia.

Nicholas Ng-A-Fook is a Professor of Curriculum Theory and the Director of the Teacher Education program at the University of Ottawa, Canada. He is also the Co-Director of the Equity Knowledge Network for the Province of Ontario. He has published several award-winning edited collections such as, but not limited to *Provoking Curriculum Studies: Strong Poetry and Arts of the Possible in Education*, and *Oral History and Education: Theories, Dilemmas, and Practices*.

Alyssa D. Niccolini's research focuses on affect and its intersections with secondary education. She is a recent graduate of Columbia University's Teachers College where her doctoral dissertation focused on censorship events in US secondary schools. Her scholarship has been published in peer-reviewed journals, including *Gender and Education* and *Knowledge Cultures*.

Cynthia Nicol is Associate Professor in the Department of Curriculum and Pedagogy at the University of British Columbia.

Mohamud Olow is a fourth-year student at University of British Columbia studying Geography, majoring in Environment and Sustainability.

Dr. Russell Pickell is the Superintendent of the Riverview Community School District, Riverview, MI 48193. He earned his Ed.D. in Educational Leadership and Policy Studies at Wayne State University, Detroit, MI. His research focus is on the impact of high school scheduling model changes on student achievement. He received his master's degree at Wayne State University, Detroit, MI, and bachelor of science degree from the University of Michigan, Dearborn, MI.

Molly Quinn is Professor of Curriculum Studies, Co-Director of the Ed.D. Educational Innovation Program, and Chair of the Department of Advanced Studies and Innovation in the College of Education at Augusta University. She is also founding member of the International Institute for Critical Pedagogy and Transformative Leadership, and president of the American Association for the Advancement of Curriculum Studies; she is author of: *Going Out, Not Knowing Whither: Education,* *the Upward Journey and the Faith of Reason; Peace and Pedagogy;* and *Theorizing Justice, Justly Theorizing in Education* (forthcoming); as well as editor of: *Complexifying Curriculum Studies: Reflections on the Generative and Generous Gifts of William E. Doll Jr.* (forthcoming). Much of her scholarship engages "spiritual" and philosophical criticism toward embracing a vision of education that cultivates wholeness, beauty, compassion, and community.

Linda Radford is a long-term appointment Professor at the University of Ottawa's Faculty of Education. Recent and ongoing research projects address the interdisciplinary and agentive possibilities of digital citizenship, digital pedagogies that foster self-reflexive reading practices, and the empowerment of marginalized youth through engaging literacies in critical ways.

Rosane Karl Ramos holds a Ph.D. in Education (Pontifical Catholic University at Rio de Janeiro, Brazil). She carried out part of her doctoral thesis research at University of British Columbia, Vancouver, Canada, supported by Conselho Nacional de Desenvolvimento Científico e Tecnológico (CNPq) in 2016–2017. She is currently a member of the research group GEFOCC (Teacher Education, Curriculum and School Routine Study Group/PUC-Rio). She has participated in conferences, congresses, and seminars on curriculum in Brazil and abroad, such as the XXXVI International Congress of the Latin American Studies Association (Barcelona, 2018); the 3rd European Conference for Curriculum Studies (University of Stirling, 2017); the 5th Triennial Conference of the International Association for the Advancement of Curriculum Studies (University of Ottawa, 2015); SeIoC (1st Internationalization of Curriculum Seminar (Universidade do Vale do Itajaí, Brazil, 2015); VI Portuguese-Brazilian Curriculum Conference (University of Minho, 2014). She has published articles on internationalization of curriculum, educational mobility, teacher education in service, and interculturality.

Eero Ropo, Ph.D. is Professor of Education at the School of Education, University of Tampere in Finland. He heads an international M.A. program in Teacher Education in Finland and Aceh, Indonesia. Ropo pursues international research interests specializing in teacher education, narrative research on learning and identity, curriculum theory, and ICT in education. Ropo has a long international experience as a researcher, conference organizer, and professor in Europe, USA, and several Asian and South American countries. Currently, he also works as a part-time Professor at the Nord University, Norway.

Muhammad Hassan Said is a third-year undergraduate student from Simon Fraser University in British Columbia studying Kinesiology and International Studies.

Carmen Shields is Professor of Education in the Schulich School of Education at Nipissing University, North Bay, Ontario. She teaches courses at the graduate level in research and curriculum development. Her own research is based on qualitative methodologies, most particularly in Narrative Inquiry Self-Study and Case Study Research. Her published writing is focused on inquiring into lived experience as foundational for understanding curriculum as personal and storied. She divides her time between Ontario and Nova Scotia, both of which she calls home.

Bryan Smith is a Lecturer at James Cook University in Townsville, Australia. His research explores social studies, anti-racism, and decolonizing theory and practice with a specific focus on their application in social studies pedagogy. As part of this research, he explores the (im)possibilities of using custom web and mobile technologies to facilitate critical anti-racist and decolonizing conversations about place, history, and subjectivities within and outside of the social studies classroom. His work can be found in the *Journal of Curriculum and Pedagogy, Transnational Curriculum Inquiry, In Education, Critical Literacy: Theories and Practices,* the *McGill Journal of Education,* the *Citizenship Education Research Journal,* and the *Nordic Journal of Digital Literacy.*

Fr. Nicholas Sseggobe-Kiruma is a Ph.D. candidate in the Educational Leadership and Policy program at Wayne State University in Detroit, Michigan. He also holds a master's degree in Educational Leadership and Planning from the Catholic University of Eastern Africa in Nairobi, Kenya, and a post-graduate diploma in secondary education with a major in Religious and Social Studies from the Catholic University of Eastern Africa. He has taught in high schools In Uganda since 1992 and has served as a member of school boards and as superintendent in the Archdiocese of Kampala in Uganda.

Hongyu Wang is a Professor in Curriculum Studies at Oklahoma State University. She received her Ph.D. in curriculum theory from Louisiana State University and master's degree in comparative curriculum theory from East China Normal University. She has authored books and published numerous articles both in Chinese and in English. Her most recent books are *Nonviolence and Education: Cross-Cultural Pathways* (Routledge, 2014) and *From the Parade Child to the King of Chaos: The Complex Journey of a Teacher Educator, William Doll* (Peter Lang, 2016). Her research interests include nonviolence education, cross-cultural dialogues, social justice education, international studies, subjectivity and curriculum, and college curriculum and teaching.

Reta Ugena Whitlock is Professor of Curriculum and Instruction and Chair of the Department of Educational Leadership at Kennesaw State University. She is the author of *This Corner of Canaan: Curriculum Studies of Place and the Reconstruction of the South* (Peter Lang, 2007) and editor of *Queer South Rising: Voices of a Contested Place* (Information Age Press, 2013). She is co-editor of the book series from Palgrave Macmillan, *Queer Studies in Education*. In addition to her continued writing on co-construction of self and place, her latest work explores how theology, particularly queer theology, informs curriculum and how we make meaning of it.

CHAPTER 1

Internationalizing Curriculum Studies: Histories, Environments, and Critiques

Cristyne Hébert, Awad Ibrahim, Nicholas Ng-A-Fook and Bryan Smith

How do we internationalize that which is deeply provincial and national? Situating our focus on and interest squarely within curriculum studies, how do we internationalize without imperializing or imposing old, colonial, and so-called "First World" conceptualizations of education on teaching, learning, and curriculum? Let us not anticipate simple answers to such complex questions. Being under no illusion that we hold Solomonic wisdom, we editors turned to the wisdom of others. A curricular response to such pedagogical questions is this edited volume. In it, we called on contributors

C. Hébert (✉)
Faculty of Education, University of Regina, Regina, SK, Canada

A. Ibrahim · N. Ng-A-Fook
Faculty of Education, University of Ottawa, Ottawa, ON, Canada
e-mail: aibrahim@uOttawa.ca

N. Ng-A-Fook
e-mail: nngafook@uottawa.ca

B. Smith
College of Arts, Society and Education, James Cook University, Townsville, QLD, Australia

© The Author(s) 2019
C. Hébert et al. (eds.), *Internationalizing Curriculum Studies*,
https://doi.org/10.1007/978-3-030-01352-3_1

2   C. HÉBERT ET AL.

to speak and write from their cultural, linguistic, and national locations, from the places they know best. We invited them to grapple with these questions in an increasingly globalized world while also *thinking through* the general and particular tasks of curriculum theorists (Derrida 2000).

We present this volume as a dialogic tapestry where our discursive exchanges are taken up as *complicated conversations* (Pinar et al. 1995). In turn, such conversations, as the chapters in the volume make clear, are suggestive of two dialogic frameworks. The first uses history to complicate local and global understandings of curriculum theorizing. The second involves a radical push of curriculum theorizing toward (re)imagining a better future that promises, without promise, bringing into existence that which is yet to come. Internationally oriented conversations start, as Pinar (2010) suggests elsewhere, at the national level where the "nation-state" continues to be a territorial and political domain from which important and consequential educational reforms are made and in turn need to be understood. For Pinar, the project of "internationalization denotes the possibility of nationally distinctive fields in complicated conversations with each other" (p. 3). But why understand the tasks of curriculum theorists in relation to internationalization versus globalization?

In *Curriculum Studies as an International Conversation*, Johnson-Mardones (2018) reminds us that the potential of thinking through the concept of internationalization "is not limited to 'moving beyond the nation' in order to reconstruct the national narrative or to reformulate a national cannon; it also includes the exploration of international conversations as in-between scholarly spaces" (p. 5). Despite the critiques, Hardt and Negri (2000) tell us, globalization cannot be reduced to not one thing. For them, "the multiple [curricular and pedagogical] processes that we recognize as globalization are not unified or univocal" (p. 219). With this in mind, this collection seeks to understand the local—with its history, environment, and critique—as the starting point for different disciplinary—vertical and horizontal—dimensions of an internationalization of curriculum studies in relation to globalization (Pinar 2015). How might we recognize the analytical and synthetical tensions and possibilities between internationalization and globalization, and how can we root (route) our differing international approaches for studying, or better yet understanding, a concept we call curriculum? This is what we are calling, to lean on Huebner's term, "the task of the curriculum theorist": to *think through* and re/direct the familiar into new, and more hopeful educational and societal directions.

In a time of uncertainty, as education becomes increasingly corporatized, monetized, and de-intellectualization, in the form of alt-right politics, continues to grow and be further embedded in public consciousness, the need to *think through* the task of the curriculum theorist is becoming more urgent than ever (Epstein 2016; Spring 2015). In light of (or sitting in the dark shadows caused by) Islamophobia, police brutality, hate-fueled attacks, and refusals to respond to the injustices that have been inflicted upon Indigenous communities across the globe, we began this work in careful consideration. We came together, from different parts of the world, to attend the International Association for the Advancement of Curriculum Studies Conference (IAACS) in May 2015. People spoke from their own accentuated political stances, listened to one another with a sense of loving humility, and tried to rearticulate and reimagine what Huebner (1975/1999) calls *language forms* and their respective radical possibilities.

It is worth noting that the Ottawa IAACS conference was the fifth iteration of our gathering together. The first iteration of this conference began 15 years ago at Louisiana State University. At that time, a community of curriculum scholars congregated to "talk about issues in curriculum, hearing what people do, how they do it, [and] how they think about things" with the hope that we could learn from each other (Trueit 2003, p. ix). Like Aoki (2000/2005) suggested then, the IAACS and its associated conference provided a potential space to "generate newness and hope" (p. 457). Then titled *The Louisiana State University Conference on the Internationalization of Curriculum Studies*, it was organized with the intention of both "encourag[ing] the internationalization of curriculum studies" and calling on curriculum theorists to "contribute to the formation of a world-wide field of curriculum studies" (Pinar 2003, p. 1). At this first gathering, Pinar (2003) offered the following cautionary note:

> Despite the bitterness and our despair over the development in the schools, many of us Americans still exude a naïve, if more than occasionally imperialistic, confidence that "the world is ours." Of course this is nonsense, but somewhere in the American unconsciousness such nonsenses is it seems, always at work. (p. 4)

Since then, the conference has been held triennially, hosted by universities in China (2003), Finland (2006), South Africa (2009), and Brazil (2012). In December of 2018, the conference will be held in Australia.

4   C. HÉBERT ET AL.

Forty-five years prior to this triennial gathering, in his groundbreaking article, Dwayne Huebner (1975/1999) first thought through *The Tasks of the Curriculum Theorist*. Huebner challenged readers to reconceptualize the field of curriculum studies as a space for multiplicity, recognizing the variety of shapes and forms various curricular phenomena, research about said phenomena, and the language we ascribe to them could assume. He tasked us with the following three areas for our future field of study: history, the environment, and critique. This collection is organized around these three areas, and we expand upon each briefly. First, when it came to history, Huebner argued, process and continuity were at the forefront of our conversations. And in many ways, they still are. For Huebner, we always need to ground ourselves in a time and a place so that we know where we come from and where we are going. This is what we are calling "histories," in the plural, because history can never be singular interpretation of our relationships with the past. Consequently, there are as many histories as there are interpreters and interpretations. Huebner stressed then, that what has begun is never quite finished, while at the same time reminding us of our allegiances to the past, in terms of tracing our intellectual histories within their particular and partial contextual states.

Huebner (1975/1999) also warned against a tendency toward ahistorical curriculum studies, a proneness for being "messianic" in the adoption of "new and permanent vehicles of salvation" positioned as "the only and only best way to talk about curricular phenomena" (p. 218). "To be aware of our historical nature," he continued, "is to be on top of our past, so we can use it as a base for projection into the future" (p. 218). Considering his comment in light of current global challenges, this projection need not be linear; tracing a clear line from past to present may not be possible, or indeed, desirable. Instead, projection might be interpreted as a metaphysical force, a movement or motion that disrupts certain ascendant historical logics while advancing alternative narratives. Here, we are looking not to "draw forth old solutions" but rather to be pushed as he put it, "to new levels of awareness" (p. 221).

Second, beyond a more general grounding of curricular work, Huebner's (1975/1999) tasks for curriculum theorists extend to an engagement with what he labels the "environment" of education, consisting of both the places of education—inside and outside of the school—and subjective experiences within these spaces. To fully understand Huebner's approach to the "environment," which is the second pillar of this book, we need to distinguish between the "school" (as the place, the geography, the building) and "schooling" (as the experiences people have in that place, what they do in it, and in turn what the place does to them). The building does not determine people's lived experiences but rather is directly related to them. Situating curriculum theory, in part, within Huebner's "environment" might help us understand and in many ways reverse the process of alienation that detaches "the individual from the history of the situation" and makes challenging the aforementioned process of change and growth (p. 223). Locating our selves in relation to others and spaces aids in the recognition of curriculum as a "form of human praxis, a shaping of the world" (p. 226) that requires reaching out, drawing from, and contributing to an active, political, and aesthetic community committed to imaging the world around us anew.

The third and final pillar of the book is centered around what Huebner calls "critique." Huebner (1975/1999) tasks curriculum theorists with a continued responsibility for conducting research as a means of determining the viability and vitality of institutions by "subjecting [them] to empirical and social criticism appropriate to given historical communities" (pp. 227–228). Apart from institutions, we might consider Huebner's move toward research as an effort to ground the field in a type of critique, wherein its language, form, and function are placed under the microscope. As he explains, "the empirical critique determines the adequacy of the form for the facts [and] the social critique determines the adequacy of the form in terms of the logical, esthetic, economic, and political values of users" (p. 227). Today, such callings upon curriculum theorists may ground our curriculum inquiries, while also moving them toward a reconceptualization of our practices and policies in particular spaces, opening up larger theoretical questions of how we might create spaces, in curriculum studies, for new ways of sitting with and *thinking through* both general and particular curricular issues.

Inspired by Huebner's (1975/1999) call to reconsider the tasks of the curriculum theorist, the 2015 meeting of IAACS provided an opportunity for our community to examine more closely what it might mean to curriculum theorize in the present time, in a moment of crisis; to reconsider what it might mean to live hopefully, radically, ethically, and lovingly with one another, across borders that are becoming increasingly real and more difficult to traverse (Lear 2008); to imagine what it might mean to open up new spaces, and to "look at things as if could be otherwise" (Greene 1995, p. 19). These complicated conversations were conducted through a variety of ever-expanding interpretive traditions:

historical, political, racial, gendered, phenomenological, post-structural/deconstructive/postmodern, (auto)biographical, aesthetic, theological, institutional, international, environmental, indigenous, postcolonial, and cosmopolitan. The chapters offered in this collection represent a move to ground curriculum studies as an international conversation. While *grounding* connotes a certain permanence when considering the etymology of the term—solidifying a foundation, constructing a firm basis, or rooting down—the chapters call attention to the possibilities for multiplicity suggested through rerouting (re-rooting) our conceptions of curriculum studies.

TURNING TO OTHERS: WHAT TO EXPECT IN WHAT FOLLOWS

In the first section, "Grounding Curricular Histories," the authors invite us to reconsider different historical conversations within the field of curriculum studies. Christou and De Luca offer a brief history of the movement in curriculum studies frequently referred to as reconceptualization. Identifying three tensions in the current state of the field—contemporaneity, discursive balkanization, and methodological diffusion—they challenge curriculum scholars to open up curricular spaces, to consider "who is able to participate in the conversation, how that conversation is referenced, the degree of coherence within the conversation, and the value and function of the conversation" (p. 29). Quinn and Christodoulou unearth curriculum by constructing an alternative world devoid of curriculum theory, examining its presence through absence. Describing curriculum theory as "the interdisciplinary study of educational experience, involving [an] extraordinarily complicated conversation," they recount their histories in curriculum theory, calling attention to both the historical roots that ground them in particular spaces and time and the fecund "cross-fertilizing" space between them (p. 36). In so doing, curriculum theory becomes a generative force of nourishment, one that has the potential to both maintain and transform.

Moreira and Ramos provide an important historical overview of the field of curriculum studies in Brazil that centers on the shift from educational transfer to mobility in light of internationalization. They draw on interviews from scholars in the USA, Canada, China, Finland, Great Britain, and Brazil to ground an inquiry into internationalization, arguing that scholars view internationalization as: a path toward homogenization, an attempt to understand how countries have grappled with globalization, and as a means for "changes and exchanges of experiences" (p. 63). Fleming offers a history of second language education in contention, drawing on a disagreement between scholars to shed light on the second language education in relation to the hidden curriculum and as a complicated conversation, highlighting the active nature of the curriculum. Focusing on the Canadian Language Benchmarks in particular, Fleming argues for an expansion of curricular implementation models, noting that language curricula might be developed both relationally and in consideration of current classroom contexts.

Ebenezer, Harden, Sseggobe-Kiruma, Pickell, and Hamden explore phenomenography and self-reflective journaling in the context of a doctoral seminar. After offering a comprehensive history of curriculum knowledge development, the authors turn to student voices to demonstrate how curriculum is conceptualized by doctoral students as a means of promoting openness and flexibility, listening to students' voices, and engaging in reflective thinking. Their chapter calls on educators to think about curriculum as dispersion of theories existing at a given time in history rather than a progression of theories that is getting better and better and will ultimately lead to the most plausible theory as in science. Meyer, Nicol, Maalim, Olow, Ali, Nashon, Bulle, Hussein, Hussein, and Hassan bring an end to this first section by examining curriculum within the context of refugee camps, highlighting the tensions of working with students in long-term and yet also emergency situations, where "the opportunity for education in a long-term refugee situation but [working] with curriculum that has limitations, perhaps barriers, for transition and life after returning to their homeland" (p. 108). The text offers a series of narratives that explore what it means to learn and teach in a refugee camp in northeastern Kenya. The authors call for curriculum theorists, to "rethink emphases and create pedagogical possibilities commensurate with: the exigency of time in long-term displacement situations; the implications of crossing physical, social, and cultural borders; the losses endured by marginalized communities; and the problematics of adaptation in lieu of choice in the daily life of displaced people" (p. 120).

In "Grounding Educational Environments," the authors attempt to answer our opening questions in relation to Huebner's conceptualization of "environment." They investigate conceptions of selves, others, and place in relation to curriculum studies. Aitken and Radford call our attention to the subjectivities of future teachers, drawing on a psychoanalytic framework to consider how students in a capstone course took up environmental stewardship. More specifically, they explore tensions that emerged as students grappled with socio-environmental equity, arguing for the value of "attending to psychic dynamics" that emerge within the classroom while challenging curriculum theorists to "renew attention to the significance of psychic dynamics in education." Ropo takes up autobiographical narratives as a means of grounding the self in particular temporal and locational contexts. Reviewing identity through the lenses of psychology, sociology, and philosophy, he uses Cote's epistemological and individual/social classifications to make a case for the significance of taking up identity in school contexts. Woven into the text is Ropo's own autobiographical writing, offered as a way to demonstrate how narratives can serve as "tools for repositioning," "anchor[ing] to place one's life course in chronological time and contexts, geographical places and environments, and the conditions of everyday lives" while at the same time constructing new "reflected narratives [that] comprise the capital for identity repositioning as a resource for future life contexts" (pp. 145–146).

Dernikos, Lesko, McCall, and Niccolini ground their curriculum theorizing within the psychic dimensions of affect. Beginning with the affective turn, they argue in favor of affect's focus on the body, thus disrupting the ever-present legacy of dualism. Highlighting the "creative, unpredictable, and vital force" of affect as "a means of interrupting and remodulating dominant moves of power and rigid normativities," Dernikos, Lesko, McCall, and Niccolini provide a series of vignettes as "affective encounters" that serve to "push against dominant configurations of power in schools" (p. 162). Shields ends this second section through a self-study that works to "unpack ... seminal experiences that inform and guide our definitions of curriculum" (p. 177). Using both Pinar and Clandinin and Connelly's work as a basis for her inquiry, she stresses the significance of "com[ing] to know the roots of our own perceptions about what is important to promote in our curriculum theorizing and teaching," highlighting narrative as a place for inquiry, recovering and reconstructing meaning, and building personal power (p. 178). In addition to uncovering her own roots through narrative writing, Shields also describes a series of methods used in teaching and supervising students that are helpful for thinking through how we might aid others, as curriculum scholars, in the process of collectively coming to know the grounding of our own ways of knowing and being in the world.

We end our collection in the final section thinking through Huebner's concept of "critique." In this third section, "Grounding Curricular

Critique," authors call attention to a series of theoretical moves that might open up new spaces for working within/through curricular issues. Wang invites us to rethink nonviolence in relation to curriculum theorizing. She describes such thinking through as an:

> organic relationality that transcends dualism, non-instrumental engagement that engages students' growth without trying to control the outcome, playfulness that decenters fixity and allows emergence in teaching and learning, the necessity of the inner work simultaneous with the outer work, a radical denouncement of violence in all forms, and the feminist advocacy of peace are all important aspects of nonviolence. (p. 195)

Understanding nonviolence as engagement with self, relationship with difference, and as an essential task of the curriculum theorist, Wang suggests that nonviolence is "not a destination or ideal to reach, but an ongoing process of daily work to unlearn the mechanism of domination internally and relate compassionately externally to others and the world" (p. 204). In this respect, grounding our critiques as nonviolence is both an inward and an outward move. Le Grange writes about the potential of the African concept of Ubuntu as a means for thinking through our becoming in relation to others, or others' becoming in relation to us. After providing a history of education in South Africa, his text offers a skillful braiding of *currere* and Ubuntu, as Le Grange weaves the practices together, offering Ubuntu-*currere* as anti-humanist, relational, and post-anthropocentric critique of the very concept we call curriculum. In our collection's concluding chapter, Whitlock situates her curriculum inquiries and critiques within theology. She examines the theological/theoretical works of Bonhoeffer through the lens of queer theology, alongside narrative accounts of a Southern place, Christian fundamentalism and losing one's religion in order to return one's self to theology and its respective study. Whitlock also proposes placing theology in conversation with education. She asks us to reconsider that "there is no human apart from the power-less, emptied, suffering God" (p. 243). What Whitlock offers here is a means of thinking through curriculum in relation to God, a "theological curriculum framework [that] presents God as a lived curriculum, as radical love, as *currere*" (p. 243).

Thinking through the tasks of curriculum theorists, it seems, is a call to write and re-write our complicated international conversations, while also questioning the quotidian of our live(d) experiences as curriculum

10 C. HÉBERT ET AL.

scholars, teachers, and human beings. The authors in this collection therefore call on each of us, like Huebner (1999) before them, to use "the unformed to create form; as a focusing on the unconditioned in order to develop new conditions" (p. 227). Even as we face what some might call a world in political, environmental, economic, existential, and so on crisis, the "radical" concept of hope continues to sustain the conditions that inform are past, present, and future tasks as international curriculum theorists. To this curricular and pedagogical end, this collection represents an evocative conceptualization of the challenging histories, environments and critiques international curriculum theorists continue to take up in their groundbreaking intellectual work.

REFERENCES

Aoki, T. (2005). Postscript. In W. F. Pinar & R. L. Irwin (Eds.), *Curriculum in a new key: The collected works of Ted. T. Aoki*. Mahwah, NJ: Lawrence Erlbaum Associates.

Derrida, J. (2000). *Of hospitality*. Stanford: Stanford University Press.

Epstein, J. (2016). *Here's the proof of Donald Trump's racism, sexism & anti-gay rhetoric you've been asking for, trolls*. Retrieved from http://www.thenewcivil-rightsmovement.com/joshuaepstein/trump.

Greene, M. (1995). *Releasing the imagination*. San Francisco: Jossey-Bass.

Hardt, M., & Negri, A. (2000). *Empire*. Cambridge, MA: Harvard University Press.

Huebner, D. (1975/1999). The tasks of the curricular theorist. In V. Hillis (Ed.), *The lure of the transcendent: Collected essays by Dwayne E. Huebner* (pp. 212–230). Mahwah, NJ: Lawrence Erlbaum Associates.

Johnson-Mardones, D. F. (2018). *Curriculum studies as an international conversation: Educational traditions and cosmopolitanism in Latin America*. New York: Routledge.

Lear, J. (2008). *Radical hope: Ethics in the face of cultural devastation*. Cambridge, MA: Harvard University Press.

Pinar, W. F. (2003). Toward the internationalization of curriculum studies. In D. Trueit, W. Doll, H. Wang, & W. Pinar (Eds.), *The internationalization of curriculum studies* (pp. 1–14). New York: Peter Lang.

Pinar, W. F. (2010). Introduction. In W. F. Pinar (Ed.), *Curriculum studies in South Africa: Intellectual histories and present circumstances* (pp. 1–18). New York, NY: Palgrave Macmillan.

Pinar, W. F. (2015). *Educational experience as lived: Knowledge, history, alterity*. New York, NY: Routledge.

Pinar, W., Reynolds, W., Slattery, P., & Taubman, P. (1995). *Understanding curriculum*. New York: Peter Lang.

Spring, J. (2015). *Economization of education: Human capital, global corporation, skills-based schooling.* New York: Routledge.

Trueitt, D. (2003). Democracy and conversation. In D. Trueit, W. Doll, H. Wang, & W. Pinar (Eds.), *The internationalization of curriculum studies* (pp. ix–xvii). New York, NY: Peter Lang.

PART I

Grounding Curricular Histories

CHAPTER 2

Toward a Complex Coherence in the Field of Curriculum Studies

Theodore M. Christou and Christopher DeLuca

The field of curriculum is ripe with tensions. Since the 1960s, scholars have repeatedly defined these and identified how they might mitigate inclusivity and coherence within the field (Connelly 2013; Hlebowitsh 2012; Reid 1999; Westbury 1999; Wraga 1998; Young 2013). These tensions are largely referenced to a growing group of curriculum theorists who have been acculturated within a reconceptualist framework of curriculum thinking (Tanner and Tanner 1979; Wraga and Hlebowitsh 2003a). While scholars who have been part of the evolving conversation about curriculum will recognize these tensions, new scholars may not. Accordingly, in this chapter, we consider the current state of curriculum studies within its present context by identifying three tensions within the field. In articulating these tensions, we aim to provide emerging curriculum scholars with three contemporary, though historically referenced,

---

T. M. Christou (✉) · C. DeLuca
Queen's University, Kingston, ON, Canada
e-mail: theodore.christou@queensu.ca

C. DeLuca
e-mail: cdeluca@queensu.ca

© The Author(s) 2019
C. Hébert et al. (eds.), *Internationalizing Curriculum Studies*,
https://doi.org/10.1007/978-3-030-01352-3_2

16 T. M. CHRISTOU AND C. DELUCA

heuristics intended to provoke progressive curriculum scholarship characterized by greater coherence.

The editors of this collection challenged us to write about the internationalization of curriculum studies while situating our work within the context in which we pursue our scholarship. They drew our attention to the seminal work of Dwayne Huebner (1999), who noted the importance of grounding in time and place. Here, while we talk about curriculum studies as a field, it is more akin to a polyvocal space, one which, as we note below, does not always involve shared understandings and open dialogue involving all scholars.

We acknowledge that we have particular worldviews that permit us to see, make sense of, and write about what curriculum has been, is, and may be. We are white males, Canadian, of European descent. We work primarily in English. The readings that shaped our thinking and the audience that we address are both shaped by our context, intellectual and material.

Again, we look to Huebner, as the editors of this collection do, who calls us to attend to the historical nature of our scholarship. As we argue for complex coherence in curriculum studies, we are historically mindful. In fact, we open here by noting two pivotal moments in the late twentieth century that led to revolutions within the field of curriculum studies. First, in 1969, Joseph Schwab characterized the field as moribund, arguing that extant methods and principles of curriculum inquiry were insufficient for significant curriculum reification. Then, nearly a decade later, Pinar (1978) declared that curriculum theory was renewed through the efforts of reconceptualist scholars who promoted curriculum inquiry as interpretive, value-laden, and biographic. Curriculum scholars were called to attention. They were challenged to delineate and justify their methods of inquiry and to establish their significance within the broader discipline of education. In this chapter, we consider the future of curriculum studies 35 years after Pinar's declaration on the reconceptualization of the curriculum field.

Since 1978, theorists have worked to articulate methodological and epistemological frameworks for the sustainability, utility, and value of curriculum studies. Significant works include *Understanding Curriculum* (Pinar et al. 1995), *What Is Curriculum Theory?* (Pinar 2004/2012), *International Handbook of Curriculum Research* (Pinar 2003), *Cognition and Curriculum* (Eisner 1982), *Curriculum Theory* (Schiro 2013), *Forms of Curriculum Inquiry* (Short 1991), *Handbook of Research on*

Curriculum (Jackson 1992b), *Curriculum* (Schubert 1996), and *The Sage Handbook of Curriculum and Instruction* (Connelly et al. 2008). The field of curriculum has been characterized differently across these, and many other, sources. These characterizations have been made in relation to the reconceptualist movement, which has emerged as a dominant framework within North American curriculum theory (Pacheco 2012; Pinar 2004). Despite its critics (e.g., Hlebowitsh 2012; Westbury 1999; Wraga 1998), the reconceptualist paradigm remains ubiquitous although not homogenous. The reconceptualists have evolved from Pinar's initial declaration in 1978 to now encompass varied scholarship predicated on diverse methodologies, interests, and traditions. The notion of a reconceptualist framework is always shifting and evolving. As scholars, we were raised within its culture. In this chapter, we address our contemporaries. While our arguments may parallel past critiques, we assert them anew in relation to the current culture of North American curriculum studies, and in relation to current socio-political contexts and international influences.

Within the current culture of curriculum studies, *conversation*—complicated, complex, or otherwise framed—is arguably the most pervasive metaphoric anchor for contemporary curriculum scholarship and serves as a framework for the eclectic nature of curriculum inquiry (Pacheco 2012; Pinar 2004). For the purposes of our argument within this chapter, we identify three caveats related to the use of *conversation*. We find the metaphor useful for the future of curriculum studies, yet it is one that demands ongoing consideration.

First, there are multiple conversations coexisting under the broad banner of curriculum studies. These refer to curriculum theory, development, evaluation, history, and other discipline-specific and practical contexts of study. Below, we will characterize this multiplicity of conversations as the tension of discursive balkanization. While our argument has implications for all of the communities of scholarship, it is most pertinent to curriculum theorists. Second, our use of conversation within this chapter should not be conflated with its use in cultural, environmental, or discursive studies. Third, the use of conversation is neither meant as an uncritical adoption of the metaphor, nor is it a criticism of those curriculum scholars who employ it in their scholarship. In exploring the current state of curriculum studies, the conversation metaphor is not only unavoidable with respect to North American curriculum studies but also useful to our argument that inclusive and coherent are fundamental to good curriculum scholarship.

Introducing conversation as a metaphor for curriculum theory, Pinar (2004) states, "curriculum becomes a complicated, that is, multiply referenced, conversation in which interlocutors are speaking not only among themselves but to those not present, not only historical figures and unnamed peoples and places they may be studying, but to politicians and parents alive and dead, not to mention to the selves they have been, are in the process of becoming, and someday may become" (p. 43). Pinar (1974, 1994, 2004) further advanced the notion of *currere* as a method. It can be understood as a methodology for engaging systematically in curriculum conversations within a reconceptualist framework (Pinar and Grumet 1976). Four steps delineate the method of *currere*: (1) regressive, (2) progressive, (3) analytical, and (4) synthetical. Taken together, these steps provoke academic inquiry into the socio-personal and systemic conditions that shape possibility as well as limitation within curricular moments (Pinar et al. 1995). They have framed, explicitly and implicitly, engagement in complicated curricular conversations:

> the method of *currere* reconceptualizes curriculum from course objectives to complicated conversation. It is conversation with oneself (as a 'private' person) and with others threaded through academic knowledge, an ongoing project of self-understanding in which one becomes mobilized for engagement in the world. (Pinar 2012, p. 47)

In this way, curriculum as conversation is meant to engage social reconstruction through a dialectic process that connects private and public spheres, historical and contemporary contexts, as well as theoretical and practical concerns.

While curriculum scholarship since 1978 has led to an eclectic, and theoretically and methodologically engaging field (Ng-A-Fook 2014), we raise important tensions that drive the future of curriculum studies. In advancing these tensions, we aim to be forward-thinking: Our interest is to envision the health, sustainability, and utility of curriculum studies while heeding and integrating previous characterizations of contemporary curriculum inquiry. Underpinning these tensions is our desire to increase the validity and the utility of curriculum studies for the greater good—to consider these tensions as generative spaces that can provoke greater inclusivity and coherence within our field. Specifically, we identify and explore the following three interconnected tensions within the field of curriculum studies: (a) contemporaneity, (b) discursive balkanization, and (c) methodological diffusion.

CONTEMPORANEITY

The first tension is what we refer to as the grip of contemporaneity; the locating of contemporary studies in relationship to historical groundings is alarmingly sparse. This tension is symptomatic of a broader trend within curriculum studies, which situates the historical roots of curriculum theorizing strictly within the early twentieth century (Pinar, 2008). It is problematic, we argue, to ignore broader and deeper traditions of curriculum history that extend into antiquity. While it is both commonplace and justifiable for contemporary curriculum scholars to link their work to John Dewey, for instance, rare is the framing of Dewey in terms of his own intellectual influences and precursors, Hegel, Pestalozzi, Herbart, Quintillian, Jane Addams, Montessori, et al. This tension again contributes to diminished coherence, resulting in fragmented tangents of thought that are tenuously linked, if at all, to previous, notable, and useful, theoretical frameworks. Drawing explicit linkages to those historical and philosophical influences that inform our line of thinking is important, yet the delimiting of curriculum studies to a twentieth-century phenomenon severs us from the continuity of thought that stretches into antiquity.

Pinar's (2008) introduction to the re-issuing of George Tompkin's *A Common Countenance* is a plea to curriculum studies scholars to be historically minded. History plays a seminal role in our search for meaning in the present. Our hopes and plans for the future depend upon our articulation of past to present and upon our understanding of what it means to *be* within the landscape of educational thinking and theorizing. "To understand one's own situation," Pinar (2008) states, "requires close attention to its history (p. 142)." This history is often engendered and partial (Hendry, 2011). There are limits that one must attend to when tracing such genealogies, and yet it is inconceivable to frame curriculum as a mere product of the twentieth century. As long as societies have sought to question what must be taught and how it can be taught, the curriculum of schools—however these may be conceived—has been subject to inquiry, speculation, vision, and revision.

This sentiment echoes the work of Kliebard (1995), who argues that the history of education enables us to engage more critically with contemporary educational contexts. When curriculum scholars are informed by the past and situate current rhetorical, reformist, and conceptual

20   T. M. CHRISTOU AND C. DELUCA

trends in their historical precedents, they neither revel or exaggerate the benefits of future reform (i.e., neophilia), nor cower in the face of it (i.e., neophobia). Rather, they see the reconfiguration of logic in their own work by relating it to the ongoing conversation in increasingly connected and coherent ways. This is the via *media* between two extreme reformist positions: "the consideration of curriculum theory and practice in historical perspective may serve to curb the field's persistent but uncritical penchant for novelty by tracing the course of ideologies and movements and analyzing their consequences in curriculum practice" (Kliebard 1976, p. 247). While history does not offer answers to curriculum studies scholars about the present and the future it does challenge us to interrogate the questions that we ask, while putting these into a broader perspective:

> Perhaps, more than anything, what the study of the history of education can provide is not so much specific lessons pertaining to such matters as how to construct a curriculum or how to run a school as it is the development of certain habits of thought, and the principal one among these is the habit of reflection and deliberative inquiry. It is the habit of holding up the taken-for-granted world to critical scrutiny, something that usually can be accomplished more easily in a historical context than in a contemporary one. Ideas and practices that seem so normal and natural in a contemporary setting often take on a certain strangeness when viewed in a historical setting, and that strangeness often permits us to see those ideas and practices in a different light. (Kliebard 1976, p. 2)

In 1968, John Goodlad penned a provocative piece that invoked the Roman god, Janus. Janus, the namesake of the month January, who bridges new years with the ones past, was represented as having two heads. Janus looked forward, even as he looked back. He was the god of archways and of doorways. Goodlad, with rare prescience, contextualized the ideology and rhetoric of 1960s progressive education in light of its earlier incarnation, which would serve as a tour de force in North American schooling, particularly during the interwar period (Christou 2008). Goodlad's (1968) article documented continuities and changes between present and past; he sought, ultimately, to temper his contemporaries' neophilia by drawing out cautionary examples of the pitfalls that might arise from running headlong and enthusiastically into progressivist reforms:

The future, like the past, must have its excesses. Excesses are the creative thrusts of individuals and of society, the counter-cyclical reactions to yesterday's excesses. But let us temper them with our lessons from the past so as to forestall crippling neuroses. Our excesses make of this sober educational pursuit our sport, our recreation. (p. 46)

Curriculum studies, Goodlad argued, is the working out of a path between our present situation and a projected future, informed by the past and infused with equal parts hope and caution.

Hope is rooted in a growing awareness of the possibility of change, which history repeatedly documents. Curriculum scholars are—and we know this because they have been—agents of change. Looking at the matter somewhat differently, curriculum history is a series of cautionary tales; it can cause contemporary heads to shake with dismay at the realization that many of our most pressing problems are persistent. Some of these are profound and yoked to our human existence in a modern age—i.e., equity, justice, concern for the individual learner, fears about the ability of schools to meet the challenges that an uncertain future will bring—and some of these are historical relics, which are no longer useful. Drawing on an evolutionary model introduced by Dewey (1910), Kliebard (1976) notes:

Intellectual progress usually happens through the sheer abandonment of questions together with both the alternatives they assume—an abandonment that results from their decreasing vitality and a change of urgent interest. We do not solve them, we get over them. (p. 248)

In other words, we do not "solve" educational problems as much as we evaluate them in context. As the context changes, questions may become vestigial. They served some purpose in the past, but they merit no further inquiry in the present. Historical work in the curriculum field helps us to identify these and to contextualize them properly.

The irony embedded in the tension of contemporaneity is that it, in itself, has been a persistent historical concern of curriculum studies scholars. This is evident from the sources discussed above and epitomized by the 1974 ASCD publication, *The Curriculum: A Field Without a Past* (Ponder 1974). This report conducted an expansive survey of literature published in the curriculum studies field and noted a dearth of historical scholarship or reference to the historical. The opening lines are damning:

The curriculum field has witnessed reform after reform in its brief history, each new generation of curriculum workers has attempted to answer continuing and recurring questions with little regard for their historical antecedents. This characteristic stance has given rise to the charge that curriculum specialists are "ahistorical" in outlook, in that their theories and proposals suffer both from a lack of knowledge of the curricular past and from selective and superficial understandings of the work of curriculum predecessors. (Ponder 1974, p. 461)

The report cites a survey of doctoral dissertations in curriculum conducted by Wick and Dirkes (1973), which found no studies of a historical nature. This survey would substantiate Goodlad's (1966) critique of curriculum reforms and rhetoric that permeated the educational landscape in the 1960s; his analysis led him to the conclusion that "a substantial number of the new crop of reformers have approached the persistent, recurring problems of curriculum construction in the naive belief that no one had looked at them before" (p. 91).

This points to a generational breach in the field of curriculum studies. In each generation, Kliebard (1968) argues, "issues seem to arise ex nihilo; each generation is left to discover anew the persistent and perplexing problems that characterize the field" (p. 69). Various scholars have taken up the subject of a generational divide that separates each new group of curriculum scholars from those who preceded them within a broader historical context. Most notably, there have been two extended discussions hosted in *Curriculum Inquiry*. Hlebowitsh prompted both of these discussions with the publication of two provocative articles, first in 1999 (Hlebowitsh 1999a, b; Pinar 1999), then again in 2005 (Hlebowitsh 2005a, b; Westbury 2005; Wright 2005). We return, in other words, to the idea of curriculum as conversation that is inclusive, not only of our contemporaries, but also of our past and our prospective future.

Discursive Balkanization

The second tension evident in curriculum scholarship squarely addresses the blurred and disparate boundaries of what (and who) constitute curriculum studies. We refer to this tension as discursive balkanization. Borrowing from Pinar (2008), this balkanization can be understood as a fracturing and diffusion of the field of curriculum, characterized by "a tendency in the field to ignore discourses, to fail to teach curriculum theory comprehensively" (p. xvii). This concern is not new: "curriculum is a complex endeavor suffering in a permanent discussion both about its theoretical state and the relationship between curriculum theory and curriculum development" (Pacheco 2012, p. 13). Since Schwab's (1970) claim that the curriculum field is moribund, scholars have sought to clarify and define the boundaries of curriculum studies (Jackson 1992a) while defining its diversity as an aspect of strength (Pacheco 2012).

As a consequence, curriculum scholars with very different interests engage in immensely different conversations all under the canopy of curriculum studies. While this diversity has generative potential, it more often creates divisive classes and scholarly factions. Egan (2003) notes that "this dividing up the field of education into many sub-fields, none of which apparently has much that is useful to say to any other, seems to me still to be the curse of the study of education" (p. 18). Egan (2003) pursues the question, "how much longer can we stagger on, producing mountains of 'knowledge' that are supposed to improve education, while patently doing nothing of the sort—and in the process earning the contempt of the wider academic world" (p. 18). While we are reticent to suggest the need for imposing boundaries on the field, we see the need to acknowledge how the diverse nature of curriculum studies can limit coherence in our conversations as well as our contribution to education as a public occupation. Moreover, we assert that curriculum scholars from various disciplines and fields should be able to engage in conversations, even when the terms and parameters are not obviously amenable (Miller 2016). These conversations ought to use consistent language and share common curricular concerns, which will enable the field to move beyond fixed debating positions championed by foils.

In the opening lines of the Introduction to *Understanding Curriculum: An Introduction to the Study of Historical and Contemporary Curriculum Discourses*, Pinar (1995) notes:

> This is an unruly book, a cacophony of voices. That is the reality and our stylistic intention. We walked a fine line, not wanting to submerge individual scholars and lines of discourse in *our* narrative. To do so would be to create a "master" narrative. What we have tried to do is represent the field as it is, not as we wish it to be, or even what it looks like from our point of view. (p. ix)

Cacophony is an appropriate adjective to represent the dispersion and variety of conversations happening concurrently within curriculum studies. In the citation above, the term has connotations of richness and diversity. Capturing the cacophony entails giving space to many perspectives, many approaches, and many voices that fall within the "fine line" that outlines the borders of curriculum studies. Etymologically, cacophony is not associated with richness and abundance; it is a compound of the Greek roots *kako* (meaning bad, evil, or discordant), and *phonē* (meaning sound, or voice). Cacophonous sounds are out of sync and dissonant. Curriculum studies may in fact be more cacophonous than conversational. While "very much in motion," this motion resembles a dispersion of sounds cast without coordination into the wind (Pinar et al. 2008, p. xiv).

Pinar (2008) astutely situated the fragmentation of the curriculum field within the reconceptualization movement, noting that even as the reconceptualist movement coalesced, it scattered: "Once that tradition had been displaced, the cohesion splintered. Now there is a certain 'balkanization' in the field, a certain tendency for student and practitioners of each discourse to act as if his or her discourse of affiliation and labor is the most important" (p. xvii). Pinar hoped that the text would serve as a correction and promote consolidation in the field; while it depicted the discursive balkanization in curriculum, its aims were, perhaps, too ambitious. We believe that curriculum scholars must seek to engage collectively in a conversation that can serve to foster some common language, definitions, or epistemologies and trespass porous borders in the curriculum field.

Kliebard's (1982) provocative perspective on the matter questions the very existence of a self-identifying definition to connect curriculum scholars:

> One of the surest ways to kill a conversation on the subject of curriculum theory is to ask someone to name one. There appears to be so much disagreement and confusion on this subject that discussions revolve not so much around the merits of rival theories as the question of what in the world we are talking about. (p. 11)

This quotation relates to the first tension noted above, jargon, but it also highlights the coexistence of distinct discursive communities that are only loosely bound and constellated. Further, this implicates the fifth tension to curriculum studies, methodological dispersion.

Methodological Diffusion

The final tension addresses the methodological diffusion within the field and refers to the dispersion of methodologies during the reconceptualist period in curriculum scholarship. Curriculum scholars have prioritized and emphasized diversification and expansion of theoretical curriculum frameworks for curriculum conversation (Hlebowitsh 2014; Ng-A-Fook 2014). The field of contemporary curriculum has achieved sufficient theoretical diversity; as Maxwell (2004) recognizes, this achievement is "fundamental and irreducible, and one that displays an 'incredulity toward metanarratives' (Lather 2004) that assert a unified, totalizing understanding of some phenomena" (p. 35). While the diversity of frameworks is useful for engaging in complex conversations, the field has largely neglected to refine these frameworks in terms of their methodological appropriation over the past 35 years. Reflecting on Schwab's second sign of crisis, Wraga and Hlebowitsh (2003b) noted, "varied forms of enquiry, including structuralism, post-structuralism, deconstructionism, and post-modernism (to name a few) have been introduced to the field, manifesting a greater commitment to talk about rather than to engage with curriculum endeavors" (p. 427). The result of this neglect is a mistaking of conceptual frameworks for methodological clarity and sufficiency.

In the absence of methodological clarity, the generation of scholarship, knowledge, and curriculum as inquiry becomes a shaky, non-transparent structure, easily discredited. If others (both curriculum scholars and other educationists from outside the field) cannot follow our methodological conversation than we not only diminish inclusivity within our conversations but limit the capacity of curriculum work for greater influence. Methodological diffusion—characterized by young methodologies and lack of comprehensive explication—jeopardizes the validity and utility of curriculum research. In calling for methodological clarity, we value Davis et al.'s (2008) notion that sufficiency-seeking inquiry involves distributed, non-centralized, but connected, scholarship; such work delves into multiple interpretations of local curricular experiences to provoke new conceptions of teaching and learning, while simultaneously considering diverse contexts and theoretical lenses. Underpinning this view of methodological clarity is (a) a commitment to diverse, rigorously articulated methodologies; and (b) a pledge to connect methodologies to both theoretical frameworks and to other methodologies to ensure commensurability across curriculum studies and to provoke coherence of a greater whole. In articulating this tension, we wish to incite curriculum scholars to seek as much coherence through the methodologies they employ as they seek through the curriculum conversations they engage.

In one of the few texts exclusively dedicated to curriculum methodologies, Short (1991) recognized that since the reconceptualist movement in curriculum studies, multiple inquiry modalities have emerged, which were highly adapted to curricular studies, and required greater attention, recognition, and articulation within the field. Short (1991) contended that not only do, "varied forms of curriculum inquiry need to be recognized and articulated within the field of curriculum studies itself, but their viability also needed to be demonstrated and legitimated beyond curriculum studies" (p. ix). Short (1991) further commented on the state of curriculum methodologies:

> In fields of inquiry that are relatively new, like the field of curriculum inquiry, it can be expected that alternative schemes for organizing the field into fairly well-established domains of inquiry will compete with each other for some time before a dominant pattern emerges. The very fluidity of a field of practical activity such as curriculum practice may also contribute to the appearance in the field of curriculum inquiry of new and competing domains of inquiry ... This whole matter of domain identity is of no great consequence unless its changing and multifarious character makes is difficult to locate related inquiry or inhibits the application of use of this inquiry. Nonetheless, it is well to know how a field of inquiry is structured and how to find one's way around in it. (p. 6)

Mapping curriculum methodologies continue to be a pressing concern given the relative renewal of the field since the 1970s and the politics of educational research (Pacheco 2012). Specifically, the *Scientific Research in Education Report* of the National Research Council (2002) asserts an overt valuing of empirical, randomized control, generalizable research for education in fulfillment of accountability and standardized frameworks (e.g., No Child Left Behind 2002). We agree with the multiple objections raised by curriculum scholars to the prioritization of this form of research (Lather 2004; Lincoln and Cannella 2004; Moss 2005; Willinsky 2005), especially as they relate to diverse forms of curriculum inquiry. We recognize that the current state of curriculum methodologies may not offer a sufficiently defensible alternative that works to establish what Lather (2004) calls the "conditions of the legitimation of knowledge in contemporary postpositivism" (p. 673). And here, legitimation does "not revert to the dominant foundational, formulaic and readily available codes of validity" (p. 676).

In particular, we attend to Lather (1993, 2004), who considers the validity of post-modern research. What are the criteria we can meaningfully use to examine validity in curriculum research, framed discursively as conversation? We begin to answer this question by positing that this conversation is necessarily dialogical and reflexive. In alignment with methodological trends toward the autobiographical and hermeneutic (Pinar et al. 1995; Slattery 2003; Smith 1991) and in relation to the dominant framework of curriculum as conversation, curricular validity is constructed as narrative that defends perspective-based evidences obtained through transparent, rigorous, and dialogical methods.

From methodological discussions outside the field of curriculum (i.e., qualitative research methods, measurement, program evaluation, feminist), dialogical and transgressive articulations of validity have begun to emerge. For instance, Cho and Trent (2006) acknowledge that validation occurs through an ongoing and recursive dialogical narrative between researchers, participants, and research consumers so that the "usefulness and validity concerns become directly connected to those in the setting" (p. 335).

Like others (Lather 2004, 2010; Lincoln and Cannella 2004; Willinsky 2005), we assert that validity remains a fundamental consideration if curriculum research is to gain influence within educational agendas and in specific contexts of practice. Accordingly, curriculum scholars might serve collectively to rationalize and explain their research methods as a contribution to some broader conversation. Further, they might explore the enabling aspects, boundaries, and limitations of this metaphor for curriculum inquiry. In short, curricular scholars need to now think as methodologists and articulate the structures that validate their practices. This involves linking methodologies within a coherent, overarching framework, and connecting methodologies to the conceptual theories that shape curriculum conversations.

Looking Toward the Future

Forty-four years ago Schwab (1970) famously argued that curriculum was moribund, yet curriculum studies as a field perseveres. Connelly (2009, 2013) has repeatedly argued curriculum maintains continued interest to education because it is deeply embedded in policy, practice, politics, and social discourse. The current state of the curriculum field is characterized by various epistemological and methodological approaches toward its theory and practice (Ng-A-Fook 2014). The reconceptualist movement, from its inception, intended to transform the field by shifting its focus from traditional concerns (i.e., curriculum development and practice) to the individual through autobiographical inquiry (Pinar 1976; van Manen 1978). As accurately predicted by Pinar (1978), "the field of curriculum studies will be profoundly different in 20 years time than it has been during the first 50 years of its existence" (p. 205).

Given this transformation, scholars have repeatedly raised concerns that curriculum theorizing has lost its moorings (Connelly 2010; Hlebowitsh 2010; Hopmann 2009). As Hlebowitsh (2014) has recently noted, "the problem ... is that the curriculum studies field still has a way to go in terms of making any difference in the lives of people" (p. 91). Despite these concerns, the reconceptualists eschew responsibility for educational practice and policy writ large and declare that their work has emancipatory and critical purposes for individuals (Pinar 1978; Pinar et al. 1995; Pacheco 2012; van Manen 1978). Herein lies a dilemma. The multiple realities currently existing in curriculum studies are divisive and lead to a general disagreement about the relationship between theory and practice. If these realities are at all overlapping, they are not engaged in a commensurable conversation.

We conclude our chapter with a call for curriculum scholars to consider the following question: What characterizes curriculum theory in a *post*-reconceptualist world? The three tensions identified in this chapter begin to shape a response to this question. While there are aspects of these tensions that may not seem new as they have been articulated by curriculum scholars in various guises over the past five decades (e.g., Bowers 1991; Hlebowitsh 1999a, b; Tanner and Tanner 1979; Wraga 1999), each generation of curriculum scholars must face its challenges anew. As Kliebard (1995) recognizes, history does not repeat itself. "At best," he notes, "historical awareness will keep us from repeating only handful of that infinitude of mistakes" (p. 194). Historical events and themes reflected in present day are always mediated by and particular to their contexts. Current curriculum scholars must be historically minded but they cannot be bound by the arguments made by their predecessors.

By endeavoring to understand what has characterized curriculum studies in a *post*-reconceptualist world, we see significant value in retaining conversation as a dominant anchor for curriculum studies. To this end, we must examine the way in which *conversation* has evolved within our field. Specifically, we must examine who is able to participate in the conversation, how that conversation is referenced, the degree of coherence within the conversation, and the value and function of the conversation. We hope that future conversations extend between curriculum scholars and between curriculum scholars and the public—students, parents, teachers, and other educationists. We acknowledge that to open curriculum conversations to others and to make them inclusive potentially challenges their coherence. Here, we draw on Taylor's (1979) notion of coherence, which involves drawing upon multiple perspectives, warrants, and interpretations that may be distinct and dissonant but that can be rationally connected through a conversation that sustains a continuity of discourse, historical, and contemporary. This form of complex coherence requires a diversity of perspectives. What is more, this conversation evolves and shifts; curriculum scholars are bequeathed the duty to incessantly examine the validity and the effectiveness of their methods in light of their contributions. Hence, curriculum as conversation entails engagement with experiences of teaching and learning as a means of understanding ourselves within the broader context of life and our relationships with others, with our environment, and with the broader world of ideas, past, present, and future. If this sense of curriculum studies is to flourish, it is only be through a conversation that is historically grounded and framed within boundaries and methodologies that enable complex coherence.

REFERENCES

Bowers, C. A. (1991). Some questions about the anachronistic elements in the Giroux/McLaren theory of critical pedagogy. *Curriculum Inquiry, 21*(2), 239–252.

Christou, T. M. (2008). *Progressive education: Revisioning and reframing Ontario's public schools, 1919–1942*. Toronto, ON: University of Toronto Press.

Cho, J., & Trent, A. (2006). Validity in qualitative research revisited. *Qualitative Research, 6,* 319–340.

Connelly, F. M. (2009). Bridges from then to now and from them to us: Narrative threads on the landscape of 'the practical'. In E. C. Short & L. J. Waks (Eds.), *Leaders in curriculum studies: Intellectual self-portraits* (pp. 39–54). Rotterdam, the Netherlands: Sense Publishers.

Connelly, F. M. (2010, May). Curriculum theory: Dead man walking? An international dialogue. In S. T. Hopmann (Chair), *International Dialogue*.

Symposium conducted at the annual meeting of the American Educational Research Association, University of Vienna, San Diego, CA.

Connelly, F. M. (2013). Joseph Schwab, curriculum, curriculum studies and educational reform. *Journal of Curriculum Studies, 45*(5), 622–639.

Connelly, F. M., Fang He, M., & Phillion, J. (Eds.). (2008). *The Sage handbook of curriculum and instruction.* Thousand Oaks, CA: Sage.

Davis, B., Sumara, D., & Luce-Kapler, R. (2008). *Engaging minds: Learning to teach in complex times* (2nd ed.). New York, NY: Routledge.

Dewey, J. (1910). *The influence of John Dewey on philosophy and other essays in contemporary thought.* New York, NY: Henry Holt and Company.

Egan, K. (2003). Retrospective on "what is curriculum?". *Journal of the Canadian Association for Curriculum Studies, 1*(1), 17–24.

Eisner, E. (1982). *Cognition and curriculum: A basis for deciding what to teach.* New York, NY: Longman.

Goodlad, J. I. (1966). *The changing school curriculum.* New York, NY: Fund for the Advancement of Education.

Goodlad, J. I. (1968). Curriculum: A Janus look. *Journal of Curriculum Studies, 1*(1), 34–46.

Hendry, P. M. (2011). *Engendering curriculum history.* New York, NY: Routledge.

Hlebowitsh, P. (1999a). More on "the burdens of the new curricularist. *Curriculum Inquiry, 29*(3), 369–373.

Hlebowitsh, P. (1999b). The burdens of the new curricularist. *Curriculum Inquiry, 29*(3), 343–354.

Hlebowitsh, P. S. (2010). Centripetal thinking in curriculum studies. *Curriculum Inquiry, 40*(4), 503–513.

Hlebowitsh, P. (2012). When best practices aren't: A Schwabian perspective on teaching. *Journal of Curriculum Studies, 44*(1), 1–12.

Hlebowitsh, P. (2014). Big ideas and dissipative effects. *Journal of the Canadian Association for Curriculum Studies, 12*(1), 90–96.

Hlebowitsh, P. S. (2005a). Generational ideas in curriculum: A historical triangulation. *Curriculum Inquiry, 35*(1), 73–87.

Hlebowitsh, P. S. (2005b). More on "generational ideas": A rejoinder to Ian Westbury and Handel Kashope Wright. *Curriculum Inquiry, 35*(1), 119–122.

Hopmann, S. T. (2009). *Out of touch: Theory and evidence in curriculum studies.* Presentation at the European Conference of Educational Research, Vienna, Austria.

Huebner, D. (1999). The tasks of the curricular theorist. In V. Hillis (Ed.), *The lure of the transcendent: Collected essays by Dwayne E. Huebner* (pp. 212–230). Mahwah, NJ: Lawrence Erlbaum Associates Publishers.

Jackson, P. W. (1992a). Conceptions of curriculum and curriculum specialists. In P. Jackson (Ed.), *Handbook of research on curriculum* (pp. 3–40). New York, NY: Macmillan.

Jackson, P. W. (1992b). *Handbook of research on curriculum: A project of the American educational research association.* New York, NY: Macmillan.

Kliebard, H. M. (1968). Curricular objectives and evaluation: A reassessment. *High School Journal, 51,* 241–247.

Kliebard, H. M. (1976). Curriculum past and curriculum present. *Educational Leadership, 33,* 245–248.

Kliebard, H. M. (1982). Curriculum theory as metaphor. *Curriculum Theory,* Winter, 11–17.

Kliebard, H. M. (1995). Why history of education? *The Journal of Educational Research, 88*(4), 194–199.

Lather, P. (1993). Fertile obsession: Validity after poststructuralism. *The Sociological Quarterly, 34*(4), 673–693.

Lather, P. (2004). This is your father's paradigm: Government intrusion and the case of qualitative research in education. *Qualitative Inquiry, 10*(1), 15–34.

Lather, P. (2010). *Engaging science policy: From the side of the messy.* New York, NY: Peter Lang.

Lincoln, Y. S., & Cannella, G. S. (2004). Dangerous discourses: Methodological conservatism and governmental regimes of truth. *Qualitative Inquiry, 10*(1), 5–14.

Maxwell, J. A. (2004). Reemergent scientism, postmodernism, and dialogue across differences. *Qualitative Inquiry, 10*(1), 35–41.

Miller, J. (2016). *Living tensions in curriculum studies: Communities without consensus in transitory times.* New York, NY: Routledge.

Moss, P. A. (2005). Toward "epistemic reflexivity" in educational research: A response to scientific research in education. *Teachers College Record, 107*(1), 19–29.

National Research Council. (2002). *Scientific research in education report.* Washington, DC: National Academy Press.

Ng-A-Fook, N. (2014). Provoking the very "idea" of Canadian curriculum studies as a counterpointed composition. *Journal of the Canadian Association for Curriculum Studies, 12*(1), 10–68.

No Child Left Behind Act. (2002). *Public Law No. 107–10.* United States Federal Education Legislation.

Pacheco, J. A. (2012). Curriculum studies: What is the field today? *Journal of the American Association for the Advancement of Curriculum Studies, 8*(1), 1–18.

Pinar, W. F. (Ed.). (1974). Heightened consciousness, cultural revolution and curriculum theory. In *Proceedings of the Rochester conference.* Berkeley, CA: McCutchan.

Pinar, W. F. (1978). The reconceptualisation of curriculum studies. *Journal of Curriculum Studies, 10*(3), 205–214.

32   T. M. CHRISTOU AND C. DELUCA

Pinar, W. F. (1994). *Autobiography, politics and sexuality.* New York, NY: Peter Lang.

Pinar, W. F. (1999). Not burdens: Breakthroughs. *Curriculum Inquiry, 29*(3), 365–367.

Pinar, W. F. (Ed.). (2003). *International handbook of curriculum research.* Mahwah, NJ: Lawrence Erlbaum.

Pinar, W. F. (2004). *What is curriculum theory?* Mahwah, NJ: Lawrence Erlbaum.

Pinar, W. F. (2008). Introduction. In G. S. Tompkins, *A common countenance: Stability and change in the Canadian curriculum.* Vancouver, BC: Pacific Educational Press.

Pinar, W. F. (2012). *What is curriculum theory?* (2nd ed.). New York, NY: Routledge.

Pinar, W., & Grumet, M. (1976). *Toward a poor curriculum.* Dubuque: Kendall/Hunt.

Pinar, W. F., Reynolds, W. M., Slattery, P., & Taubman, P. M. (1995). *Understanding curriculum: An introduction to the study of historical and contemporary curriculum discourses.* New York, NY: Peter Lang.

Ponder, G. I. (1974). The curriculum: Field without a past? *Educational Leadership, 31*(5), 461–464.

Reid, W. A. (1999). The voice of the practical: Schwab as correspondent. *Journal of Curriculum Studies, 31*(4), 385–399.

Schiro, M. S. (2013). *Curriculum theory: Conflicting visions and enduring concerns* (2nd ed.). Thousand Oaks, CA: Sage.

Schubert, W. H. (1996). *Curriculum: Perspective, paradigm, and possibility.* New York, NY: Macmillan.

Schwab, J. J. (1970). The practical: A language for curriculum. *The School Review, 78*(1), 1–23.

Short, E. C. (Ed.). (1991). *Forms of curriculum inquiry.* Albany, NY: State University of New York Press.

Slattery, P. (2003). Hermeneutics, subjectivity, and aesthetics: Internationalizing the interpretive process in U.S. curriculum research. In W. F. Pinar (Ed.), *International handbook of curriculum research* (pp. 651–666). Mahwah, NJ: Lawrence Erlbaum.

Smith, D. G. (1991). Hermeneutic inquiry: The hermeneutic imagination and the pedagogic text. In E. C. Short (Ed.), *Forms of curriculum inquiry* (pp. 187–209). Albany, NY: State University of New York Press.

Tanner, D., & Tanner, L. N. (1979). Emancipation from research: The reconceptualist prescription. *Educational Researcher, 8,* 8–12.

2 TOWARD A COMPLEX COHERENCE IN THE FIELD ... 33

Taylor, C. (1979). Interpretation and the sciences of man. In P. Rabinow & W. M. Sullivan (Eds.), *Interpretive social science: A reader* (pp. 25–71). Berkeley: University of California Press.

van Manen, M. (1978). Reconceptionalist curriculum thought: A review of recent literature. *Curriculum Inquiry, 8*(4), 365–375.

Wesbury, I. (1999). The burdens and the excitement of the "new" curriculum research: A response to Hlebowitsh's "the burdens of the new curricularist". *Curriculum Inquiry, 29*(3), 355–364.

Wesbury, I. (2005). Reconsidering Schwab's "practicals": A response to Peter Hlebowitsh's "Generational ideas in curriculum: A historical triangulation". *Curriculum Inquiry, 35*(1), 89–101.

Wick, J. W., & Dirkes, C. (1973). Characteristics of current doctoral dissertations in education. *Educational Researcher, 2*, 20–21.

Willinsky, J. (2005). Scientific research in a democratic culture: Or what's a social science for? *Teachers College Record, 107*(1), 38–51.

Wraga, W. G. (1998). 'Interesting, if true': Historical perspectives on the 'reconceptualization' of curriculum studies. *Journal of Curriculum and Supervision, 14*(1), 5–28.

Wraga, W. G. (1999). Extracting sun-beams out of cucumbers: The retreat from practice in reconceptualized curriculum studies. *Educational Researcher, 28*, 4–13.

Wraga, W. W., & Hlebowitsh, P. S. (2003a). Commentary: Conversation, collaboration, and community in the US curriculum field. *Journal of Curriculum Studies, 35*(4), 453–457.

Wraga, W. W., & Hlebowitsh, P. S. (2003b). Toward a renaissance in curriculum theory and development in the USA. *Journal of Curriculum Studies, 35*(4), 425–437.

Wright, H. K. (2005). Does Hlebowitsh improve on curriculum history? Reading a rereading for its political purpose and implications. *Curriculum Inquiry, 35*(1), 103–117.

Young, M. F. D. (2013). Overcoming the crisis in curriculum theory: A knowledge-based approach. *Journal of Curriculum Studies, 45*(2), 101–118.

CHAPTER 3

Making Manifestos in Absentia: Of a World Without Curriculum Theory

Molly Quinn and Niki Christodoulou

What if we lived in a world where there was no curriculum theory—curriculum theory had never been, or was at its end? As we consider the current, and to come, tasks of curriculum theorists (Huebner 1999) internationally, and the compelling makings of manifesto matters therein, we ponder these questions. Here, we take them up: The vital presence/movement of curriculum theory, perhaps, felt and perceived most keenly in contemplating its absence (Chambers 1999). Yet we honor living interpretation—diversity and multiplicity herein: dynamic interpretive communities (Aoki 2004), and the trajectories creatively emerging from them; counterpoint—conjuring presence/movement... Our task demands that we acknowledge, "What makes the desert beautiful...is that it hides a well somewhere" (Antoine de Saint-Exupéry 1941/2015, p. 68), just like questions that wait for us to find, unveil, unfold them,

---

M. Quinn (✉)
Augusta University, Augusta, GA, USA
e-mail: maquinn@augusta.edu

N. Christodoulou
Strovolos, Cyprus
e-mail: n.christodoulou@frederick.ac.cy

© The Author(s) 2019
C. Hébert et al. (eds.), *Internationalizing Curriculum Studies*,
https://doi.org/10.1007/978-3-030-01352-3_3

and take them up. Further, our task requires that we embrace situations that remind us what Antoine de Saint-Exupéry (1950) poetically advised, that is, learning and teaching *to yearn for the vast and endless sea*, rather than gathering, dividing, and ordering men how to build a ship.

Affirming curriculum theory as the interdisciplinary study of educational experience, involving extraordinarily complicated conversation, we do not situate ourselves within one such community, each nested deeply within some, in overlapping—even contradictory—ways, and at the expense of others (Pinar et al. 1995). Rather, dialoguing about the internationalizing work of the curriculum theorist, and way of manifesto-making for curriculum theory therein—what imagining the field's absence reveals; we watch for what emerges between us, in such "cross-fertilizing" conversation. We hope to understand more fully what the work is, should or could be by engaging both our affinities and differences, expanding our own horizons of understanding (Gadamer 1975/2004) and possibility.

We differ—in nationality, culture, language, generation; our curriculum "projects" and orientations. We both, however, studied in the USA, with scholars of the reconceptualist movement (Doll 2012; Schubert 1996). We both embrace the significance of subjectivity—lived experiences, life stories, and their educational meanings: curriculum, in relation to human potential and possibility, self and social reconstruction (Pinar 2012b). We both find ourselves recently together, in the USA in a shared context and place: the deep South, Georgia—land of guns and gardens, southern belles and civil rights. It is the land, too, where the only positions in curriculum theory were to be found. We share our personal search for curriculum theory, both migrating here—"flying South," respectively, from New York City and Nicosia—from a felt sense of "winter," the absence of curriculum theory in our work and world.

In proposing to think through such absence together, and its implications for our loyalties and labors in curriculum, we proceed autobiographically, from historical roots that have nurtured and sustained us. We also conceptualize the work as an affirmative and transformative human project—beseeching radical hope in the face of much human suffering, oppression, and injustice. We examine a world without curriculum theory through its vital thrust—a source of its generativity that if not kept alive, the work would arguably cease to exist: that of theory itself.

CHRISTODOULOU AND CURRICULUM THEORY: OF VAST AND ENDLESS SEAS

"You have reached the Schubertian Center for Curriculum Speculation where we wonder and ponder about curriculum, life, and cosmos. Please leave your message and have a beautiful day and life!" This was the voicemail greeting of my advisor and dissertation committee chair as a doctoral student at the University of Illinois at Chicago (UIC). This greeting, one of my first interactions with what I later came to contemplate as one of the deepest meanings, sources of, and resources for curriculum theory, still echoes in my ears (Christodoulou 2012). Wondering and pondering about life and cosmos, and adding curriculum to this speculation, and herein, ten curriculum questions of worth (Schubert et al. 2002), were something fascinating for me; it grabbed my attention, imagination, and started me thinking about what curriculum is, and might be, and all the possibilities that unfold when we consider it together with bigger ideas.

The ten curriculum questions, in particular, centered around the what's-worthwhile question, allow consideration of, reflection on, and an interpretation of the main questions that characterize inquiry in the curriculum field, point to alternative forms of inquiry and modes of expression as sources of insight about these matters, and offer an understanding of the potential of the many educative forces that constitute the curriculum of life, both here and abroad, as it were.

Before I met my advisor, upon obtaining my bachelor's in preprimary education, I became a kindergarten schoolteacher in my homeland of Cyprus. Having envisioned my work with children to be exciting, rejuvenating, and open up possibilities, instead, I realized that being a kindergarten teacher was practical, technical, and limiting. Theory, theorizing, pondering, and wondering were absent in the conversations with fellow teachers and the broader educational cycles. In search of meaning in education and life, then—some sort of theory and worldview, I needed to continue my studies.

Studying curriculum studies was enlightening. I felt internally alive, a spark toward broadening my perspectives, what and how I knew and understood, and the need to (de)construct ideas and worlds, to question and pose questions. Knowledge and perspectives started falling into place and context, making sense, forming a coherent whole. Such speculations included questions about life, society, school, and curriculum.

Being in an environment that cherished theory, and promoted pondering and wondering through the multitude of readings and conversations, was nurturing, I was able to theorize.

While something I have not contemplated previously, as I delve deeper into my scholarship I realize that a theory of the world cannot be a simple statement. Rather, a theory that allows for many, complex, flexible spaces is needed so that the various, complex, diverse views of, and happenings in our world(s) and universe(s) may fit, be interpreted, and understood (Doll as cited in Pinar 2012a). Like when looking at a forest from far above we only see one, unified field, yet taking a closer look we see many happenings; a theory of our world can only consist of many different theories in order to grasp and understand its complexity—and this especially in our present globalizing, internationally engaged view. Located in diverse *worldly circumstances* (Miller 2005b) and complicated conversations (Pinar 2012b), *curriculum* in the post-reconceptualization era (Malewski 2010a) must depict, represent, and draw from the world, life, cosmos, and the universe. Herein, making an analogy from quantum theory, there is a network of theories "each of which is a good description of observations only in some range of physical situations" (Hawking and Mlodinow 2010, p. 8), rather than a single theory that describes every aspect of the universe.

In such a complex universe(s) and world(s), our theories must acknowledge "the personification of the individual" and ensure "a primacy of the particular" (Pacheco 2012, p. 13). They must also include "self-knowledge that enables understanding of others" (Pinar 2009, p. 7), as we strive for meaning. Meaning, and making sense of our world, is created through a process ignited from our capacity to conceptualize our autobiography and share it with others who strive for similar understanding (Miller 2005b). Our theories, then, involve spaces wherein we explore our autobiographies, often through the biographies of others. The concepts of subjectivity, embodiment, curriculum as an inward journey, the study of internal experiences (Pinar 2012b), and their interconnectedness (Slattery 2006) are important as we delve into autobiographical and phenomenological explorations; together with language and narrative, they are to be understood as sources of meaning-making. Narrative is part of how people understand the world they live in and a way of communicating that understanding to others (Bruner 1986). Language, particularly contested language, must be viewed with a particular focus on memory, subjectivity, plurality of voices, and language terminology usage (Christodoulou 2015). In all these, interpreting lived experiences "invokes questions of the good life for individuals and matters of justice in pursuing life together" (Schubert 1996, p. 169).

My doctoral dissertation focused on uncovering teachers' lives and teaching theories as they were pondering about life events, personal experiences, and teaching through the arts they had encountered. Being in academia, back in Cyprus, it became apparent to me that teacher theorizing—what I spent time examining—and theory in general did not really matter, even in teacher preparation departments. In many such places, vision and theory were and are still absent. Sadly, not everyone understands completely, if at all, curriculum theory and theorizing; *yearning for the vast and endless sea*—a quote that had prime location on Bill Schubert's office door—is often irrelevant. Further, instead of having vibrant and alive collaborations, and promoting theory and ideas to guide practice, future educators received only fragmented, technical information about the separate subject matters they would teach. The theory, or the many theories that connect ideas into a coherent whole were, still are, often absent.

How can we not have a theory? A theory that unifies everything? How would cosmos, life, and education be without curriculum theory? A bunch of disconnected subject matters and ideas that we try to implement in education, without a coherent background vision and philosophy? There are two issues to consider here. First, the importance of procedures and the underlying theories and assumptions should not go unobserved, since to understand something at the deepest level, "we need to know not only *how* [it] behaves, but *why*" (Hawking and Mlodinow 2010, p. 9). It really is this combination of *how* and *why* that allows us to observe a procedure and then theorize and ponder possibilities. Second, everything is really not one theory and does not have one history or path, but many. Multiple theories may grasp the range of possible paths from their source to the current moment of observation to the possible futures they may form. Here, I connect curriculum theory with "alternative histories" in quantum theory, which is the idea that because the universe has no single past, or history, the way observations are made in the present allows for different interpretations of the past. As curriculum is an active force of human educational experience (Pinar 2012b), our theories must acknowledge the wide range of experiences, interpretations, and possibilities in our lives. This shall be helpful in gaining understandings and meanings toward better lives, and together in a diverse multinational world.

In curriculum studies, I came across many theories that allowed pondering on the importance of studying the wide range of people's experiences, including teachers' wisdom (Schubert and Ayers 1991), intertextuality and the transactional nature of our experiences (Varelas et al. 2005), the ideas of breaking our silences (Miller 2005a), and (un) muting the voice of the non-Western others (Spivak 1988). Narrative inquiry, phenomenology, hermeneutics, and critical theory were some of the traditions used to depict the range of such experiences. Together with these, inquiry and research enhance thinking and practice in curriculum, education, and our lives (Connelly et al. 2008).

For curriculum theory to keep informing our thoughts and practices relevant to experience and education in a variety of differing cultural and national contexts, it must have a method and rigor. Here, I consider three methods to be of profound influence in the field: reflection (Dewey 1933; Doll cited in Pinar 2012a), *currere* (Pinar 2012b), and psychoanalysis (Chodorow 1999). *Currere* is a method of autobiographical reflection, while psychoanalysis puts emphasis on the analytic encounter. *Currere* is rooted in psychoanalysis as evidenced in its regressive, progressive, analytical, and synthetical moments. These methods engage the construct of experience, and the way we observe and understand it. Both Dewey and Doll, who embraced science and scientific experimentation, emphasized the importance of method and rigor in examining experience (Pinar 2012a). For them, reflective method was a "rigorous way of '*experimenting with directing personal experience*,'" one of *transformation*, neither *transmission* nor imposition, "marked by an '*elusive* process of jumping from one stage or level to the next'" (Pinar 2012a, p. 2). Because "educational experience requires 'reflective thinking,' it is both *open* and *directed*" (p. 2). Herein, the interactive and dynamic character of the educational process is highlighted. In many ways, the methods of reflection, *currere,* and psychoanalysis embrace postmodernism, transactionalism, interactionism, chaos, and complexity theories (Doll 2012) and recognize the continuity of time in our paths and the importance of history. Time and history, in the synthetical moment of *currere*, are understood as "the confluence of past, present, and future" (Slattery 2006, p. 64).

Embracing theories about continuity, alternative histories, possible paths, experiences, the individuality of each and the interdependence of all, and the existence of everything in some balance and universe despite their complexity, helps me understand the task of curriculum theory and its internationalizing. Our stories and experiences are the molecules that make up people's lives and understandings. In seeking a more just world, then, every story and voice must be illuminated. In my scholarship on oral history and the way language terminology is used, I often discuss the educational significance of personal stories, as they uncover pathways, thoughts, actions, and potential contributions to our world. I also discuss how shifts in language terminology, memory, testimonies, and oral history can be reframed as curriculum questions, in order to explore possibilities that a rich, authentic, and subjective language can offer (Christodoulou 2014, 2015). Herein, theory becomes a method of reflection, envisioning, and speculating and allows for choices that rest logically upon premises (Ladd and Brubacher 1956). As we continue to consider the set of criteria for curriculum theory articulated by Walker (1990), namely *validity*, *serviceability*, *power*, and *morality*—i.e., how ideas are defined and presented, theory assists practice and is applicable in real-life problems, and judgments are delivered based on acceptable values—we should also consider three other criteria: *multiplicity*, inclusive of diverse (auto)biographies, alternative histories, narratives, and the ways they contradict or complement each other; *complexity*, inclusive of issues, dimensions, struggles, challenges, and successes in a sociopolitical-cultural sphere; and *flexibility*, inclusive of emergent meanings and spaces for the idiosyncratic. These manifest the manifold heights and breadths of curriculum theory.

Quinn and Curriculum Theory: Of Hidden Wells in the Dessert

Is a world of curriculum theory, and its internationalizing, without theory even possible? Heidegger (1954/1977) illumines the living contours of theory, and its deformation/demise via science from the modern age. If science is "the theory of the real" (p. 163), what is theory? His study offers us a way to rethink the place of theory in curriculum theory too. Theory emerges from *theōrein* and *theoria*, uniting *thea* and *hōrao*: Thea (*theater*)—the look that is outward, wherein something shows itself; *Hōrao*—to view attentively, to look over closely. "Thus, it follows that *theōrein* is *thean horan*, to look at attentively on the outward appearance wherein what presences becomes visible and, through such sight—seeing—to linger with it" (p. 163). Pinar's (2012b) focus on experience, study, and understanding in defining curriculum theory seems to resonate with such etymological insinuations.

"For, *theoria* is pure relationship to the outward appearances belonging to whatever presences, … that, in their radiance, concern man [sic] in that they bring the presence … of the gods to shine forth" (Heidegger 1954/1977, p. 164). *Theá*: 'goddess.' *Aleitheia*—or truth, *a-leitheia*, not hidden, out of hiding—reveals herself; *órá*: respect. "[T]hen *theōria* is the reverent paying heed to the unconcealment of what presences" (p. 164); "the *beholding that watches over truth*" (p. 165, italics in original). James MacDonald's portrayal (1995) of curriculum theorizing as a prayerful act, involving faith and a "humanistic vision" of life, bears this legacy—theory, wherein we see/think/know, unveil the spirit/truth/reality, here, of curriculum, shining through particular manifestations or imaginings thereof—openings to its not yet, to come, might be, and our relationships to such. Here, we must be present, too, to the "internationalizing" of internationalizing.

"I think, therefore I am … NOT a curriculum theorist," said my department chair to me as a doctoral student at Louisiana State University (LSU) one day. While he was making a play on Descartes's famous assertion, such a sentiment is expressed by many in education—theory ever in contested tension with practice, education deemed primarily field-based, more than scholarly. In the USA, such is pronounced, given a penchant for can-do action and pragmatic necessity—anti-intellectual proclivity as in kinship with anti-elitism. Still, theory's absence was not truly felt by me as a student during what some have described as theory's "Golden Age" at LSU. I had suffered through undergraduate study in elementary education, and later teaching, in a world where theory, if attended at all, was somehow its opposite—the mere receipt of what you needed to know to explain the recipe by which you methodologically conducted curriculum through a given technique. "*Just say 'no' to bows*," Southern Belle motto of the day—my desire to think, question, study, dream, was dismissed as "impractical."

Working in a religious community, I was able to pursue study, of a sort—entertaining questions of ultimacy, examining Greek/Hebrew etymologies—but genuine questioning was deemed dangerous: Theory had a capital "T" within this closed, fixed, unitary frame; the meta-narrative of truth never to be challenged, rethought. Whether in the name of theory or through its totalization, depreciation, or confinement to application, theory was absent: neither living nor alive. What a breath of fresh air was curriculum theory to me then, of the spirit rather than the letter—my fundamentalist frame having fractured, faltered, and fallen—and practical too! I was given a new language—new methods, questions, and possibilities—for understanding the curriculum of my own life, its educational significance: I could address the existential questions and crises of meaning besetting me, and the modern world (Quinn 2001)—heightened, too, by accelerating international and globalizing forces.

Dewey (1922/1964a, b) illuminated for me my own "cabined and cramped" experience in a spiritual community diminished by "pathologies of goodness"—freedom, thought, closed off by compulsions to carry out the will of others, or some project set out in advance of living. And I learned of another fundamentalism in the world of education, felt in my undergraduate studies—the colonizing positivism, instrumentalism, techno-rationalism, compelling the curriculum field (e.g., Doll 1993), and well beyond US borders. Here, such was interrogated within a space *for* theory, where theory breathed and flowed: of open dialogue, difference, and community (Miller 1990). Herein were entertained: inquiry, adventure, and imagination. Beholding and asking ever anew—all present, living waters, theory lived.

Then, a professor in New York, theory's waning was felt. Working in teacher education ought to present a dynamic tension through which to creatively engage theory and practice, academy and profession, and their relations (Aoki 2004). Yet, theorizing takes time and commitment, and where deemed irrelevant or extravagant, where one is compelled to contend with ever-increasing "practical" demands, the tension can all too easily turn to antagonism—theory thwarted therein or redirected simply to its useful implication. Everything measured by a "New York minute," there was no time for lingering. The history of our field suggests a perpetual vulnerability to this threat, theory ever turned into but a tool for a reckoning up of the "real" in *objectness* in order to explain, predict, order, control: Only what can be measured is real (Heidegger 1954/1977). In an international scene of global competition and capitalism, accelerating acceleration, perhaps too, only money is real, measured—the measure. The field also, born formally at the turn of the twentieth century, in kinship with psychology, has abiding affinities for this measuring credibility and mode of "beholding": eschewing or disregarding the messiness, irreplaceability, unanswerability, of human life, of our educational lives together; quick, fast sprints toward 'profitable' or productive development often valued over slow, long efforts at understanding. Is curriculum theory itself an oxymoron—in curriculum, we are asked to run, map out, and take to the course as a race, while theory asks us to attend, to behold, to tarry, to linger?

My own de-theorizing experiences—amid impact and accountability measures, certification and accreditation audits, tenure and promotion politics—are all too familiar. Taubman (2009) describes these neoliberal forces at work, involving the political control (positioned as objective, unbiased research) of education through alliances of government, business, and learning science by which teaching is turned to testing, the "gracious submission" of educators to evidence-based edicts, in the context of unflagging "educational deform" (Pinar 2012b) indelibly tied to economics and power on the global scene. Theory relegated to its shadow, my work would feel mostly in the service of legitimation: theory related to some prescribed, required standard; to demonstrate its relevance to or influence on practice. How we talk about education has even changed—a more corporate, business-minded, and outcomes-based language shapes our work and frames our theoretical efforts (Taubman 2009). Huebner (1999) called for our attention to language, its power—reflecting and shaping our imaginations, purposes, practices, and resources in education: Is the language of curriculum even our own? Embracing our many languages, the silenced and subjugated? Such reflects the "hostile *topos*" (Chambers 1999) in which curriculum theorists conceptualize/engage their work today (Ibrahim 2005; Quinn 2010).

I found theory undermined in the academy or perpetuated as a singular notion of instrumental intention or legitimizing practice. Even of social justice, subjecting theory *solely* to emancipatory/ameliorative aims deemed requisite for *all* theory is another "pathology of goodness"; constraining freedom of will, thought, imagination, through a predetermined project or meaning, perhaps as much as empiricist aims at observation for prediction and intervention (Pinar 2010); and may not serve justice at all. Despite the temptation, and need to defend theory, I am a little wary, then, of the very making of manifestos—even as we toy with such here, and in relation to the field's internationalization, unless the principles embraced constitute a play-forum rather than platform—approach "consonance" rather than consensus, a harmonizing and humanizing vision of many-colored chords (Block 2010) in affirming things like: difference, dialogue, and dynamism; inquiry, engagement, and emergence; generativity, generosity, and hospitality; *currere*, conversation, and complexity—critical to the making of genuine community and solidarity, particularly in the way of internationalizing such.

Should we traverse and visit the curricular terrain of others, we might well experience this larger *topos* as less desert-parched hostile and find for our own theorizing places more quenching waters and open-air breezes—and yearn, even hope, afresh before the deep and vast and endless. And theory itself cannot be kept alive without humble attention to the frame(s) by which we theorize and openness to engage—inter-, cross-, trans-, multinational(izing) understandings and exchanges. It is this, only to be attended in this kind of reverent—and sometimes irreverent—beholding before that which presences: the theoretical spirit itself, to which I would submit we must ever attend, and the relation of our own "letters of the law" discourses and traditions to such.

I may have returned too much to the past in an intergenerational (more than international?) contemplation of the world of curriculum theory—the presence and absence of theory therein. Yet, such historical tasks may illumine for us what is in fact indigenous to our own field (Pinar et al. 1995), well-water sources reflecting Chambers' (1999) "who are we" as related to "where is here" and "who has come before"; the places from which we speak here and now, if even as unawares or *in absentia*. Many of my own tasks of late have involved the works of my mentors—Noddings, Greene, Blumenfeld-Jones, and Doll—by which I have gleaned wisdom, remembered and renewed a love of theory—manifold theories, and realized that they speak powerfully to our present and future as to our past, and particularly regarding an internationalizing scene.

Theory here to be embraced is neither aggrandizing nor universalizing, neither singular nor complete—in fact, its incompletion is a source of hope; it is this yearning for and discovery of pure relationship to that which is before us, is other, in its presencing—vast and deep, with a stance of attentiveness, openness, even reverence, through which new truths are revealed. It is "a fascinating imaginative realm, born of the echo of God's laughter where no one owns the truth and everyone has a right to be understood" (Kundera, cited in Doll 2012, p. 231). Such theory is living, embodied, subjectively experienced, discursively and contextually engaged. It speaks meaningfully to particularity and place, generating questions from such, and yet also brings to "unconcealment"

46 M. QUINN AND N. CHRISTODOULOU

the realization that: earth, sky, wellspring, sea, "all the world is you and me ... Hope and peace and love and trust, all the world is all of us" (Scanlon 2009, n.p.), before which we each, and together, are responsible.

IN PRESENTIA: OF A WORLD WITH CURRICULUM THEORY

Spring is announcing its arrival in Augusta, Georgia, and a world of sweet garden green and vibrant flower bursts forth for visitors soon to the Masters, a sport of international attendance. Our own lives have taken on a new rhythm, as we sway on porch swings and sit in porch rockers, talking and taking in the dusk evening light—cocktails and conversations, our task. We walk down the red road along the canal as it meets up with the Savannah River, the sun already high and hot and penetrating, neither sand nor sea here in our view. We wonder why and how the offer of theory was made to us here, and we—as international companions—have been able to revive and rebuild in some way a world of curriculum theory for ourselves, one where—deep and wide—theory is here and thrives, or at least the dream and hope of it anew.

Much has been written about southern place (Casemore 2008; Pinar and Kincheloe 1991), and there is no singular, unitary South; for now, for us, it is perhaps the propensity here for *lingering* that has helped us imagine, experience, feel, this presence again. This way of being might have something to do with its "other," indirect way of knowing, of alterity, rooted in a history of oppression, and the creative resistance and response of its subjugated peoples. Influenced by its black heritage, it may be that an African epistemology dwells more deeply here, which Watkins (1993) aptly described: moving in circles, not preoccupied with verification, but rather seeking interpretation, meaning, and expression. Relocating may have enabled us to open up again to the new, a vast and endless view—(re-rooting, re-routing) tapping the wells of our capacity to begin again.

There is much that lingers here, too, one wishes wouldn't—e.g., normalizing and marginalizing frames of intelligibility involving race, gender, religion, class, and sexuality; global wrongs, to be sure, yet viscerally local and lived. Debates about confederate flags and civil war memorials raged last year, and despite so many school shootings, the Georgia legislature passed House Bill 859, which if signed by the governor would make it legal for weapons carry license holders to bring guns to public-owned facilities.

The growing influence of globalization appears too, with its complex and contradictory markings amid the "accelerating acceleration" (Hansen 2008) of human communications, migrations, dislocations, encounters, and conflicts—standardizing, diversifying, homogenizing, hybridizing; alienating, energizing, dominating, democratizing; also deeply felt, as pressure and possibility. Enormous change is anticipated with Cyber Command/Security coming to Fort Gordon. From our contemporary scene, how to make for and sustain a soil in which theory can grow? Support a sector for theory (Pinar et al. 1995) for its further development and maturation, not simply proliferation (Malewski 2010b)? Here, where we are, and there, where each of us who are taken to task as curriculum theorists is? And in complex conversations, internationalizing across, between, among, all our many places? Robinson (2001/2011) describes the time in which we are living as a social and economic revolution of unprecedented proportion and speed, wherein new technologies are rapidly transforming the way we communicate and work, our world and way of being in it. He also finds our education systems to be direly out of step, yet crucial for the realization of creative potential and cultivation of a culture of creativity this new context requires.

This global scene has made it possible for us (Molly and Niki) to be together, engaging our disparate and shared worlds, in this place. In reimagining the tasks of curriculum theory, and its internationalizing, this attention to promoting creativity within and among us may hold much promise, remembering that to foster cultures which nourish such is integral to such. Affirmed would be space for speculation and wild imagining, suspension of hierarchy or judgment in giving way to openness of inquiry, and irreverent play from which surprise and new understandings are born; for each to find the best mediums/methods for fulfilling one's creative potential, creativity constitutive of all human intelligence and activity. Relationships between and among differences, rather than the differences themselves, take on new import: e.g., challenging existing boundaries and divisions, bringing together thought and feeling, combining critique and creativity, crossing disciplinary lines, conversing across contexts and communities.

To such tasks—in addition to our own theorizing work in a world of such injustice, suffering, and sadness, yet also of much beauty, wisdom, and joy, we add our laboring together. In our Ed.D. program in educational innovation, we collaborate with others in leadership, technology, and medicine and give students opportunities to listen to their own voices, and myriad "others." As "meaning and interpretation are at the heart of all creative processes", experiences and our stories of them continue to matter deeply to us (Robinson 2001/2011, p. 153). We have also begun an oral history project here, illuminating marginalized stories and counter-narratives concerning race and education, for example; uncovering curriculum source and substance for theorizing from the place, we now inhabit—which reflect, too, Huebner's (1999) emphasis on the import of history, environment, and criticism.

Malewski (2010b), of the field, challenged the claim that we have reached the end of theory, despite shifting epistemological circumstances—citing Butler to assert there is no "'livable' life for the individual or public without theorizing such existences" (p. 7). Sometimes, such uncovers difficult knowledge (Britzman 2000) and disputed understandings. Such is always a work of "radical hope," of attuning ourselves to "the goodness of the world (that) transcends [our] limited and vulnerable attempts to understand it" (Lear 2006, p. 104). Perhaps theory itself requires this radical hope? In embracing this art of attending, 'inconvenient' truths are uncovered, felt too are the sufferings of oppression or injustice—in such, we must hope that the examination of, watching over, life can lead us to more worthwhile living, to mindfully seek "a happier life for all" (Schubert 1996). We trust, too, that such work strengthens our capacity for transformation, transcendence, loving response—that which makes wisdom, happiness, and human kindness possible.

REFERENCES

Aoki, T. T. (2004). *Curriculum in a new key: The collected works of Ted T. Aoki.* New York: Routledge.

Block, A. (2010). And they'll say it's a movement. In E. Malewski (Ed.), *A curriculum handbook: The next moment* (pp. 523–527). New York: Routledge.

Britzman, D. P. (2000). If the story cannot end: Deferred action, ambivalence, and difficult knowledge. In S. Rosenberg & C. Eppert Rog (Eds.), *Between hope and despair: Pedagogy and the remembrance of historical trauma.* Lanham, MD: Rowman & Littlefield.

Bruner, J. (1986). *Actual minds possible worlds.* Cambridge, MA: Harvard University Press.

Casemore, B. (2008). *The autobiographical demand of place: Curriculum inquiry in the American South* (Vol. 21). New York: Peter Lang.

3 MAKING MANIFESTOS IN ABSENTIA ... 49

Chambers, C. (1999). A topography for Canadian curriculum theory. *Canadian Journal of Education/Revue canadienne de l'éducation, 24*, 137–150.

Chodorow, N. J. (1999). *The power of feelings: Personal meaning in psychoanalysis, gender, and culture.* New Haven, CT: Yale University Press.

Christodoulou, N. (2012). A place full of wisdom and inspiration. In R. L. S. Harper (Ed.), *3010: Presented to William H. Schubert.* Chicago.

Christodoulou, N. (2014). Oral history and living memory in Cyprus: Performance and curricular considerations. *Transnational Curriculum Inquiry, 11*(1), 30–43. http://ojs.library.ubc.ca/index.php/tci.

Christodoulou, N. (2015). Contested language, memory, and oral history as curriculum questions: A tale from Cyprus. *European Journal of Curriculum Studies, 2*(2), 324–345. http://pages.ie.uminho.pt/ejcs/index.php/ejcs/article/view/95.

Connelly, F. M., He, M. F., & Phillion, J. (Eds.). (2008). *The Sage handbook of curriculum and instruction.* Thousand Oaks, CA: Sage.

Dewey, J. (1964a). Human nature and conduct. In R. Archambault (Ed.), *John Dewey on education* (pp. 61–69). Chicago, IL: University of Chicago Press (original work published 1922).

Dewey, J. (1964b). What is freedom? In R. Archambault (Ed.), *John Dewey on education* (pp. 81–88). Chicago, IL: University of Chicago Press (original work published 1922).

Dewey, J. (1933). *How we think.* New York: D. C. Heath.

Doll, W. (1993). *A post-modern perspective on curriculum.* New York: Teachers College Press.

Doll, W. (2012). *Pragmatism, post-modernism, and complexity theory: The "fascinating imaginative realm" of William E. Doll, Jr.* New York: Routledge.

Gadamer, H. G. (2004). *Truth and method* (J. Weinsheimer & D. G. Marshall, Trans.). London: Continuum International Publishing Group (original work published 1975).

Hansen, D. (2008). Curriculum and the idea of a cosmopolitan inheritance. *Journal of Curriculum Studies, 40*(3), 289–312.

Hawking, S., & Mlodinow, L. (2010). *The grand design.* New York: Bantam Books.

Heidegger, M. (1977). *The question concerning technology* (W. Lovitt, Trans.). New York: Harper and Row (original work published 1954).

Huebner, D. E. (1999). *The lure of the transcendent: Collected essays by Dwayne E. Huebner.* Mahwah, NJ: Lawrence Erlbaum.

Ibrahim, A. (2005). The question of the question is the foreigner: Towards an economy of hospitality. *Journal of Curriculum Theorizing, 4*(21), 149–162.

Ladd, E. T., & Brubacher, J. S. (1956, July 2). *Philosophical foundations of the curriculum: A report prepared at the request of the Secretariat of Unesco.*

Paris: International Advisory Committee on the School Curriculum, United Nations Educational, Scientific and Cultural Organization (UNESCO).

Lear, J. (2006). *Radical hope: Ethics in the face of cultural devastation.* Cambridge, MA and London: Harvard University Press.

MacDonald, J. (1995). *Theory as a prayerful act: The collected essays of James B. MacDonald.* New York: Peter Lang.

Malewski, E. (2010a). A way of knowing in the future of curriculum studies. In E. Malewski (Ed.), *Curriculum studies handbook: The next moment* (pp. 534–539). New York: Routledge.

Malewski, E. (2010b). Introduction: Proliferating curriculum. In E. Malewski (Ed.), *A curriculum handbook: The next moment* (pp. 1–39). New York: Routledge.

Miller, J. (1990). *Creating spaces and finding voices: Teachers collaborating for empowerment.* Albany, NY: SUNY Press.

Miller, J. (2005a). *Sounds of silence breaking: Women, autobiography, curriculum.* New York: Peter Lang.

Miller, J. (2005b). The American curriculum field and its worldly encounters. *Journal of Curriculum Theorizing, 21*(2), 9–24.

Pacheco, J. A. (2012). Curriculum studies: What is the field today? *Journal of the American Association for the Advancement of Curriculum Studies, 8,* 1–25.

Pinar, W. F. (2009). *The worldliness of a cosmopolitan education: Passionate lives in public service.* New York: Routledge.

Pinar, W. F. (2010). The next moment. In E. Malewski (Ed.), *A curriculum handbook: The next moment* (pp. 528–533). New York: Routledge.

Pinar, W. F. (2012a). Introduction. In D. Trueit (Ed.), *Pragmatism, postmodernism and complexity theory: The "fascinating imaginative realm" of William E. Doll, Jr.* (pp. 1–10). New York: Routledge.

Pinar, W. F. (2012b). *What is curriculum theory?* (2nd ed.). Mahwah, NJ: Lawrence Erlbaum (original published 2004, 1st ed.).

Pinar, W. F., Reynolds, W. M., Slattery, P., & Taubman, P. M. (1995). *Understanding curriculum: An introduction to the study of historical and contemporary curriculum discourses.* New York: Peter Lang.

Pinar, W., & Kincheloe, J. (1991). *Curriculum as social psychoanalysis: The significance of place.* New York: SUNY Press.

Quinn, M. (2001). *Going out, not knowing whither: Education, the upward journey and the faith of reason.* New York: Peter Lang.

Quinn, M. (2010). 'No room in the inn'? The question of hospitality in the post(partum)-labors of curriculum studies. In E. Malewski (Ed.), *A curriculum handbook: The next moment* (pp. 101–117). New York: Routledge.

Robinson, K., Sir. (2011). *Out of our minds: Learning to be creative.* West Sussex, UK: Capstone Publishing (original work published 2001).

Saint-Exupéry, A. de. (1950). *The wisdom of the sands* (S. Gilbert, Trans.). New York: Harcourt, Brace and Company (English translation of the French *Citadelle*).

Saint-Exupéry, A. de. (2015). *The little prince* (R. Howard, Trans.). New York: Houghton Mifflin Harcourt (original work published 1941).

Scanlon, L. (2009). *All the world*. New York: Beach Lane Books.

Schubert, W. H. (1996). Perspectives on four curriculum traditions. *Educational Horizons, 74*, 169–176.

Schubert, W. H., & Ayers, W. C. (1991). *Teacher lore: Learning from our own experience*. White Plains, NY: Longman.

Schubert, W. H., Lopez-Schubert, A. L., Thomas, T. P., & Carroll, W. M. (2002). *Curriculum books: The first hundred years* (2nd ed.). New York: Peter Lang.

Slattery, P. (2006). *Curriculum development in the postmodern era: Teaching and learning in an age of accountability* (2nd ed.). New York: Routledge.

Spivak, G. (1988). Can the subaltern speak? In C. Nelson & L. Grossberg (Eds.), *Marxism and the interpretation of culture* (pp. 271–313). Champaign: University of Illinois Press.

Taubman, P. (2009). *Teaching by numbers: Deconstructing the discourse of standards and accountability in education*. New York: Routledge.

Varelas, M., Pappas, C. C., & Rife, A. (2005). Dialogic inquiry in an urban second-grade classroom: How intertextuality shapes and is shaped by social interactions and scientific understandings. In R. Yerrick & W.-M. Roth (Eds.), *Establishing scientific classroom discourse communities: Multiple voices of teaching and learning research*. Mahwah, NJ: Lawrence Erlbaum Associates.

Walker, D. (1990). *Fundamentals of curriculum*. New York: Harcourt Brace Jovanovich.

Watkins, W. (1993). Black curriculum orientations: A preliminary inquiry. *Harvard Educational Review, 63*(3), 321–338.

CHAPTER 4

Curriculum Theory in Brazil: A Path in the Mists of the Twenty-First Century

Antonio Flávio Barbosa Moreira and Rosane Karl Ramos

INTRODUCTION

Globalization different meanings for different people around the world, especially to those who have access to some kind of material goods that connect them virtually. This idea may even be considered as part of a generalized common sense, and in terms of its benefits and drawbacks, definitions, effects, uses, and habits within it that allow (or do not, if we think in those who are excluded from the process of globalization for different reasons worldwide) the person to feel part of an interconnected and dynamic, ever-changing world. García Canglini (2007) wrote that "the kinds of knowledge available on globalization constitute a series of *narratives*" (p. 43), that are in turn, constructed in relation to a multiplicity of contexts, agents, and factors.

A. F. B. Moreira
Federal University of Rio de Janeiro, Rio de Janeiro, Brazil

A. F. B. Moreira
Catholic University of Petrópolis, Rio de Janeiro, Brazil

R. K. Ramos (✉)
Pontifical Catholic University, Rio de Janeiro, Brazil

© The Author(s) 2019
C. Hébert et al. (eds.), *Internationalizing Curriculum Studies*,
https://doi.org/10.1007/978-3-030-01352-3_4

We can trace processes of globalization far back in time. First in economic relationships, and gradually reaching other areas of human practices. However, the expansion of capitalism in the last century made way for the idea of globalization in a more comprehensive scope, which surpassed the economic realm and now influences other aspects of societies, like the social, political, cultural, and educational fields. It aims at global standards of behavior, economy, culture, and politics, and although it acknowledges the differences among the countries, it searches for common regulations and standards to all—it is majestic in its scope and desires.

Internationalization, on the other hand, is a conceptual segment of globalization. It is a less comprehensive concept, since it does not necessarily involve the idea of the global, but rather it may concern the relations between two countries, for instance. It presupposes the strength (and not the dilution) of each nation-state, the interchanges and exchanges among them, and, also the existence of borders, whether they are geographical or symbolic. It unfolds itself in different processes, like the internationalization of culture, higher education, and curriculum. Internationalization does not have the aspirations of homogeneity or of the establishment of certain patterns and standards strictly speaking. Nevertheless, in the process of internationalization there is acknowledgment of asymmetrical relationships among the various nation-states as far as hegemonic and/or (still) colonial relations and powers are concerned. There is a search for interculturality and dialogue to a certain extent, which is not always visible in terms of conceptualizations of globalization. Besides, the importance of the local is paramount, since it is from local standpoints that the "complicated conversation" with the Other (not local) is made possible (Pinar 2003).

In regard to curriculum studies, internationalization involves different important current issues that must be considered, like the new educational configurations in education (Knight 2004, 2014), the expanding educational market ruled by rankings and by international business corporations and agencies around the world (Ball and Junemann 2011), and also the consumerist turn in higher education (Naidoo et al. 2011). However, what seems to be not fully considered in all of these scenarios is the fact that curriculum is a collective *constructo*, which also takes into account all the subjectivities, personal experiences, local contexts, bodies, dreams, and desires of the agents involved in the process. Curriculum should not determine a set of rules to be followed, like in a prescription, but should be created in consonance with the variety of factors and, most of all, applied to a similarly large variety of actors.

Bearing these ideas in mind, we present in this chapter a gathering of different voices that think and discuss the history of curriculum making in Brazil. Moreover, our chapter seeks to decipher our way through the epistemological mists in which we find ourselves in this twenty-first century. We assume the commitment of the editors of this volume to the full: Make our contribution a dialogic space and a tapestry where our discursive exchanges may occur. This chapter intends to defend a place that has been under construction for quite a while. It does not intend to be a mere apologia for the field per se. It does intend, though, to come in defense of the place for an idea, and the idea is that there are in curriculum theory counter-hegemonic discourses and actions involving the internationalization process in education that should be brought to further debate, so as to live up to the whole political nature involved in such an issue.

This chapter has three sections. In the first, we present a brief history of the educational transfer process that we had in Brazil, moving to the current perspective of educational mobility that seems to best suit the internationalization of curriculum. In the second, based on data gathered from a previous research conducted by one of the authors, we present and discuss three views on the internationalization of curriculum. Finally, in our conclusions, we suggest that the internationalization of curriculum should ask for a critical understanding of the local in the context of the global and vice versa, and also for a critical perspective on the relevance of local contents and practices alongside—and not to the detriment of—global ones.

From Transfer to Mobility

The interest in this theme goes back to a research carried out more than twenty years ago, in which one of the authors analyzed the emergence or the curriculum field in Brazil from the 1920s to the late 1980s under heavy North American influence (Moreira 1997). Conceiving the process of *educational transfer* as the movement of ideas, institutional models and practices from one country to another (Ragatt 1983), the author argued that, in the first stages of this process—from the 1920s to the late 1970s of last century—what occurred in Brazil was predominantly an instrumental adaptation of the North American curricular discourse, in an attempt to provide local colors to the transferred material and to best suit it to our reality.

During the ensuing decades, when there were significant changes in politics, economics, and culture, both at national and international levels, a critical adaptation of the received materials from different countries was promoted with the intention to create a more autonomous development in curriculum field. Moreira (1997) maintained then that the reception of foreign material involved exchanges, readings, confrontation, and resistance, with varying levels of intensity and subversive potential according to local and international circumstances:

> There is not a mechanical transport of knowledge from one country to another. Between transfer and reception, there are mediating processes (among which the dynamics and the specificities of the receptive context, as well as the agents' will and practices involved in the transfer) that affect the way in which determined theory or foreign practice is received, propagated and applied.[1] (p. 206)

The category educational transfer was, then, reconceptualized by Moreira (1997) as overcoming simplified models that reduced the phenomenon to a mere instrument of control and domination to be used by developed countries[2] and to be easily imposed on and received by the developing countries. On that occasion, Moreira (1997) also proposed an alternative focus constituted by three elements.

The first element corresponded to the international context, which proved itself to be indispensable to the understanding of foreign influence in the Brazilian education in general, and to the curriculum field in particular. The second element covered the Brazilian socioeconomical and political contexts, always having in mind that educational decisions and activities are never isolated from economic, political, and ideological struggles that take place in society. The last element—the process context—involved institutional and interactional aspects. The latter was paramount to understand how the development in the field has been affected by institutions, curricular proposals, meetings, discussions, conflicts, and alliances among researchers.

---

[1] All the translations from Portuguese have been made by the authors.

[2] Although we are aware of the studies on post-colonial theories that question the use of binary terms like Developed and Non-developed countries, First and Third Worlds, Central and Peripheral Countries, we have decided to maintain such terms on the basis of the socio-economic, political, and cultural aspects in which they were historically created.

In the text subsequent to the research carried out with the support of *Conselho Nacional de Desenvolvimento Científico e Tecnológico (CNPq/Brasil)* in 1994 (Moreira and Macedo 2006), Moreira suggested that the contradictory and complex character of our contemporary societies in this globalized world does not allow for a view of educational transfer based merely on the transmission and reception of cultural contents produced in the industrialized West. Analyses of the process of globalization completed on that occasion highlighted the intense movement of information and knowledge facilitated by unprecedented technological advancements that were and still are taking place, albeit unevenly among the different parts of the world. Although there is the possibility (and eventual purposes) of cultural homogenization, there is also evidence of clear tension in an extremely complex process. Moreira and Macedo (2006) explain:

> At the same time that the benefits from the wide mobilization of all kinds of scientific knowledge are spread, the risks arising from translations and pasteurized interpretations made by a globalized media are delineated, in which the transmitted images of the reality and the world views are the ones that benefit the powerful social groups. Thus, different ways of knowledge, life styles and world views face themselves, discord within themselves, confront themselves, subordinate one another, renew themselves. If the process may cause homogenization, invasion, destruction of cultural manifestations, it may also, on the other hand, stimulate a critical appropriation of ideas and theories formulated by the "other." (pp. 18–19)

Taking up this perspective, Moreira and Macedo (2006) questioned the possibility of ideas and cultural manifestations in a pure state, not contaminated by others, liable to be translated from a place into another. It might be considered that the concept of educational transfer, such as it was used in the 1980s, should be reworked so as to be useful to analyze the multiple and intense changes that happen today. Moreira and Macedo (2006) proposed, then, that the categories *cultural hybridization* and *cosmopolitanism* were used in an attempt to rethink and deepen the notion of educational transfer.

According to Robert Cowen (2012), the concept of educational transfer refers to an idea, or practice, or educational institution that moves from one place to another beyond international limits and frontiers. As a complement to this idea, the concept should also be considered under the perspective of the internationalization of educational policies. Educational transfer has been presenting in the last two decades different characteristics from those traditionally relevant to the field of curriculum studies. To name but a few, borrowing and lending and the existence or non-existence of international convergence in educational are phenomena of transnational transfer (Steiner-Khamsi 2004).

The educational systems of peripheral countries have been affected and severely influenced by the flux of ideas that migrate acrossborders. However, the global diffusion of ideas is not a recent phenomenon. Rather, it is a continuous process that dates back to the time of the creation of the first universities in Europe, circa the thirteenth century.

According to Elizabeth Macedo, the curriculum studies field has been international since its emergence: "My proposal (...) would be to reverse the logic that the international presupposes the national, trying to defend that an international curriculum studies field precedes the national fields" (n.d., p. 3). That is, since its beginning, the curriculum studies field in a peripheral country has been under the direct and/or indirect influence of central countries that have already been developing their theories in the area. Here, we understand that Macedo refers to the emergence of the field in peripheral countries, since central countries were where the field of curriculum studies was created and historically developed.

From the 1950s to 1960s, there were two prevailing tendencies on educational transfer. One of these suggested that educational transfer was not only possible but also desirable, since it assumed that education was an independent aspect or social reality, thus able to be analyzed separately from its sociohistorical context. Consequently, educational "improvements" could be transported directly from one country to another. Moreover, for the followers of this tendency, educational tenets were universal and general. There was an ideal of universal education that, once established, could be applicable to distinct demands and to implement improvements anywhere in the world (Jullien, Mann, Griscom, Arnold, Kay-Shuttleworth, Tolstoy, and Sarmiento). Education was understood as nearly a positive science when framed through this perspective.

The main thinkers of this tendency framed their theories in as a linear notion of progress and an evolutionary conception of the educational systems. They believed that by borrowing the educational system from another country they would avoid the same mistakes committed by the pioneer theorists and practitioners of a determined curriculum, taking a shortcut so as to reach that ideal model of education in a shorter period of time. Nevertheless, these thinkers also believed that the selection process needed to go through a certain degree of adaptation to the new contexts.

According to this perspective, pedagogical institutions and practices were regarded as potentially neutral technologies that could be used in different contexts, including having distinct objectives. The other tendency on educational transfer, however, emerged in the middle of the nineteenth century from the works of the Russian author K. D. Ushinky, and a little later, in 1990, with Sadler (Beech 2009). This tendency stresses the importance of context in the educational institutions and practices. If the sociohistorical context was more important than the institutions and practices themselves, specific aspects of an educational system could not be transferred successfully to a different context. Sadler's (1979) view was that the context is the most relevant in the definition of educational systems:

> In studying foreign systems of Education we should not forget that the things outside the schools matter even more than the things inside the schools, and govern and interpret the things inside. We cannot wander at pleasure among the educational systems of the world, like a child strolling through a garden, and pick off a flower from one bush and some leaves from another, and then expect that if we stick what we have gathered into the soil at home, we shall have a living plant. A national system of Education is a living thing, the outcome of forgotten struggles and difficulties, and of 'battles long ago.' (as cited in Beech 2006, p. 7)

Nevertheless, to study and analyze a foreign educational system would still be valid for a better understanding of one's own system. One of the positive aspects of transfer is, thus, to use the foreign educational system as a parameter, not as a paradigm.

Gita Steiner-Khamsi (2004) and some other contemporary authors in comparative education defend that research should suspend the issue as to whether transfer is possible or not; instead, one should examine the process through which ideas and practices are transferred from an educational context to another. Jason Beech (2009) argues for the growing importance of multilateral international agencies as essential actors in the educational field as a whole, and this importance should be considered in light of the new complexities of the social space involved in the concept of transfer.

Our contemporary life has been fundamentally constituted by a great variety of kinds of mobility: of people, goods, services, and information. The access to all these possibilities should be granted to all, indistinctively. Zygmunt Bauman (1999) explains it thus:

> Mobility climbs to the highest level among the most desired values – the freedom of movements, an always scarce and unevenly distributed good, and which has soon become the main stratifying factor of our late modernity or post-modernity. ... Being local in a globalized world means social deprivation and degradation. ... A specific cause of worrying is the progressive communications rupture between extraterritorial elites increasingly more global, and the rest of population, increasingly more local. (pp. 8–9)

Cowen (2009) suggests the concept of *educational mobility* to describe the present phenomenon. Since one must take into account the fact that this concept, is a historical consequence—although not necessarily a linear one—of educational transfer, it seems to be more adequate to the curriculum theory in this twenty-first century if one considers all the agents and complexities involved in this process.

Academic mobility involves people, institutions, and programs in these new configurations present in the educational internationalization field. However, as Bauman mentioned above, mobility implies processes that engender and/or maintain inequalities of opportunities, access, information, and so forth. Mobility also implies changes and interchanges among colleagues beyond direct subjection resulting from differentiated relationships of power, even at a symbolic level.

Facing the globalized scenario in which we live, we can notice great mobility of people—researchers, professors, and students—and alongside it, a mobility of concepts, theories, practices, and policies among nations and their educational systems: "Not only peoples move, but also their models of society" (Madeira 2009, as cited in Cowen 2009, p. 318). An interchange, a sharing among colleagues from different nations that, for reasons that go beyond the aims of this chapter, see themselves subjected to global determinations and demands from multilateral agencies: standards of excellence, quality, assessment, and performance, to name but a few, requested from all the countries alike despite their particularities.

In this sense, we would like to highlight academic institutional mobility. Phillip Altbach and Jane Knight (2007) affirm that the international dimension of higher education includes many new configurations, among which are internationalization at home and abroad; the growing demand for higher education has led to a greater expansion of academic mobility; and an unprecedented interest in cross-border education. Moreover, international institutions themselves have developed new educational configurations, like merging with local institutions, adapting curricula, offering online courses, opening branches and overseas campuses, and so forth, which bring to the educational field new services in an international level. Consequently, one can observe a new form of transfer through which not only knowledge, information, practices, and theories are transferred, but also educational goods and services, attending to the logic of consumerism (Naidoo et al. 2011).

The logic of neoliberal discourses on globalization, broadly speaking, "stresses global regimes of 'free trade,' applying to both goods and services, even to services such as health and education that were traditionally marked by their highly national character" (Rizvi and Lingard 2010, p. 32). In other words, according to the hegemonic discourses, everyone is submitted to this process, despite their countries or educational systems, since it is regarded as "historically inevitable and irreversible … and [a] benefit[s] [to] everyone" (Rizvi and Lingard 2010, pp. 32–33). We are all subject to global market logic and must then comply with it. In curriculum theory, it implies moreover the idea that cultural differences among countries are to be thought in the abstract, with the incorporation of the idea of interculturality in official discourses, rather than in practical political actions or educational policies. That is, by and large, the interculturality discourse is used in favor of the institutionalized power as a strategy to reinforce social cohesion by assimilating sociocultural subaltern groups into the hegemonic culture without the proper critical perspective and respectful attitude that should come with the idea of interculturality.

However, there should be place for a counter-hegemonic discourse, one that comes in defense of those who are left behind in this globalized, overwhelming state of affairs, which as a "juggernaut" destroys everything it meets (Rizvi and Lingard 2010, p. 32). And the field of curriculum studies is a territory where this counter-hegemonic principle may expand, since it is where it is possible to take political action against the system. In Pinar's (2003) words,

> frank and ongoing self-criticism must be the reinvigoration of our professional commitment to engage in "complicated conversation" with our academic subjects, our students, and ourselves. Such "complicated conversation" requires the academic – intellectual – freedom to devise the courses we teach, the means by which we teach them, *and* the means by which we assess students' study of them. We must fight for that freedom as individuals in classrooms and as a profession. (p. 15)

FINDING OUR WAY THROUGH THE MISTS

In Brazil, we have been passing by a moment of suspension and suspicion: On the one hand, we must tackle issues of a local, everyday curriculum practice; on the other, we tackle issues of a curriculum that is demanded mostly by international agencies and assessment processes, in order not to be excluded from the major international educational scenario. Our latest qualitative research focused on published texts, in both Brazilian and international journals dedicated to curriculum studies tried to understand how the internationalization of curriculum has been understood by different researchers. As part of the research, interviews were conducted with researchers from the USA, Canada, China, Finland, Great Britain, and Brazil who have been supporting the internationalization of curriculum. In these non-structured interviews, the researchers were asked to talk freely about their views in relation to the process—their strategies, advancements, difficulties, and challenges. We have opted to not identify the interviewees, or to quote them directly, in order to provide them with as much freedom to talk as possible.

We have noticed from their testimonies that the process of internationalization has been differently understood. By and large, we can group their positions into three views. The first corresponds to a perspective of convergence of the curricula proposed in schools, supported both by the process of globalization and by the international assessment systems. According to this view, the path leads to a homogenization rather than to a shared vision of an internationalization of the field.

Such perspective is liable to criticism, since homogenization corresponds to a production that occurs in a globalized world: It is the result not of a necessity, but of a standard that is generalized, of a good that is serial produced. It expresses the principle of functionalists. According to François Jullien (2009), homogeneity comes from imitation: "there is no rational argument that justifies it; only its recurrence seems to authorize it. Besides globalization, world-scale assessment also imposes homogenous models of education, which are considered to be the *only imaginable path*" (p. 33). Thus, curricula result from a "discreet dictatorship" presenting superficial variations that tend to give some local color to curriculum. However, in Jullien's terms (2009), "while homogenization anesthetizes because of its regularities, diversity can create tension, debate, creative action. The uniform, in short, contributes to devaluation to the point that the richness found in different cultures is lost" (p. 102).

The second view that emerged from the interviews is that internationalization implies the effort to understand how, in different countries, issues or emerging themes have been dealt within the major globalization process. According to such a perspective, it is imperative to discuss different views of schooling, curriculum, curriculum policies, school knowledge, culture, teaching and learning, teachers, professors and students, skills, competences, and attitudes, that is, all of the critical components that permeate curriculum theory and practice.

Underpinning this view is the thematic of the relative autonomy of curriculum. Is this autonomy defended or is it taken as an instrument to fulfill wider political, social, and economical purposes? Such questioning is present in the views of those who worry more about understanding and interpreting the effects and dilemmas of the process of internationalization, examining the impact of globalization in curriculum, instead of encouraging debates, meetings, and associations, as we can see in the next view.

The third view on internationalization of curriculum implies changes and exchanges of experiences, points of view, and ideas. It implies, for instance, a greater amount of congresses, publishing, readings, and collaboration among researchers from different countries. The main objective is the mutual enrichment of knowledge, and not homogenization. In such attempt, there must be a constant pursuit of articulation between local and global, without hindering or extinguishing national histories and interests. Yet, the risk that in this process the local ends having a null effect due to a supposedly scientific stance on the search for universal knowledge has been pointed out by one of the interviewed researchers, for whom strategies for internationalization should include the fostering of joint researches and publications, debates, and events that promote the meetings of different perspectives.

Moreover, it is important that powerful voices do not dominate dialogues and debates. It is necessary that the attraction for theories produced in hegemonic countries do not blind the critical view that should be kept. One should not let thought surrender itself to homogenization, impoverishment, and contamination by less noble interests that may, even if unconsciously, underlie efforts toward cooperation. In future collaborative research, there should be space for problem-solving processes in relation to the needs present in local educational scenarios. Besides, it is important to hold a cautious attitude when dealing with themes, methodologies, and theoretical references in order to avoid exclusion or the muting of less powerful voices.

CONCLUSION

Educational mobility implies, among other things, exchanges and discussions between colleagues, that extend beyond influencing each other or direct subjection resulting from differentiated relationships of power, even at a symbolic level. In order to achieve it, it is necessary that a sort of intercultural competence among the actors involved in the process of internationalization of curriculum is constantly and permanently pursued. Promoting intercultural competence is, according to Betty Leask (2009),

> The incorporation of an international and intercultural dimension into the content of the curriculum as well as the teaching and learning arrangements and support services of a program of study.[...] Internationalization of the curriculum as a component of both the formal and the informal curriculum. (p. 209)

The internationalization of curriculum, in other words, for us, should ask for a critical understanding of the local in the context of the global and vice versa, and also a critical perspective on the relevance of local contents and practices alongside global ones.

Although we have already seen a few changes, we are still trying to find a way to develop a curriculum theory in partnership and collaboration with the international dimension, rather than in a mere transfer process. We believe that educational mobility and the development of an intercultural perspective, based on dialogue and not on power relations, can contribute to the curriculum field as a whole. Internationalization is an ongoing process that demands constant dialogue, negotiation, and openness to the new, while holding on dearly to the local. Our chapter intends to defend, with a certain impetus and to a certain symbolic extent, a demarcation of a territory for a counter-hegemonic discourse on internationalization, whether it be the curriculum praxis field or the curriculum theory field. This place should be filled with that "complicated conversation" so much defended by Pinar and various curriculum researchers so as to live up to the whole political nature involved in the internationalization process. Since a written manifesto is but halfway through; we should dedicate ourselves to more political action even if in the mists of the curriculum path, in an attempt to go beyond the text.

Finally, in relation to internationalization of curriculum in Brazil, we can posit that the process is still marked with uncertainties, as researchers have been trying their best to exchange ideas inside the country as well as across different borders, and that we still have a long way to go. Despite uncertainties and apparent divergent opinions, we must insist on the effort for the engagement of us all, researchers on curriculum, both in dialogue and in developing this intercultural competence, which will certainly allow us to find new paths together.

References

Altbach, P., & Knight, J. (2007). The internationalization of higher education: Motivations and realities. *Journal of Studies in International Education, 11,* 290–305.

Ball, S., & Junemann, C. (2011). Education policy and philanthropy—The changing landscape of English educational governance. *International Journal of Public Administration, 34*(10), 646–661.

Bauman, Z. (1999). *Globalização: as consequências humanas.* Rio de Janeiro: Jorge Zahar.

66 A. F. B. MOREIRA AND R. K. RAMOS

Beech, J. (2006). The theme of educational transfer in comparative education: A view over time. *Research in Comparative and International Education, 1*(1), 2–13.

Beech, J. (2009). Redefining educational transfer: International agencies and the (re)production of educational ideas. In J. Sprongoe & T. Winther-Jensen (Eds.), *Identiy, education and citizenship: Multiple interrelations* (pp. 172–188). Frankfurt and Main: Peter Lang.

Burke, P. (2003). *Hibridismo cultural.* São Leopoldo: Editora UNISINOS, Coleção Aldus 18.

Cowen, R. (2009). The transfer, translation and transformation of educational processes: And their shape-shifting? *Comparative Education, 45*(3), 315–327.

Cowen, R., Kazamias, A., & Ulterhalter, E. (Orgs.). (2012). *Educação Comparada. Panorama internacional e perspectivas* (Vol. 1). Brasília: UNESCO/CAPES.

García Canglini, N. (2007). *A globalização imaginada.* São Paulo: Iluminuras.

Harris, S. (2011). *The university in translation: Internationalizing higher education.* London: Continuum.

Jullien, F. (2009). *O diálogo entre as culturas: do universal ao multiculturalismo.* Rio de Janeiro: Zahar.

Knight, J. (2004). Internationalization remodeled: Definition, approaches, and rationales. *Journal of Studies in International Education, 8*(1), 5–31.

Knight, J. (2014). *International education hubs: Student, talent, knowledge-innovation models.* New York: Springer.

Leask, B. (2009). Using formal and informal curricula to improve interactions between home and international students. *Journal of Studies in International Education, 13*(2), 205–221.

Macedo, E. (n.d.). *The internationalization of curriculum studies.* Rio de Janeiro: PROPED. http://www.curriculouerj.pro.br/imagens/artigos/THE_INTERN_6.pdf.

Moreira, A. F. B. (1997). *Currículos e Programas no Brasil.* Campinas: Papirus.

Moreira, A. F. B., & Macedo, E. F. (2006). Faz sentido ainda o conceito de transferência educacional? In A. F. B. Moreira (Org.), *Currículo: Políticas e práticas* (pp. 13–29). Campinas: Papirus.

Naidoo, R., Shankar, A., & Veer, E. (2011). The consumerist turn in higher education: Policy aspirations and outcomes. *Journal of Marketing Management, 27*(11–12), 1142–1162.

Pinar, W. F. (2003). *The internationalization of curriculum studies.* http://www.riic.unam.mx/01/02_Biblio/doc/Internationalizaton_Curriculum_W_PINAR_(MEXICO).pdf.

Ragatt, P. (1983). One person's periphery. *Compare, 13*(1), 1–5.

Rizvi, F., & Lingard, B. (2010). *Globalizing education policy.* New York: Routledge.

Sadler, M. (1979). How far can we learn anything of practical value from the study of foreign systems of education? In R. Cowen & A. Kazamias (Eds.) (2009), *International handbook of comparative education* (Vol. 22, pp. 341–357). London: Springer.

Steiner-Khamsi, G. (2004). Globalization in education: Real or imagined? In G. Steiner-Khamsi (Ed.), *The global politics of educational borrowing and lending* (pp. 201–220). New York and London: Teachers College Press.

CHAPTER 5

Talking Back to Second Language Education Curriculum Control

Douglas Fleming

In 2014, the Director of the *Canadian Centre for Language Benchmarks* emailed me about a presentation I had recently given at the *Centre Canadien D'études et de Recherche en Bilinguisme et Aménagement Linguistique* regarding the qualitative research I had conducted pertaining to the *Canadian Language Benchmarks* (Hajer and Kaskens 2012; Pawlikowska-Smith 2000). He stated:

> I asked a colleague who is a university-based language expert to review your presentation. The review is attached. We would be grateful if you would take the necessary steps to correct the inaccuracies in your work so that those attending your presentations or reading your work are not misled regarding the CLB.

The subsequent email exchange we had revolved around my contention that he was using the prestige of his position to put pressure on a scholar to suppress work he found threatening. He, on the other hand, contended that he was not attempting to "silence [my] opinions" and that in any case it was "not a question of opinions here, but facts."

D. Fleming (✉)
University of Ottawa, Ottawa, ON, Canada
e-mail: dfleming@uottawa.ca

© The Author(s) 2019
C. Hébert et al. (eds.), *Internationalizing Curriculum Studies*,
https://doi.org/10.1007/978-3-030-01352-3_5

In this chapter, I outline some of the political implications of the reviewer's comments in view of current linguistic theory and make the case for how curricular practices within second language education (SLE) can be better understood through a greater consideration within the field of two concepts from general education: the *hidden curriculum* (Jackson 1968) and the notion of viewing curriculum development at a *complicated conversation* (Pinar 2012) that converts these documents from nouns to verbs (*currere*).

In what follows below, I first provide a brief overview of the significance of the CLB as represented from a policy viewpoint. My original critique of the 2000 version of the CLB then follows. This leads to an assessment of the 2012 version of the same document. I then proceed to give an overview various curriculum implementation models as they apply to SLE. Special attention is given to Jackson's (1968) notion of the *hidden curriculum*. My chapter concludes with a discussion of how these curriculum implementation models can be expanded and enhanced through the use of Pinar's (2012) notion of a *complicated conversation*.

The Significance of the CLB

As I have discussed elsewhere (Fleming 2007), the CLB represents the culmination of SLE policy changes initiated by the Canadian federal government with the release of its four-year *Immigration Plan* (Citizenship and Immigration Canada 1990). The *Plan* was a major change in direction for the federal government and came at a time when important demographic changes in Canadian society were becoming more evident. The document talks explicitly about how second language immigration was becoming more and more economically significant in the face of a declining national birthrate and how this immigration should be consistently managed in the interests of "nation-building" and the "building a new Canada" (p. 3). The *Plan* identified immigrant language training as a major national priority for the first time.

The official character of the *CLB* is attested to the fact that it was painstakingly developed in a long series of consultations and draft formulations facilitated by federal agencies who explicitly referred to the 1990 *Immigration Plan* (Norton Pierce and Stewart 1997). Significantly, the further development of the CLB has been overseen by the *Centre for Canadian Language Benchmarks* (CCLB), a nonprofit organization founded in 1998 and funded by the federal government.

Both versions of the CLB comprise over 200 compact pages. It consists mainly of a set of language descriptors arranged in 12 levels, from basic English language proficiency to full fluency. As Norton Pierce and Stewart (1997) noted, the federal government-initiated initiatives that gave rise to this text were framed around the need to develop a systematic and seamless set of English language training opportunities out of the myriad of federal and provincial programs that existed previously.

The bulk of the content found in the actual *Benchmarks* (both in the 2000 and 2012 versions) is arranged for each level in a series of matrixes to correspond to the four language skills. Each benchmark found within the CLB contains a general overview of the tasks to be performed upon completion of the level, the conditions under which this performance should take place, a more specific description of what a learner can do, and examples and criteria that indicate the task performance has been successful.

My Critique of the 2000 CLB

The expert the Director consulted, who has remained anonymous, had evidently read one of my peer-reviewed articles that explored the links between citizenship and race in SLE (see Fleming 2014a). In their review, I "rave" and show "bias" in my "attack" against this key federal document.

The article in question updated the analysis from my doctoral research that compared the way in which citizenship was conceptualized within the CLB with a sampling of adult second language learners in a federally funded English as a Second Language (ESL) program. The participants in the qualitative study from which this data is drawn described becoming Canadians predominantly in terms of human rights, multicultural policy, and the obligations of being citizens. I found that the CLB rarely referred to citizenship in these terms and instead described being Canadian in terms of normative standards that implied the existence of a dominant and singular culture to which second language learners had to conform. This was true even for the 2012 version of the CLB. I argued that these normative standards had the effect of racializing second language learners in this context.

In the entire 2000 document, there were only three references to tasks or competencies that could be said to be broadly associated with citizenship. These were "understand rights and responsibilities of client,

72   D. FLEMING

customer, patient and student" (p. 95); "indicate knowledge of laws, rights, etc." (p. 116); and "write a letter to express an opinion as a citizen" (p. 176). Unfortunately, these competencies were not elaborated upon and remained rather vague and incomplete.

In many ways, in fact, it is even more revealing to note what was missing, especially in terms of how language was connected to exercising citizenship. The word *vote*, for example, did not appear in the document. In addition, the document represented (through admission and omission) good citizens as obedient workers. This could be seen in the fact that issues related to trade unions and collective agreements were given next to no attention in the document. Labor rights, such as filing grievances or recognizing and reporting dangerous working conditions, were nonexistent. Employment standards legislation was covered in a singular vague reference to the existence of minimum wage legislation. The 2000 version of the CLB had no references to understanding standards of employment legislation, worker's compensation, employment insurance, or safety in the workplace. At the same time, however, a lot of space in the document was devoted to participating in job performance reviews, giving polite and respectful feedback to one's employer, and participating in meetings about trivial issues, such as lunchroom cleanliness.

The 2000 version of the document did represent language learners as having rights and responsibilities. However, these were almost exclusively related to being good consumers. Learners understood their rights and responsibilities as a "client, customer, patient and student" (Pawlikowska-Smith 2000, p. 95), but not as a worker, family member, participant in community activities, or advocate. As I have discussed elsewhere on the basis of empirical evidence, adult English language learners enrolled in the programs informed by the CLB often complain about being consistently denied overtime pay and access to benefits, being forced to work statutory holidays, or being fired without cause (Fleming 2010). In short, the document emphasized the virtues of being an obedient and cooperative worker and a good consumer who can return flawed items for refunds.

It was also disconcerting to note the limitations placed on the few references to citizenship noted above and the manner in which they had been couched. In the entire document, there are only three references that I consider being associated with citizenship. These are: "understand rights and responsibilities of client, customer, patient and student" (p. 95); "indicate knowledge of laws, rights, etc." (p. 116); and "write a letter to express an opinion as a citizen" (p. 176). It is very noteworthy that no content is linked to collective action, group identity, debate, or investigation to citizenship rights.

What is even more significant was the way in which forms of exercising citizenship were connected to levels of English language proficiency. All three of the above competencies that referred to citizenship occurred at the very highest benchmark levels, at the point at which one is writing research papers at universities. In this way, the document implied that opinions not expressed in English had little value in terms of Canadian citizenship.

My Critique of the 2012 CLB

The Canadian Language Benchmarks 2012: ESL for Adults is a revised version of the original 2000 publication (Hajer and Kaskens 2012). It was the result of an extensive series of processes designed to establish the validity and reliability of descriptors found within the document. The authors and a set of consultants hired by the CCLB compared the document to the *Common European Framework of Reference*, the *American Council for the Teaching of Foreign Languages Guidelines*, and the *Échelle québécoise*. The document was then subjected to field validation and checked against the *American Education Research Association Standards for Educational and Psychological Testing*.

In contrast to the introduction found within the 2000 version, the new version is more forthright about claims that it is designed to be "a national standard for planning curricula for language instruction in a variety of contexts" (Hajer and Kaskens 2012, p. v). However, the document still claims not to endorse a specific instructional method. In my estimation, this is somewhat disingenuous since the new version, like the previous, exhibits many hallmarks of the communicative approach, including task-based exemplars and an explicit endorsement of Bachman's (1990) model of communicative language ability. In my estimation, much of my critique of the 2000 version of the document from a language-testing standpoint is still valid here.

I have argued previously that exemplar tasks within assessment and curriculum documents in this context should be scrutinized carefully since they contain and represent privileged orientations that influence how teachers approach the treatment of curriculum content (Fleming 2008). Content that is held up as exemplars in such documents is

74   D. FLEMING

privileged in the sense that it encourages particular orientations toward themes and discourages others. Exemplar tasks that deal with citizenship represent privileged content that a teacher or curriculum writer is encouraged to reproduce and elaborate upon, and are not innocent of ideology (Shohamy 2007).

Although the focus on consumer rights is as dominant within the new version of the CLB as it was in the old, there has been a significant addition of content that refers to labor rights. Benchmark 5, for example, contains an exemplary task that requires an understanding of employment standards legislation. Within Benchmark 7, there is a reference to pedagogical tasks in which one discusses wages and working conditions. These are marked improvements for which the authors should be commended. However, in my estimation, there are still problems within the new version of the CLB in terms of citizenship rights. As a way of illustration, I shall discuss the use of the word "vote," which I believe is of pivotal importance when discussing notions of citizenship. As mentioned above, the word did not occur within the 2000 version. Voting is mentioned twice in the new document. One of these references is within the exemplar task when a learner is expected to evaluate the arguments presented by candidates during an election. The other reference to voting is almost identical in content and appears on the same page. This is an improvement over the previous version of the CLB. Unfortunately, both of these references within the new version of the CLB are found in the listening framework at benchmark 12, the highest in the document. My previous criticism that the document links citizenship rights to high levels of English language proficiency still holds. This is a significant problem, since this implies that citizenship rights are tasks that can only be fully realized once one is at the level of writing graduate-level assignments, another exemplar task found within level 12.

Politics, Culture, and Language Assessment

There were a number of complaints from the Director and his anonymous reviewer that questioned my qualifications to make critiques and denigrated qualitative research methodology. I have dealt with these complaints elsewhere and do not believe that they are worth going into here (Fleming 2014b). However, there were other complaints that had political and cultural ramifications and illustrate how bureaucratic control operates in the field through linear conceptions of curriculum development. The most important of these was the reviewer's claim the CLB "strips languages of any political agenda and contains and construct of language learning [that] is the same [and] remains the same regardless of what language is being learned, and where it is learned."

The contention that a set of competency descriptors can remove the political or cultural content from language flies in the face of linguistic theory and practice since the time of Saussure's insights over a century ago. This is regardless of whether one takes a generative (Chomsky 1965) or a functional approach (Halliday 1985) in terms of theory. As Saussure (1916/1983) noted, there are no easy comparisons that can be made between specific languages. One doesn't even have to go to the post-structural literature to support this claim. To give Saussure's most famous example, the conception of a "river" is different in French (a "flueve" ends up in the ocean; "rivière" ends up in a lake) than it is in English ("creek" and "river" are different solely in terms of size). Now, I do not wish to replicate the long-standing debates within linguistics and anthropology regarding the connections between specific cultures and languages (Feuerverger 2009, provides a comprehensive review of this). However, I think that it is clear from any perusal of the academic literature that one doesn't need to be a radical "raver" to regard as illogical, not to say ridiculous, an attempt to describe a specific language (in this case English) as some kind of innocent universal standard that can be applied to all others.

A perusal of the academic literature also shows that individual approaches to language learning are highly varied and not universal. Learning content is selected through the consideration of a set of factors, such as learner needs, programming goals, or pertinent linguistic elements. Language learning itself, as Oxford (1990) has shown, is influenced by such factors as motivation, subject position (e.g., gender), cultural background, attitudes and beliefs, types of tasks involved, overall learning styles, and deep-seated cognitive styles (e.g., tolerance of ambiguity). Despite the implicit claims made by my anonymous reviewer, the second language field, as Pennycook (2007), Canagarajah (1999), and Norton (2000) have shown, has long moved away from the notion of the "good language learner" who uses singular learning strategies.

Even though the reviewer claims that the CLB is a neutral document that has no political import, in the text that the CLB cites as one of its principal theoretical resources, Bachman and Palmer (2010) state "we must always consider the societal and educational value systems that

76 D. FLEMING

inform our test use [and that] the values and goals that inform test use may vary from one culture to another" (p. 34). Do not social values constitute a form of politics? Does not variance between cultures invalidate a "one size fits all" approach? I might add rhetorically: Does what appears to be an attempt to suppress my work on the part of the Director constitute a political agenda?

My chief complaint about CLB, simply put, is related to the lack of citizenship content found within the document, especially at the lower levels of English language proficiency. The publication that the reviewer critiqued is centered on how the exemplars within the CLB emphasize the virtues of being an obedient and cooperative worker and a good consumer. I argue that the content of these pedagogical tasks is highly significant. In contrast to the claims of my reviewer, politics are inevitably contained within this content in the sense that they reflect the societal and educational value systems that Bachman and Palmer (1996/2010) talk about above. In effect, these exemplars infantilize and even racialize second language learners.

In short, if you do not have exemplars that cover the topic of citizenship at the lower levels of language proficiency, you imply that this topic is not for the learners at these levels. If you emphasize consumer rights within your document at the expense of worker rights, you imply that this is where we place our priorities and values as a society. What could be more political?

GOING BEHIND THE HIDDEN CURRICULUM

The CLB is meant to strongly inform curriculum development. This is made clear in a key implementation document officially associated with the CLB (that provides explicit guidelines and examples of how teachers are to implement the document into their program Holmes et al. 2004). These guidelines recommend that teachers first determine how the CLB fits into the purpose and goals of their program and then identify and prioritize the possible initiatives that would correspond to appropriate CLB learner-centered competencies.

This orientation toward curriculum implementation reflects a *progressivist value system* (Clark 1987), in which teachers are expected to design their own school-based curricula. In Clark's (1987) framework, this is in contrast to *classical humanism,* in which teachers are expected to implement the curricula recommended by administrators and *reconstructionism*, in which teachers are expected to implement curricula designed by experts. By adopting a *progressivist* orientation, the CLB and its associated documents *have the appearance* of avoiding the perpetuation of curriculum-planning hierarchies that maintain inequalities between ESL theorists, curriculum experts, and practitioners (Pennycook 1989).

However, as Giroux (1981) points out, one must go beyond the rhetoric and platitudes commonly found in pedagogical processes and examine concrete particularities if one is to see clearly see how they operate as "agents of legitimation, organized to produce and reproduce dominant categories, values, and social relationships" (p. 72). In other words, we must go beyond appearance and examine what is hidden.

Through this examination of the concrete aspects of the CLB, I argue that a hidden curriculum is at work in this instance that realizes and reinforces a hierarchical paradigm of citizenship (Jackson 1968). It does this by privileging particular aspects of curricular content that infantilizes second language learners and utilizing a hierarchized orientation toward the roles that teachers play in curriculum development. To reiterate, there are very few references to citizenship within the entire document. And, those that do exist link high levels of English language proficiency to trivialized forms of citizenship.

In terms of concrete practice, I think that the challenge is to develop curriculum processes that allow students and practitioners to "talk back" to language policy implementation documents such as the CLB. It is not enough to simply "start with" or "modify" a document such as this for one's own classroom. Students and practitioners should be able to expand on Clark's (1987) notion of a *progressivist* orientation toward curriculum so that they are helping design curriculum guidelines (in whatever guise they take: even as assessment instruments). In this way, the ground could be clear to develop curriculum content that contains equitable citizenship content and avoids the infantilism so evident in documents such as the CLB.

Morgan (2002) provides a detailed and concrete account of how alternative forms of classroom practice can avoid infantilism by recounting a lesson that he himself conducted that was focused on a referendum on Quebec separatism. Rather than avoiding the dangers involved in handling the issues related to a very controversial issue then raging in the media, Morgan made this topic the focus of his lesson. He drew upon bilingual dictionaries and various decoding strategies to enhance the abilities of his learners to engage in debates surrounding the topic. The result was that his learners were able to deeply engage in what it meant to be a Canadian citizen in the context of a then current political crisis. As Fleming and Morgan (2012) describe it in a subsequent treatment of the data, this example:

> of participatory citizenship in a L2 was enabled by L1 use and traditional L1 literacy strategies, a classroom approach notably absent in the *CLB* document. What might be observed, indeed stigmatized, as methodologically and acquisitionally remedial (i.e. bilingual dictionary translation), or indicative of a lower-order cognitive task (i.e. decoding) through a *CLB* framework, was re-contextualized in ways that enhanced critical engagement and an understanding of language and power around the Quebec referendum that could exceed the ideological awareness of native speakers and long-standing citizens. (p. 9)

VIEWING CURRICULUM AS A COMPLICATED CONVERSATION

Transmission linear process models based on preconceived pedagogical objectives dominate the curriculum models currently in SLE (Aguilar 2011; Arnfast and Jorgenson 2010; Gunderson et al. 2011). In these models, content is selected through the consideration of a set of factors, such as learner needs, programming goals, or predetermined linguistic elements. The content is formulated into sets of summative objectives. These processes are linear in the sense that the curriculum content is not modified once determined. These processes are transmission-based in the sense that course content, once determined, is transmitted in one direction from the teacher to the learner. The task of the teacher, in these models, is to impart the predetermined course objectives as definitive versions of knowledge.

This type of process can be seen concretely in the model provided in a recent overview of curriculum design by Nation and Mcalister (2010), two highly cited seminal theorists in the field. In their text, they outline sets of inner and outer circles that provide a model for language curriculum design. The outer circles are a range of factors (principles of instruction, teaching environment, and learner needs) that effect the overall course production. The sets of inner circles (course content and sequencing, format and presentation of materials, and monitoring and assessment of student progress) are centered on the overall goals of the course in question. In this model, course content consists primarily of linguistic elements such as vocabulary, grammar, language functions, discourse, and learning skills and strategies.

Whether linguistic elements can truly be represented in the language classroom as sets of predetermined and definitive course objectives ("facts") is a matter for another debate elsewhere. What is of importance here is the way non-linguistic course content is incorporated into this model. Borrowing from Cook (1983), Nation and Mcalister (2010) describe non-linguistic content as "ideas that help the learners of language and are useful to the learners" (p. 78). These ideas can take the form of imaginary happenings, an academic subject, "survival" topics such as shopping, going to the doctor or getting a driver's license, interesting facts, or a set of subcategories pertaining to culture.

It is process of determining cultural content within this model that interests me particularly. Nation and Mcalister (2010) argue that a curriculum should move learners "from explicit knowledge of inter-related aspects of native and non-native cultures, to markedly different conceptualizations between the cultures, to understanding the culture from an insider's view and gaining a distanced view of one's own culture" (p. 78). In other words, course content moves in a linear fashion that first explicitly contrasts static versions of the first and target cultures and then acculturates learners into that target culture, turning them away from their first culture. Nothing in this model suggests the possibility of equitable or dual cultures or the notion of a fluid hybridity between or within various cultures. The implied goal in this model is to transmit the target (i.e., socially dominant) culture as a set of pedagogical objectives.

This linear and transmission model is the way, in fact, that the citizenship content operates within the CLB. As mentioned above, the CLB privileges rights and responsibilities that pertain almost exclusively to being good consumers and not to being workers, family members, participants in community activities, or advocates. These are explicitly started as objectives pertaining to the pedagogical tasks contained throughout the document. Thus, the CLB, through admission and omission, implicitly defines citizenship in a particular way and transmits this definition through privileged content to the learner. The teacher is admonished to develop specific learning objectives that frame the classroom activities and content.

80   D. FLEMING

Instead of the dominant linear transmission model that is expressed as pedagogical objectives, I advocate that ESL practitioners explore viewing language curricula as *complicated conversations* (Pinar 2012). Based on the notion that education is centered on transdisciplinary conversations (Oakeshott 1959) that are animated (Bruner 1966) and within the contexts of action and reflection (Aoki 2005), Pinar argues that curriculum is not a set of narrow pedagogical tasks and objectives, but lived experience. As he puts it, "expressing one's subjectivity … is how one links the lived curriculum with the planned one" (p. xv). In such a conception, curricula are ongoing co-constructions between teachers and students that are always becoming. Individual curriculum documents are never fully realized, but are continually in transition.

Moreover, this "conversation between teachers and students [is] over the past and its meaning [is] for the present as well as what both portend for the future" (Pinar 2012, p. 2). In other words, curriculum construction takes into account previous knowledge but dialogically examines it from the current and future perspectives. In terms of my discussion about citizenship, this would mean that classroom activities take into account received interpretations of what it means to be a citizen but examine these interpretations of citizenship from the viewpoint of the concrete present realities and the imagined future of those engaged in the conversation. It is this "conversation with others that portends the social construction of the public sphere," Pinar (2012) argues, because this form of subjective engagement combats passivity and political submissiveness. The key, as he makes clear, is "self-knowledge and collective witnessing [which] reconceptualizes the curriculum from course objectives to complicated conversation" (p. 47).

REFERENCES

Aguilar, J. (2011). Teachers knowledge of second language curriculum: A narrative experience. *Profile, 13*(1), 89–110.

Aoki, T. (2005). *Curriculum in a new key.* New York: Routledge.

Arnfast, J., & Jorgenson, J. (2010). Second language learning. In V. Aukrust (Ed.), *Learning and cognition* (pp. 205–211). Amsterdam: Elsevier.

Bachman, L. (1990). *Fundamental considerations in language testing.* Oxford: Oxford University Press.

Bachman, L., & Palmer, A. (1996/2010). *Language testing in practice: Designing and developing useful language tests.* Oxford: Oxford University Press.

5 TALKING BACK TO SECOND LANGUAGE EDUCATION ...   81

Bruner, J. (1966). *Towards a theory of instruction*. Cambridge, MA: Belknap.

Canagarajah, A. S. (1999). The politics of English language teaching. In S. May & N. H. Hornberger (Eds.), *Encyclopedia of language and education* (2nd ed.). Volume 1: *Language policy and political issues in education* (pp. 213–227). New York: Springer.

Chomsky, N. (1965). *Aspects of the theory of syntax*. Cambridge, MA: MIT Press.

Citizenship and Immigration Canada. (1990). *Immigration plan for 1990*. Ottawa: Communications Branch, Citizenship and Immigration Canada.

Clark, J. (1987). *Curriculum renewal in school foreign language teaching*. Oxford: Oxford University Press.

Cook, V. (1983). What should language teaching be about? *ELT Journal, 37*(3), 229–234.

Feuerverger, G. (2009). Jewish-Canadian identity and Hebrew language learning in Montreal and Toronto: Belonging (or not belonging) in diaspora. In J. Zajda, H. Daun, & L. Saha (Eds.), *Nation-building, identity and citizenship education: Cross-cultural perspectives* (pp. 117–130). New York: Springer.

Fleming, D. (2007). Adult immigrant ESL programs in Canada: Emerging trends in the contexts of history, economics and identity. In J. Cummins & C. Davison (Eds.), *The international handbook of English language teaching* (pp. 185–198). New York: Springer.

Fleming, D. (2008). Becoming citizens: Punjabi ESL learners, national language policy and the Canadian language benchmarks. In M. Manteno, P. Chamness, & J. Watzke (Eds.), *Readings in language studies: Language across disciplinary boundaries* (pp. 143–158). St. Louis, MO: International Society for Language Studies.

Fleming, D. (2010). Racialized forms of citizenship and the *Canadian language benchmarks. Canadian Journal of Education, 33*(3), 588–616.

Fleming, D. (2014a). Citizenship, race and second language education. In R. Kubota (Ed.), Race and language learning in multicultural Canada: Towards critical antiracism. *Journal of Multilingual and Multicultural Development* (Special Issue), *36*, 42–52.

Fleming, D. (2014b). Encounters with SLE bureaucrats: Misunderstandings and misgivings. *Citizenship Citizenship Education Research Journal, 1*, 80–88.

Fleming, D., & Morgan, B. (2012). Discordant anthems: ESL and critical citizenship education. *Citizenship Education Research Collection, 1*, 28–40.

Giroux, H. (1981). *Ideology, culture and the process of schooling*. London: Falmer Press.

Gunderson, L., Murphy Odo, D., & D'Silva, R. (2011). Assessing the English language learner. In D. Lapp & D. Fisher (Eds.), *Handbook of research on teaching English language arts* (3rd ed., pp. 343–349). New York: Routledge.

Hajer, A., & Kaskens, A. (2012). *Canadian language benchmarks 2012*. Ottawa, ON: Centre for Canadian Language Benchmarks.

82 D. FLEMING

Halliday, M. A. K. (1985). *Spoken and written language.* Geelong, VIC: Deakin University Press.

Holmes, T., Kingwell, G., Pettis, J., & Pilaski, M. (2004). *Canadian language benchmarks 2000: A guide to implementation.* Ottawa: Centre for Canadian Language Benchmarks.

Jackson, P. (1968). *Life in classrooms.* New York: Holt, Rinehart and Winston.

Morgan, B. (2002). Critical practice in community-based ESL programs: A Canadian perspective. *Journal of Language, Identity, and Education, 1,* 141–162.

Nation, I. S. P., & Macalister, J. (2010). *Language curriculum design.* New York: Routledge.

Norton, B. (2000). *Identity and language learning: Gender, ethnicity and educational change.* Harlow, UK and New York: Longman.

Norton Pierce, B., & Stewart, G. (1997). The development of the Canadian language benchmark assessment. *TESL Canada Journal, 8*(2), 17–31.

Oakeshott, M. (1959). *The voice of poetry in the conversation of mankind.* London: Meuthen.

Oxford, R. L. (1990). Language learning strategies and beyond: A look at strategies in the context of styles. In S. S. Magnan (Ed.), *Shifting the instructional focus to the learner* (pp. 35–55). Middlebury, VT: Northeast Conference on the Teaching of Foreign Languages.

Pawlikowska-Smith, G. (2000). *Canadian language benchmarks 2000.* Ottawa: Centre for Canadian Language Benchmarks.

Pennycook, A. (1989). The concept of "method", interested knowledge, and the politics of language teaching. *TESOL Quarterly, 23*(4), 589–618.

Pennycook, A. (2007). *Global Englishes and transcultural flows.* London and New York: Routledge.

Pinar, W. (2012). *What is curriculum theory?* (2nd ed.). Mahwah, NJ: Lawrence Erlbaum.

Saussure, F. (1916/1983). *Course in general linguistics* (C. Bally & A. Sechehaye, Eds., R. Harris, Trans.). La Salle, IL: Open Court.

Shohamy, E. (2007). The power of English tests, the power of the English language and the role of ELT. In J. Cummins & C. Davison (Eds.), *The international handbook of English language teaching* (pp. 521–532). New York: Springer.

CHAPTER 6

A Phenomenography of Educators' Conceptions of Curriculum: Implications for Next Generation Curriculum Theorists' Contemplation and Action

Jazlin Ebenezer, Susan Harden, Nicholas Sseggobe-Kiruma, Russell Pickell and Suha Mohammed Hamdan

A task of the curriculum theorists for the twenty-first century is to engage educators in critiquing the various ways theorists conceptualize curriculum. Educators need opportunities in curriculum studies courses to critically analyze and assess the relative worth of the underlying assumptions and values of curriculum theories. Teacher educators are responsible for enabling the next generation of educators in curriculum studies

---

J. Ebenezer (✉) · S. Harden · N. Sseggobe-Kiruma · R. Pickell ·
S. M. Hamdan
Wayne State University, Detroit, MI, USA
e-mail: aj9570@wayne.edu

S. Harden
e-mail: susan.harden@wayne.edu

N. Sseggobe-Kiruma
e-mail: fn8034@wayne.edu

© The Author(s) 2019
C. Hébert et al. (eds.), *Internationalizing Curriculum Studies*,
https://doi.org/10.1007/978-3-030-01352-3_6

to experience curriculum "*in particular ways*" (Marton and Booth 1997, p. vii). Consequently, we must understand the various ways in which we conceptualize curriculum. In this chapter, we discuss how a phenomenographic eye can discern the different historical and contemporary conceptions of curriculum and highlight them in curriculum studies courses.

Phenomenography is an empirical approach that originated in Sweden (Marton and Tsui 2004). It is a research tradition in which the qualitative differences of how people experience, perceive, conceptualize, and understand the same event are inductively analyzed to determine their influence on an individual's reality (Akerlind 2008). This approach has been one of the most influential developments in higher teaching and learning in the past three decades (Bradbeer 2004). Within the framework of phenomenography, "qualitative changes occur through learning to transform an individual's reality" (p. 53). Thus, phenomenography is grounded in a theory of learning can serve as an analytical tool to describe, interpret, and represent categories of curricular conceptions (Ebenezer and Fraser 2001). Although curriculum courses may carry out rich discourses about curriculum and engage educators in reflective practice, there is no study to our knowledge that has mapped the variations of educators' conceptions.

This research took place in the context of the doctoral seminar: a curriculum and instruction course at Wayne State University, Detroit, Michigan, in the fall of 2014. The course was 15 weeks long. The lead author has taught this course for many years. Twelve doctoral students (educators) from diverse educational and ethnic/racial backgrounds were in the doctoral seminar. Some of them are the co-authors of this chapter. The prescribed textbook for the course was *Pragmatism, Post-modernism, and Complexity Theory: The "Fascinating Imaginative Realm" of William E. Doll, Jr.*, edited by Donna Trueit (2012). During the doctoral seminar, we discussed Dolls' reflections on his experiences in becoming a curriculum theorist; the process of transformation of learning theorists such as Dewey, Piaget, Bruner, and Whitehead; structures, forms, and organization of modernism and postmodernism; and teaching.

R. Pickell
e-mail: rpickell@riverviewschools.com

S. M. Hamdan
e-mail: suha.mohammed.hamdan@wayne.edu

The research focused on the educators' reflections on the classroom discussion of curriculum issues via Blackboard's discussion board. The outcome of this research is the educators' conceptions of curriculum. At the outset, we discuss the different conceptions of curriculum theorists over time.

A Phenomenography of Curriculum

Internationally, curriculum theorists conceive curriculum differently regarding its content, aims, and the process of enactment in different philosophical, socioeconomic and political contexts. The theorists' conceptions of curriculum engender the metaphors that they posit in theorizing about curriculum to find answers to curriculum questions. For instance, Pinar and Grumet (1976) situate curriculum as an autobiographical text and posit narrative as the theoretical basis for its conceptualization, whereas Schwab (1983, 2013) conceptualizes curriculum as a communal and participatory process that leads to bodies of knowledge. This view of the curriculum is rooted in understanding the learners' communities and contexts for making decisions about what constitutes legitimate knowledge concerning who should teach it and to whom. Hurren (2003) theorizes curriculum as "the medium that creates the space for telling" (p. 120), where curriculum occurs within contextual stories. And Norman (2003) takes up curriculum and its theorizing as a dream work embedded within the mystical and metaphysical realm.

Dillon (2009) underscores the fact that the incoherence and divergence of opinions among scholars render the strict definition of curriculum futile. However, in response to Schwab's seven curricular elements, Dillon proposes seven corresponding curricular questions. Dillon argues that these "seven elements constitute an entity or enterprise called curriculum" (p. 348). Dillon further notes that "practice in *the curriculum* field is not a matter of brute action but thinking-in-action" (p. 349). The study of the ways to think and act through curriculum enactment has been a domain of curriculum development, which has morphed into curriculum studies.

In retrospect, Hlebowitsh (2005) hails Schwab for keeping what Hlebowitsh calls, generational ideas, that is, focusing on "the development of the school experience and on the relevance of local school authority" (p. 73), and for his new outlook at curriculum. He showed us the way toward a more participatory process in curriculum decision making. This commitment "kept the school close to the hands of the people and the practitioners that produced better teacher ownership of and investment in school reforms" (p. 86).

As Westbury (2005) makes clear, contemporary curriculum studies now focuses on understanding curriculum itself rather than on the "traditional narrow focus of doing curriculum work" (p. 89). Understanding curriculum, as Weenie (2008) asserts, "is about acknowledging lived pedagogy" (p. 549), or, as Aoki (2003) puts it, acknowledging "the site[s] of chaos in which dwell transformative possibilities" (p. 6). Understanding the historical foundations of curriculum studies and its theorizing is crucial for scholars and practitioners to situate themselves as active enactors who can contribute to the growth of our curriculum field.

Bellack (1969) notes that the purpose of a historical inquiry into curriculum thought "should not be viewed as a search in the past for solutions in present-day instructional problems" (p. 291). Rather we should perceive curriculum as a narrative "to help make us aware of the possibility and complexity of curriculum change, and conscious of the carryover of past doctrines and practices into the present situations" (p. 291). Further to this, curriculum scholars should not separate the history of curriculum thought and practice from the general history of American education. The curriculum knowledge development should be part of "the broader stream of cultural and intellectual history" (p. 291).

HISTORICAL MOMENTS IN CURRICULUM KNOWLEDGE DEVELOPMENT

According to Pinar (2014), there have been three historical moments in the development of curriculum as a field of study in the USA, which have had a significant influence on its public school system and education systems across the globe. For us, the first moment, which lasted five decades (1918–1969), was the inauguration of the curriculum field and its stabilization as curriculum development. The first part of the second moment was a decade long (1969–1980) during which scholars focused on re-conceptualizing curriculum development into curriculum studies. During the second part of the second moment (1980–2001), curriculum scholars aimed at understanding curriculum as an interdisciplinary and paradigmatically organized academic field.

Emerging in 2001, a third moment, characterized by the internationalization of curriculum studies, is what we call the postmodern era (Ropo and Autio 2009; Sohoni and Petrovic 2010). The overarching curricular concerns among scholars during the third moment included the nature of knowledge, the process of knowing, the professional status of the new specialty of curriculum making, and procedures for introducing new curriculum insights into educational practice on a broad scale. Caswell (1966) observes that the 1920s through 1930s were the years of the organized curriculum movement. During this period, curricular specialists focused on guaranteeing sound sequence in the curriculum, establishing consistent relationships between general goals of education and specific objectives that guide curricula design and enactment. The trend of curricular thought in the 1920s through 1930s, according to Pinar (1977), was the fruit of the practical concerns of curriculum specialists working with school personnel to revise the school curriculum. Curriculum specialists at that time, Pinar (1977) argues, were "former school people whose cultural and intellectual ties *tended* to be with the practitioner" (p. 3). They were "less interested in basic research, theory development, [and] parallel theoretical movement in other fields than in the reality of the classroom and school settings" (p. 3). Kliebard (1968) described this social efficiency movement as an educational moment in time, which sought to hold "up all school subjects, indeed all school activity, against the criterion of social utility" (p. 75).

According to Pinar (2014), Ralph Tyler's (1950) *Basic Principles of Curriculum and Instruction* ushered in the first paradigmatic movement. Doll (1972) reminds us that Tyler's *Rationale rested* on four fundamental questions: What goals should a school seek? What means should it use? How should these means be organized? How should the effectiveness of these means be organized? In his criticism of Tyler's *Rationale*, Doll notes that the preset, standardized, and goal-oriented curriculum fell short of engaging the learner in the determination of the objectives or ends of the learning process. Arguably, Tyler's conception of curriculum influenced his focus on its enactment. Tyler's view of the learner as a product of a preset process in which the learner was a passive consumer of the curriculum laid the foundation of his curriculum theorizing. Tyler seems to have borrowed the concept of behavioral objectives from behavioral psychologists such as, but not limited to, Edward Lee Thorndike (1874–1949), Burrhus Frederick Skinner (1904–1990) and Robert Gagne (1916–2002). From a behaviorist's perspective, knowledge is finite while learning is overt, measurable, and observable through behavioral changes in the learner (Cunningham et al. 2007). The teacher then determines the objectives that the learner should achieve ahead of the lesson. Curriculum practice based on Tyler's principles, and as influenced by behaviorist learning theories, was—and still is—rooted, in linearity and a step-by-step approach to teaching.

During the 1950s, the criticisms of the quality of the US public school system intensified and even more so after the Soviets launched Sputnik. "Sputnik launched," as Pinar (2014) makes clear, "a persisting curricular obsession with science and technology" (p. 521). Such educational obsessions lead to curriculum reforms that "yielded a quasi-official doctrine of rational curriculum planning embedded in large-scale curriculum projects ... notable for their global orientation, teacher-proofing and discipline-specificity" (Sears and Marshall 2000, p. 200). For Pinar (2014), the charge that the quality of the US public school system needed revamping was the irrationality, which politicians deployed to wrestle the curriculum away from teachers and university curriculum development specialists. Further to this, Cornbleth (2008) notes that even though external events (Sputnik, 1957 and the Vietnam War, 1965–1975), internal events (US Census, 2000 and the Terrorist Attack on the World Trade Center, September 11, 2001), and sociopolitical economic forces (the Great Depression of 1930s; the Civil Rights Movement of the 1950s–1960s; the Bush administration, 2001; the Economic Depression, 2007; the Obama administration, 2008–2016) seem to have influenced US curricular thought over the decades, "there has been relatively little systematic examination of what makes a difference, when, where and how" (p. 144). Sears and Marshall (2000) observe that during the 1950s, conceptualizing curriculum the Tylerian way dominated the field and behavioral objectives became the mantra for curriculum enactment. However, Sears and Marshall also report the existence during this period of a dichotomy among curriculum specialists where one group focused on "curriculum in a pure or theoretical sense" (p. 201) and another group emphasized "life in schools as their starting point" (p. 201).

A generation of curriculum theorists came of age during the 1960s era of "political activism, civil rights marches, anti-war rallies and acts of civil disobedience" (Sears and Marshall 2000, p. 201). At that time James Macdonald, a curriculum generalist, argued that education should be grouped within the humanities and not the sciences (Sears and Marshall 2000). The discipline "is made up," Macdonald (1971) told us then, "of problems in social policy, social decision making and social action" (p. 121). According to Wraga and Hlebowitsh (2013), a different generation of curriculum scholars emerged at the beginning of the 1970s that "pronounced the historic curriculum field 'dead' and launched a self-styled reconceptualization of curriculum studies" (p. 426). In 1973, William F. Pinar planned a landmark conference, which in turn was attended by a growing band of new curriculum revolutionaries who provoked the "re-conceptualization of the curriculum studies as political, historical and autobiographical" (Sears and Marshall 2000, p. 204). Pinar brought to the fore a reconceptualization of curriculum which engendered a new path to curriculum theorizing. Pinar's reconceptualization of curriculum, now rooted in politics, history, and autobiography, pronounced life narrative as the new way of conceptualizing curriculum. Davis and Sumara (2000) describe their frustrations as student teachers during the 1970s when a behaviorist doctrine still reigned:

> As we each learned more about working with different groups of students, in different schools and communities, amid tremendous social, economic, and political change, it became obvious that learning outcomes could not be contained by orderly boxes, and teaching intentions refused to be bounded by the tidy grids we had been asked to create. (p. 822)

Evidently, until the 1970s, the knowledge that would lead to social efficiency underlay curriculum theorizing, inquiry, and practice as the goal of the educational enterprise. The most effective way to enact the curriculum was the Tylerian preset-behavioral-objectives-step-by-step approach.

The identification of curriculum workers in the curriculum field and their respective roles in curriculum development characterized the latter part of the second moment. Sears and Marshall (2000) observe that curriculum specialists at this time "continued to borrow freely from a variety of academic disciplines while focusing on the cultural struggle and everyday life, the competitive ethos, and the moral and spiritual crises in education" (p. 208). Hilda Taba's (1902–1967) hallmark book, *Curriculum Development: Theory and Practice* (first published in 1962), drew significant attention in curriculum theorizing, inquiry, and practice during this moment. Taba's philosophical ideas on curriculum theory and curriculum development embraced four principles (Krull 2003). First, social processes are nonlinear, and sequential planning cannot model curriculum. Second, social institutions, among them school curricula and programs, are more likely to be defensibly rearranged if the leaders can use a reliable and coordinated system of development from bottom to top.

Third, the development of new curricula and programs is more effective if democratic principles guide the distribution of work. Fourth, the renovation of curricula and programs is not a short-term effort but a long process, lasting for years.

Having worked with John Dewey, Ralph Tyler, and Benjamin Bloom, Taba's work not only furthered some of her colleagues' ideas but also put forth some modifications. One of Taba's major contributions to curriculum theorizing was her conceptualization toward understanding curriculum about nonlinearity. Taba explained that ends and aims were not simple and easily comprehensible units. Therefore, it was unreal and impossible to set up rigid educational goals to develop specific objectives for a concrete plan (Krull 2003). Taba's bottom-up efficiency approach to curriculum theory, inquiry, and practice was also key toward re-conceptualizing and democratizing the processes of curriculum development (Krull 2003). Taba's metaphorical language included notions such as a "spiral curriculum"; "a multiplicity" of learning objectives; "strategies of learning"; and "inductive teaching," all of which were rooted in her conception of a flexible and nonlinear curriculum.

The mid-1980s witnessed the development of *Naturalistic Inquiry*, published by Lincoln and Guba (1985), who propounded a new research paradigm that challenged the dictatorship of the popular rationalistic or scientific method. Naturalistic inquiry emphasized research in natural settings, qualitative research methods, the human as a research instrument, purposive sampling, grounded theory, emergent design, inductive data analyses, negotiated outcomes, case study reporting, idiographic interpretation, tentative applications, special criteria for trustworthiness, and focus-determined boundaries. A naturalistic paradigm intended to aid social scientists in investigating behavioral and social issues. The paradigm brought about a new conversation not only to the landscape of curriculum research, inquiry, and practice but also to research and inquiry in various fields (Lin 2012). A naturalistic approach moved hand in hand with the social constructivist view of reality advanced by Berger and Luekmann (1967). Social constructivists posited that individuals develop subjective meanings of their experiences to understand reality in the world. The subjective meanings are negotiated socially and historically within the individual's life settings through interaction with others (Creswell 2014). Social learning theorists including Lev Semavovich Vygotsky (1896–1934), Albert Bandura (1925–present), and Michael Eraut espoused the concept of learning as social interaction and knowledge as co-creation through cooperation, interaction, and negotiation among individuals (Cunningham et al. 2007). According to Wertsch (1985), the constructivist movement re-emphasized the active role the students play in acquiring knowledge and in the social construction of knowledge as an important principle in sociocultural theory. The interfacing and intermingling of social constructivist concepts and those of social learning theorists rooted in the milieu of naturalistic inquiry ushered in a new and different way of engaging with curriculum theorizing, inquiry, and practice.

Curriculum scholars of the second moment of the curriculum field also borrowed some concepts and principles from the proponents of the humanistic theory of learning including John Dewey (1859–1952), Alexander Sutherland Neill (1883–1973), Carl Rogers (1902–1987), and Abraham Maslow (1908–1970). Knowledge, for the humanists, is deemed infinite with limitless possibilities. The learner's potential for growth is considered to be boundless. Therefore, learners only need to be empowered to take charge of the learning process for them to unleash their potential for growth. The teacher then is a facilitator of the learning process and is responsible for creating an enabling environment in which the learner explores new ideas through reflection and critical inquiry (Cunningham et al. 2007). The metaphors of the humanistic language included words such as "self-worth," "self-esteem," "self-actualization," "reflection," and "self-analysis" pointing to the centrality of the learner's engagement in the learning process and of meeting the learner's needs. The individual learner and the learners' social, political, economic, and cultural context or setting became central to curriculum theorizing and enactment in an endeavor to answering the call for "learner-centeredness."

The third moment of curriculum, which we date back to 2001, is characterized by the internationalization of our field and is a process that promises another paradigmatic shift. This third moment sought to invite "cosmopolitan curriculum research" and challenge "the disabling provincialism of American exceptionality" (Pinar 2014, p. 525). Among the outstanding curriculum theorists of the third moment is William E. Doll (1931–2017). Rooted in John Dewey's belief in science and the methodology of experimentation and the interactional concept of change (Schecter 2011), Doll delves into "devising a curriculum that is dynamic, emergent, transformative and non-linear" (Trueit 2012, p. 1). Like Dewey, Doll believes that it is through reflection and interaction on situations in the present and those in the past that individuals grow intellectually. According to Trueit (2012), Doll underscores the importance of reflective thinking as a process that brings about transformation within the individual and in the environment through the subject's interaction with other subjects in that particular environment. Doll borrows concepts and ideas from various curriculum theorists and educational philosophers in an eclectic fashion while modifying some and creating new ones to propose a "new" conceptualization of curriculum and the entire education enterprise. Doll puts forth the idea that nature is complex, fractal, self-organizing, and turbulent, drawn from contemporary science, complexity theory, chaos theory, and fractal geometry. His complex conceptualizations of curriculum underlie his fervent proposal for the urgency to follow a new path of curriculum conceptualization, inquiry, and practice.

In 1967, Whitehead observed "the problem of keeping knowledge alive, of preventing it from becoming inert ... is the central problem of all education" (as cited by Doll 2005, p. 5). Reflecting on Whitehead's assertion, "ideas," Doll argues, "are inert when they are disconnected, atomistic, isolated" (p. 111). Ideas are not related to the practicalities of life, an individual's interests, or the field of which they are part. Doll's view of curriculum as dynamic, emergent, nonlinear, and transformative influences his perception of the kind of knowledge that is of greatest worth and how that knowledge should emerge during the teaching and learning experience. For Doll (2002), teaching is journeying with others on "a path of learning engagement and personal transformation" (p. 97). Doll employs several sets of metaphors in advancing curriculum theorizing, inquiry, and practice. Doll proposed a curriculum that is rich, relational, recursive, and rigorous (the 4Rs). The 4Rs were supplemented by the 5Cs, namely currere, complexity, cosmology, conversation, and community that engendered complex thinking. Doll also proposed play, precision, and pattern (the 3Ps) as methods for curriculum enactment. Lastly, Doll espouses spirit as curriculum in the third space; science and story are the first and second spaces, respectively.

Some contemporary situational learning theorists including Etienne Wenger, Jean Lave, Paul Hager, and Stephen Billet share some of the concepts that Doll propounds for the curriculum in the third space. Situational learning theory emphasizes the integral link between learning and the social environment (Cunningham et al. 2007). Here, knowledge is meaningful in a particular context in which it is learned, and social interaction is a fundamental part of situated learning. Social learning theorists use metaphors such as sharing ideas, views, and opinions, the co-creation of knowledge, and interactive negotiation during the learning experience. Doll with Trueit (2012) and Mason (2008) warn that a complex relationship in curriculum cannot be reduced because the whole is greater than its parts. Thus, discerning curriculum complexity requires a balance of intellectual struggle and understanding that can be achieved reflectively (Rasmussen 2012). Instead of taking what someone else says to be true, reflection allows thinkers to generate their own "truth." Dewey calls this process reconstruction or reinvention of knowledge, a by-product of humans reflecting on their experiences (Doll 1993). Knowledge is the interaction of thinking and experience; it does not exist independent of human experience; it exists through acting reflectively. Reflection on any past or present situation allows one to grow intellectually (Doll 1993). It is through reflective practice that individuals are persuaded to transform their thinking and commit to renewed practice. For this imperative, curriculum theorists should not only theorize about curriculum but also take on the task of doing empirical research at the intersection of theory and practice.

Such assumptions of curriculum knowledge growth persuaded a teacher educator to engage her students (referred to as educators in this study) to reflect on curriculum through reading and face-to-face classroom interaction. Thus, the following research question framed the study at hand: What are educators' qualitatively differing conceptions of curriculum?

METHODOLOGY

All twelve students, three males, and nine females enrolled in the doctoral seminar (curriculum and instruction course) participated in the study. There were four African Americans, seven Caucasians, three people who identified as Middle Eastern, and one Asian American, with diverse experiences from various countries. The educators represented varying professions with the majority in an educative role.

Each week two or three educators led the class discussion about the complexities of curriculum discourse. Throughout the semester, as part of their assignment, the educators were expected to keep a reflective journal to explore their and peers' evolving thoughts, questions, and ideas of curriculum theory. With the aid of their journal writing, they also dialogued on Blackboard. Based on their journal writing and e-dialogues, each educator wrote two sets of reflective papers consisting of five pages.

All twelve educators consented to use their reflective papers and Blackboard dialogues for this study. We downloaded e-dialogues from the system. For ethical reasons, data analysis began only after the course was complete, and the marking period was over.

We assigned a letter code and a pseudonym to each educator. All twenty-four reflective papers and discussion board dialogues were carefully read and critically analyzed using phenomenography. Through an iterative process, each author of this study color coded and labeled the common conceptions to develop the descriptive categories. To agree upon the descriptive categories for ensuring inter-rater reliability and validity, we held three one and one half hour meetings. These results were subsequently presented to two researchers within the curriculum field to critically analyze the match between the descriptive categories of educators' conceptions, excerpts of educators' reflections as evidence, and researchers' interpretations.

RESULTS AND DISCUSSION

Based on educators' reflections, we depicted three descriptive categories of conceptions of curriculum theory focusing on student learning. They are as follows: promoting openness and flexibility, listening to students' voices, and engaging in reflective thinking.

Promoting Openness and Flexibility

A curriculum that promotes openness and flexibility for student learning was the focus of educators' discussion. For example, Aaliyah reflected on Randall's comments about students needing the freedom and encouragement to think outside the existing paradigms.

> Randall stated that the current educational models are framed with no realistic expectations of students' needs and growth in mind. We must, therefore, encourage students to reinvent the wheel and work outside the given paradigms. Randall's comments are in line with what Doll speaks about regarding [the] learners' reinventing the wheel. Doll believes learners should be helped to transform and blossom their intellectual powers and creativity through the interaction and the connection of their learning to the real-life contexts. (Aaliyah, November 10, 2014)

Randall, according to Aaliyah, is of the view that current educational models neglect students' need and growth. Pointing to Randall's connection to Doll's notion of "reinventing the wheel" rather than thinking about it in a traditional sense and not requiring students to reinvent what has been known, Aaliyah states that a child's learning should involve connections to and interactions with real-life contexts that will transform "intellectual powers and creativity."

Kristen notes that the notion of "reinventing the wheel" for students is likely only in an educational system where administrators, teachers, and students are in synchronicity and are adaptable (Doll 1993, p. 193).

> This ability to reinvent the wheel and allow the educational experience to progress organically is only possible when all parties recognize its importance and allow[s] the programming to be adaptable at the administrative, teacher, and student level. Curriculum focused on the intellectual and emotional relationships becomes less objective and deterministic. This promotion of creative thinking and freedom breathes new life to Doll's "spirit" and "story" in an educational setting. Teacher adaptability and flexibility is how curriculum can become rich and full of possibilities. (Kristen, October 6, 2014)

Kristen notes, reinventing the wheel is possible only when programming can be adaptable "at the administrative, teacher and student level." The curriculum can become less "objective and deterministic" when it focuses on "intellectual and emotional relationships." Creative thinking and freedom breathe life into Doll's spirit and story for learning allowing critical thoughts to emerge from interactions, not impositions. When the teacher qualities of "adaptability and flexibility" to make the curriculum rich with possibilities are absent, a student learning to think critically would be hampered. Thus, teachers should be allowed the flexibility to model traits of adaptability in the classroom.

Educators highlighted situations where teachers strive to be adaptable, but administrators restrict deviations from programming.

> Melissa feels that the curriculum she is teaching is more passive, and certainly more restrictive. She is asked to follow scripted lessons and not deviate from the given scripts. This is extremely restrictive for both the teacher and the learner. (Sarah, November 10, 2014)
>
> If teachers are not given space, trust, and respect, they will be like obedient servants. (Saina, October 6, 2014)

Educators need the freedom to promote abstract thinking and creativity in curriculum. When educators are placed in a facilitative role, learners can craft their own experience and advance to a more experiential learning style. (Kristen, October 6, 2014)

In essence, educators' reflective thoughts as revealed by the above excerpts suggest that they do not have the autonomy to adapt and create their curriculum, but must follow "scripted lessons and not deviate" as mentioned by Sarah. Saina's image of this restriction is that of an "obedient servant" to a master. Kristen highlights the need for teacher "freedom" to promote thinking and creativity to design a curriculum that will facilitate "experiential learning." Thus, it is necessary for administrators to be more cognizant of teachers' notions of teaching and learning rather than focus on their programming.

In contrast, situations might characterize administrators who are open to change that empower and encourage teachers to try new teaching strategies only to find teachers' reluctance to abandon old strategies.

Randall stated, "What happens if your set objectives are not being met and your instructional methods are not getting students to learn?" A good teacher should be adaptable. We need teachers to be creative people who discover the learner's path. (Noah, October 6, 2014)

If the teacher is not adaptable enough to change instructional methods to promote students' learning needs, the class agreed with Noah that instruction and student learning would be limited. Teacher buy-in, or rather lack of buy-in, may be one reason for inflexibility in teaching. Akerlind (2008) suggests that learning should be student centered and teachers should turn their attention to what students are experiencing in class and how their actions impact student learning.

In analyzing the different dynamics of an administrator/teacher relationship, there exist situations of synchronicity, but both are unadaptable to the needs of students according to the following excerpts:

Sarah stated, it would be nice if all teachers had the opportunity to be creative and drive curriculum in a creative way, but in a system of high accountability teachers and administrators are afraid to try. (Randall, November 10, 2014)

To have all students do the same problem, text, exercise in the same uniform manner is an inefficient way to teach and a poor way to learn

(Noah, November 10, 2014). In discussing current educational conditions in urban public schools, Trisha said it seems that the art of teaching has been abandoned and teachers have been replaced with technicians. (Randall, November 10, 2014)

The accountability expectations of current teaching might be a leading cause for creating a system of restriction and frustration for both teachers and administrators. In this situation, both teachers and administrators do not feel empowered to provide what is necessary to educate students. In an era of high accountability, teachers and administrators find it easier to follow the status quo and not adapt. In urban public schools, teachers have been reduced to mere "technicians" according to Randall. Unfortunately, such constraints do not allow teachers to promote abstract thinking within the lesson, to give students an opportunity to craft their own experience, and to explore the "spirit" of the subject (Doll 1993).

Discussion occurred around the idea that teachers take responsibility for continuous learning to be adaptable to meet curriculum challenges. Dana and Melissa reflected on the preceding issue:

> Kristen expressed her view by stating that we do not shape curriculum, curriculum shapes curriculum and that we are bound to make mistakes because we are always faced with challenges. It is our responsibility to learn. (Dana, October 6, 2014)
>
> Teaching is not a set process, it's about your interaction. Let's use rigor, let's play, and let's make mistakes because we are shaped by curriculum. We don't make it. It's about being and it's our responsibility to go out there and learn. (Melissa, October 6, 2014)

Dana reminds us that "curriculum shapes curriculum" and teachers are "bound to make mistakes." She takes up the responsibility to learn, a trait of teacher adaptability. Melissa states that curriculum shapes teachers because they "don't make it." Like Dana, Melissa also understands that making mistakes is normal and teachers take the "responsibility to go out and learn." Teacher concern is caused by a continuous change in the profession and teachers are continually operating in an atmosphere of chaos (Doll 1993). For instance, contemporary curriculum and teacher professional changes include instructional technology advances, instructional best practices, and school climate and demographics. As well, the strength of the teacher is measured by their ability to learn and adapt to

98   J. EBENEZER ET AL.

meet curricular and professional challenges. For this reason, Dana and Melissa bargain for making mistakes and taking responsibility to learn new knowledge advancements and meet new curricular expectations (the attributes of teacher adaptability).

Listening to Students' Voices

During the doctoral seminar, discussion revolved around the notion of considering students' voices as curriculum frameworks. This view is evident in the following excerpts.

> The idea of teachers relinquishing power to students is a change oppositional to the current curriculum pattern. Essentially, the students' ideas would be used in the construction of curriculum or added into the existing curriculum. Furthermore, the teacher would sacrifice the power of being the expert and join the students in their world to create experiential learning. (Kristen, November 10, 2014)
>
> A complex curriculum designed by teachers with student input would most likely benefit the students more than a linear program that has goals set by someone other than the intended user. (Thea, November 10, 2014)

To incorporate students' ideas into existing curriculum and to join with students to create experiential learning were viewed by Kristen as a sacrifice of expert power. Thea points to the complexity of curriculum with students' input and suggests that such a curriculum will benefit students more than a linear one. As Doll (1993) contends, when power lies outside the entity, the rules are designed and enforced by the powerful. In our postmodern era, the current methods dictate that the teacher is in power and will control the learner's thinking. The systematic and explicit use of students' conceptions in curriculum redesign supports Doll's notion of power, which was emphasized by the teacher educator of the doctoral seminar course based on the "variation theory of learning" underpinning phenomenography (e.g., Wood et al. 2013). These authors contemplate on the need for teachers to relinquish power to students by incorporating students' conceptions of natural and social phenomena and negotiating expert explanations with them. The educators' conceptions of the curriculum are rich with examples of the usefulness of encouraging student power over curriculum content. One way of releasing teacher power resides in viewing curriculum, not as a set of pre-determined structures and goals but as a way to provide freedom of learning:

Freedom of learning must come into play to help children be creative, ask questions, inquire, and look for answers. (Noah, November 10, 2014)

Teaching students how to think and make real connections between knowledge and real-life experiences should be one of the main themes in curriculum development. In this approach, learners are motivated to make their own reflections, understanding and learning, and raise questions. (Saina, November 10, 2014)

The discourse in class challenged how educators may work with the existing curriculum although they felt constrained by it. One way of overcoming their challenges is to incorporate students' ideas into the curriculum. Another way to work with the curriculum is not to view the curriculum as a set of rigid guidelines to be covered, but to uncover the core ideas and standards using a more inquiry-based approach.

Noah and Saina point to elements of inquiry. An authentic inquiry process is the exploration of ill-structured problems, open to variations of meaning and solutions. The inquiry-based curriculum allows for reflective practices requiring the learner to interact with concrete experiences and find a relationship with abstract thought (Patary-Ching and Roberson 2002). These authors state that inquiry provides a learner-centered, curricular framework that ensures learners see the world through a lens of questioning which allows them to make changes and adjustments to their thinking, experiment with tools in their environment, invent new tools, and venture further into their inquiries. Such an inquiry process does not lend itself to certainty and precision. Doll (1993) likens inquiry curriculum to an ecological view, rich with ambiguity and uncertainty and evolving. This image of learning enables a teacher to take the back seat and provide students the driver's seat for learning.

Engaging in Reflective Thinking

Several educators focused on reflective thinking for learning within today's educational system. Excerpts follow:

Children need to be reflective in order to learn. Being reflective allows students the opportunity to assess what they do well and what improvements they need to make. It is seeing relationships between materials being presented and making connections with real-life situations and experiences. It is creating new and original expressions of what is known and understood. (Melissa, October 6, 2014)

A true learning experience is one that is naturally felt and reflected upon, analyzed, and compared. The purpose of growth should be further growth. Constraining, or molding, the minds of the youth is not an option in this era. (Aaliyah, October 6, 2014)

Reflective thinking invites subjectivity into the classroom which opens up spaces for multiple opinions; consequently, students are exposed to various points of view, open-mindedness, deeper understanding, and much growth. It is important for teachers to support students in order to engage them in a constant reflective process that allows room for broader, nonlinear development. (Saina, November 10, 2014)

Aaliyah suggests that "true learning experience" has several characteristics and one of them is reflection. Melissa and Saina observe distinct values of reflecting thinking. Saina calls teachers to open up space to invite variations in views and to be open minded so that students will develop a deeper understanding and grow intellectually. Saina admonishes teachers who constantly engage students in reflection that "allows room for broader, non-linear development." While some educators reflect on the importance of students' reflecting on their learning, Noah places the responsibility on parents and teachers to be reflective and to bring reflective thinking to student awareness.

Families and schools are not attuned to reflective thinking. Perhaps, the discourse on reflective thinking was not and is not pervasive enough to inform and influence teacher training programs and teacher practice. (Noah, November 6, 2014)

There is a need to bring reflectiveness to the children in order to facilitate their journey to intellectual growth. We must engage parents and teachers in reflectiveness if children are to engage in reflective thinking in the learning process. (Noah, November 10, 2014)

Noah alludes to the idea that families and schools are not attuned to reflective thinking. He blames the discourse of reflective thinking itself, suggesting that it did not have a powerful influence on teacher preparation and teacher practice. Noah argues that student reflectivity is important for their intellectual growth, but this can be accomplished if parents and teachers engage in reflection. In line with Noah's concerns on teacher reflections, Latta and Kim (2011) make a similar case. Not only can the student learn from reflective practices, but the teacher can learn and improve on their practice through inquiry, specifically narrative inquiry that allows teachers to interrogate their teaching and learning by negotiating how the past, present, and future recursively interact with each other.

CURRICULAR IMPLICATIONS

This study used phenomenography as a learning theory and an analytical tool espoused by international scholars to identify descriptive categories of educators' conceptions of curriculum theory, all concerning learning (Ebenezer and Fraser 2001; Marton and Tsui 2004). Thus, this phenomenographic research has implications for curriculum theorists, practitioners, and researchers. Educators are admonished to practice adaptability to embrace openness, nonlinearity, and complexity in the curriculum. They are encouraged to explore students' conceptions to incorporate into the curriculum for explanatory transformation and shaping inquiry. Teacher educators need to model such practices in their university classroom to deepen their students' understanding of curriculum and to promote reflective thinking for learning. For continued growth, our doctoral students need to build knowledge through reflection and interactive discourse.

In this study, the educators focused on the conditions for quality learning, perhaps because most of them were classroom teachers and student learning was crucial to them. Exploring educators' conceptions of curriculum theory in the university classroom is important to understand the curricular issues that confront them. Furthermore, educators have the time and opportunity to engage in discourse with peers at a similar knowledge level. There is also increased likelihood for educators to undergo transformative experience based on the exposure to the curriculum theorists' tasks from the perspectives of their interpretive communities to advance knowledge.

Based on the variation theory of learning, this study provides educators the context to contemplate on various curriculum views. The reason is that they think about curriculum as the dispersion of perspectives existing at a given time in history rather than a progression getting better and better to find the most plausible theory as in science. The preceding argument is vital to narrowing the disconnect between curriculum theory and practice, and between universities and schools because practitioners do not believe in curriculum theorists or have confidence in adopting what they have to say (Petrina 2004; Pinar et al. 1995).

Curriculum theories are also often dismissed because of the enactment of standards, increased accountability, and high-stakes testing (Au 2011). Thus, this study gives the educators an alternative focus through the variation theory of learning to contemplate on one interpretive community of curriculum, a postmodern perspective, so that it becomes a part of their professional repertoire. Perhaps the kind of curriculum theorizing, inquiry, and practice that Doll (2003) proposed is the new direction for international curriculum scholars to reconsider. Curriculum, as Doll succinctly puts it, "honors, *and* utilizes the ineffable, the aesthetic, the creative, the passionate, the awe-inspiring ... *while* engaging difference with a sense of passion, play reverence, *and* respect" (p. 103). Curriculum so conceived is a space where science, story, and spirit interact toward teachers and students living, learning, and creating knowledge together.

References

Akerlind, G. (2008). A phenomenographic approach to developing academics' understanding of the nature of teaching and learning. *Teaching and Learning in Higher Education, 13*(6), 633–644.

Aoki, T. (2003). Postscript c. In W. F. Pinar & R. L. Irwin (Eds.), *Curriculum in a new key: The collected works of Ted T. Aoki* (pp. 453–457). Mahwah, NJ: Lawrence Erlbaum Associates.

Au, W. (2011). Teaching under the new taylorism: Standardization of the 21st century curriculum. *Journal of Curriculum Studies, 43*(1), 25–45.

Bellack, A. A. (1969). History of curriculum thought and practice. *Review of Educational Research, 39*(3), 283–292.

Berger, P. L., & Luekmann, T. (1967). *The social construction of reality: A treatise in the sociology of knowledge.* Garden City, NJ: Anchor.

Bradbeer, J. (2004). Undergraduate geographers' understandings of geography learning and teaching: A phenomenographic study. *Journal of Geography in Higher Education, 28*(1), 17–34.

Caswell, H. L. (1966). *Emergence of the curriculum as a field of professional work and study: Precedents and promises in the curriculum field.* New York: Teachers College Press.

Cornbleth, C. (2008). Climates of opinion and curriculum practices. *Journal of Curriculum Studies, 40*(2), 143–168.

Creswell, J. W. (2014). *Research design: Qualitative, quantitative, and mixed approaches* (4th ed.). Los Angeles, CA: Sage.

6 A PHENOMENOGRAPHY OF EDUCATORS' CONCEPTIONS ... 103

Cunningham, T., Gannon, J., Kavanagh, M., Greene, J., Reddy, L., & Whitson, L. (2007). *Theories of learning and curriculum design key positionalities and their relationships.* Dublin Institute of Technology [Online]. Available at http://level3.dit.ie/html/issue5/tony_cunningham/cunningham.pdf.

Davis, B., & Sumara, D. J. (2000). Curriculum forms: On assumed shapes of knowing and knowledge. *Journal of Curriculum Studies, 32*(6), 821–845.

Dillon, J. T. (2009). The questions of curriculum. *Journal of Curriculum Studies, 41*(3), 343–359.

Doll, W. E. (1972). A methodology of experience. In D. Trueit (Ed.). (2012), *Pragmatism, post-modernism, and complexity theory: The "fascinating imaginative realm" of William E. Doll, Jr.* (pp. 49–65). New York: Taylor and Francis.

Doll, W. E. (1993). *A post-modern perspective on curriculum.* New York: Teachers College Press.

Doll, W. E. (2002). Beyond methods. In D. Trueit (Ed.). (2012), *Pragmatism, post-modernism, and complexity theory: The "fascinating imaginative realm" of William E. Doll, Jr.* (pp. 81–97). New York: Taylor and Francis.

Doll, W. E. (2003). Modes of thought. In D. Trueit (Ed.). (2012), *Pragmatism, post-modernism, and complexity theory: The "fascinating imaginative realm" of William E. Doll, Jr.* (pp. 103–110). New York: Taylor and Francis.

Doll, W. E. (2005). Keeping knowledge alive. In D. Trueit (Ed.). (2012), *Pragmatism, post-modernism, and complexity theory: The "fascinating imaginative realm" of William E. Doll, Jr.* (pp. 111–119). New York: Taylor and Francis.

Ebenezer, J. V., & Fraser, D. (2001). First year chemical engineering students' conceptions of energy in solution process: Phenomenographic categories for common knowledge construction. *Science Education, 85,* 509–535.

Hlebowitsh, P. (2005). Generational ideas in curriculum: A historical triangulation. *Curriculum Inquiry, 35*(1), 73–87.

Hurren, W. (2003). Auto'-geo'-carto'-graphia' (a curricular collage). In W. Hurren & E. Hasebe-Ludt (Eds.), *Curriculum inter-text: Place/language/pedagogy* (pp. 111–121). New York: Peter Lang.

Kliebard, H. (1968). The curriculum field in retrospect. In P. W. F. Witt (Ed.), *Technology and the curriculum* (pp. 68–84). New York: Teachers College Press.

Krull, E. (2003). Hilda Taba (1902–1967). *Prospects, 33*(4), 481–491.

Latta, M., & Kim, J. (2011). Investing in the curricular lives of educators: Narrative inquiry as pedagogical medium. *Journal of Curriculum Studies, 43*(5), 679–695.

Lin, A. M. Y. (2012). Towards transformation of knowledge and subjectivity in curriculum inquiry: Insights from Chen Kuan-Hsing's "Asia as method". *Curriculum Inquiry, 42*(1), 153–178.

Lincoln, Y. S., & Guba, E. G. (1985). *Naturalistic inquiry.* Beverly Hills, CA: Sage.

Macdonald, J. B. (1971). Curriculum theory. *Journal of Educational Research, 64*(5), 196–200.

Marton, F., & Booth, S. (1997). *Learning and awareness.* Mahwah, NJ: Lawrence Erlbaum Associates.

Marton, F., & Tsui, A. (2004). *Classroom discourse and the space of learning.* Hillsdale, NJ: Lawrence Erlbaum.

Mason, M. (2008). Complexity theory and the philosophy of education. *Educational Philosophy and Theory, 40*(1), 4–18.

Norman, R. (2003). Whispers among places: Teaching and writing in-between past, present and future. In W. Hurren & E. Hasebe-Ludt (Eds.), *Curriculum inter-text: Place/language/pedagogy* (pp. 243–258). New York: Peter Lang.

Patary-Ching, J., & Roberson, M. (2002). Misconceptions about a curriculum-as-inquiry Framework. *Language Arts, 79*(6), 498–505.

Petrina, S. (2004). The politics of curriculum and instruction design/theory/form: Critical problems, projects, units, and modules. *Interchange, 35*(1), 81–126.

Pinar, W. F. (1977). *The re-conceptualization of curriculum studies.* A paper presented to the annual meeting of the American Educational Research Association. New York City.

Pinar, W. F. (Ed.). (2014). *International handbook of curriculum research* (2nd ed.). New York: Routledge.

Pinar, W. F., & Grumet, M. R. (1976). *Toward a poor curriculum.* Dubuque, IA: Kendall Hunt.

Pinar, W. F., Reynolds, W., Slattery, P., & Taubman, P. (1995). *Understanding curriculum: An introduction.* New York: Peter Lang.

Rasmussen, H. (2012). Wrestling with data. *Instructional Leadership, 33*(5), 46–49.

Ropo, E., & Autio, T. (2009). *International conversations on curriculum studies: Subject, society, and curriculum.* Rotterdam, the Netherlands: Sense Publishing.

Schecter, B. (2011). "Development as an aim for education": A reconsideration of Dewey's vision. *Curriculum Inquiry, 41*(2), 250–266.

Schwab, J. (1983). The practical 4: Something for curriculum professors to do. *Curriculum Inquiry, 13*(3), 239–265.

Schwab, J. J. (2013). The practical: A language of the curriculum. *Journal of Curriculum Studies, 45*(5), 591–621. Retrieved from http://dx.doi.org/10.1080/00220272.2013.809152.

Sears, J. T., & Marshall, D. (2000). Generational influences on contemporary curriculum thought. *Journal of Curriculum Studies, 32*(2), 199–214.

6 A PHENOMENOGRAPHY OF EDUCATORS' CONCEPTIONS ... 105

Sohoni, D., & Petrovic, M. (2010). Teaching a global sociology: Suggestions for globalizing the U.S. curriculum. *Teaching Sociology, 38*(4), 287–300.

Trueit, D. (Ed.). (2012). *Pragmatism, post-modernism, and complexity theory: The "fascinating imaginative realm" of William E. Doll, Jr.* New York: Taylor and Francis.

Tyler, R. (1950). *Basic principles of curriculum and instruction.* Chicago: University of Chicago Press.

Weenie, A. (2008). Curricular theorizing from the periphery. *Curriculum Inquiry, 38*(5), 545–557.

Wertsch, J. V. (1985). *Vygotsky and the social formation of mind.* Cambridge, MA: Harvard University Press.

Westbury, I. (2005). Reconsidering Schwab's "practicals": A response to Peter Hlebowitsh's "generational ideas in curriculum: A historical triangulation". *Curriculum Inquiry, 35*(1), 89–101.

Whitehead, A. N. (1967). *The aims of education and other essays.* New York: The Free Press (Original publication, 1929).

Wood, L., Ebenezer, J., & Boone, R. (2013). Effects of an intellectually caring model on urban African American alternative high school students' conceptual change and achievement. *Chemistry Education Research and Practice.* https://doi.org/10.1039/c3rp00021d.

Wraga, W., & Hlebowitsh, P. (2013). Toward a renaissance in curriculum theory and development in the USA. *Journal of Curriculum Studies, 35*(4), 425–437.

CHAPTER 7

Crossing Borders: A Story of Refugee Education

Karen Meyer, Cynthia Nicol, Siyad Maalim, Mohamud Olow,
Abdikhafar Ali, Samson Nashon, Mohamed Bulle,
Ahmed Hussein, Ali Hussein and Muhammad Hassan Said

Moulid Iftin Hujale, a freelance writer, describes his experience growing up in a refugee camp:

> Throughout my ... education, I rarely heard about my home country. Most of my history classes were about Kenya and when we learned about East Africa, Somalia was a side note. I can list all the different tribes of Kenya and explain the country's history and political system, but I know almost nothing about the people, history and politics of my native soil. We memorized the Kenyan national anthem. I forgot that of my motherland. (IRIN 2011)

K. Meyer (✉) · C. Nicol · S. Nashon
Faculty of Education, University of British Columbia, Vancouver, BC, Canada
e-mail: karen.meyer@ubc.ca

C. Nicol
e-mail: cynthia.nicol@ubc.ca

S. Nashon
e-mail: samson.nashon@ubc.ca

© The Author(s) 2019
C. Hébert et al. (eds.), *Internationalizing Curriculum Studies,*
https://doi.org/10.1007/978-3-030-01352-3_7

107

Refugee camp communities value and take responsibility for the education of their children. Given the urgency and structure of "emergency education," outside authority and agencies conceive and control choices related to curriculum and its language of instruction. Adapting to the educational system of the host country appears as a viable solution alongside its currency of benefits (national certification, diplomas, and scholarships). In this case, however, students do not "see" themselves—their culture, language, and history—in the host country's curriculum, which impacts imagining a future beyond the camp borders. Herein lies contradiction: the opportunity for education in a long-term refugee situation but with a curriculum that has limitations, perhaps barriers, for transition and life after returning to the homeland. The implication of knowing one's homeland as a "side note" remains a complicated challenge for curriculum theorizing when considering choice, participation, and possibility for education in refugee lives, and in view of the "social, political and economic contradictions" (Freire 2000, p. 35) displaced people around the world face.

S. Maalim · M. Olow · A. Ali · M. Bulle · A. Hussein
Vancouver, BC, Canada

M. Olow
e-mail: m.olow@alumni.ubc.ca

A. Ali
e-mail: abdikhafar.ali@alumni.ubc.ca

M. Bulle
e-mail: mohamed.bulle@alumni.ubc.ca

A. Hussein
e-mail: a.hussein@alumni.ubc.ca

A. Hussein · M. H. Said
Surrey, BC, Canada

M. H. Said
e-mail: hassanh@sfu.ca

Our research is part of a larger project dedicated to living, learning, and teaching in a refugee camp. Our findings indicate the importance of paying attention to perspectives relevant and unique to refugee communities. Firstly, distinctions between immediate and long-term solutions for education need critical scrutiny. The exigency of time plays out in immediate solutions becoming fixed, long-term conditions wherein refugee communities have no choice but to adapt (e.g., to encampment and provision of rations). Secondly, historical, local, and global contexts matter to understanding the conditions and difficulties displaced communities have experienced and still face. Life-threatening situations that lead people to cross borders and disconnect from their homeland happen under the auspices of intact global, economic, and political agendas or conflicts. Thirdly, in the context of emergency education, the weaknesses of an inherited curriculum warrant critique. Such review opens thinking to new possibilities, leading to different courses of responsive action. Fourthly, significant leadership in curriculum decisions and practices should come from within the refugee community and thereby create a legitimate voice in educational discourses. Sharing experiences particularize a meaningful whole of refugee lives.

In this chapter, we open narrative and dialogical spaces based on stories and interpretations of living, learning, and teaching in Dadaab Refugee Camp in northeastern Kenya. As a research team and authors of this chapter, seven of us grew up in the Dadaab Refugee Camp, became teachers in secondary schools there, and currently are studying in or graduated from Canadian universities. Three of us who have taught secondary teachers within a teacher education diploma program in the camp are curriculum researchers in a Canadian university.

In our research, we spend considerable time engaged in dialogues around stories and experiences, including our own, gathered from practicing teachers inside the camp. Between story lines, we negotiate meaning through reaffirming and elaborating our own experiences within Dadaab, much like a "hermeneutical conversation" between story and interpreters (Gadamer 1975, p. 388). Further analyses of our dialogues have led to identifying conditions and contradictions across the stories, related to border, temporality, loss, and choice. For example, we take up the concept of "border" as a critical referent that marks the dynamics of borderlands people cross and inhabit.

Two questions guide our intent of this chapter. How might "refugee education" be inscribed in curriculum studies and its emphases? What do marginalized narratives of education among displaced peoples offer the conversation on internationalizing curriculum? This chapter comprises three parts. In the first part, we introduce Dadaab Refugee Camp in the wider context of crossing borders. Specifically, we provide brief summaries of the situation leading to the construction of the camp, as well as challenges regarding the provision of education, beginning with primary and later with secondary schools. We then turn to three stories drawing upon the experiences of our research team: leaving the homeland, being a student in school, and being a secondary teacher in the camp. Excerpts from our data-analysis meetings follow, written as a conversation with examples of further interpretation, particularly around "border." We end the chapter by posing questions and discussion relevant to displaced people and critical to the study of curriculum and internationalization.

CROSSING BORDERS

Within our work, we found Henry Giroux's use of "border" particularly fruitful toward our interpretations of struggles refugee communities face upon leaving their homeland and living in an encampment situation.

> Thinking in terms of borders allows one to critically engage the struggle over those territories, spaces, and contact zones where power operates to either expand or shrink the distance and connectedness among individuals, groups, and places. (Giroux 2005, p. 2)

For people forced to seek asylum, national borders become primary challenges. Leaving one's homeland manifests as both a traumatic and risky endeavor. Survival and a future depend upon decisions whether or not to cross as a refugee. Those who cross physical borders still encounter cultural borders, wherein social codes, experiences, and language differ. They meet boundaries between themselves and the host population based on fear that those seeking asylum threaten "the well-being of a state or the character of a nation" (Zembylas 2010, p. 33).

Once inside the borders of the camp, refugee communities meet with loss. In her essay, "We Refugees" (1994), Hannah Arendt's description of loss is compelling: Daily life within the familiarity of home becomes a memory; confidence and expression fade when leaving one's occupation and language; private lives rupture from the loss of loved ones.

7 CROSSING BORDERS: A STORY OF REFUGEE EDUCATION   111

The refugee camp itself has sociopolitical agendas, organization, rules and regulations, and a culture of refugeeness with particular ways people connect and live together. One's cultural practices and values become difficult or impossible to sustain. Imagine the change to the everyday life of a Somali pastoralist who comes from generations of nomadic life, herding livestock in a constant search of pasture and water, whereby "pasturage is regarded as a gift of God" (Lewis 2002, p. 9). Cultural practices are situated differently outside the homeland. For example, girls and women face cultural contradictions when NGO-driven interventions arise to counterbalance perceived gender inequities, such as the privilege for boys and the absence of girls/women in attaining education. Dependency on camp aid compromises traditional roles of men as patriarchs and providers for their families.

Life in a refugee camp turns more complex when prolonged conflict back in his/her homeland means few prospects of returning home and the continuation of new arrivals. In such time, camps remain holding centers for survival, rather than places of residence and education (Crisp 2003). Even though most refugee camps become protracted situations (five years or longer), the provision of education falls behind priorities related to security, shelter, food, and health. UNESCO (2015) reports that a mere 2% of humanitarian assistance goes to education.

Dadaab Refugee Camp

The United Nations High Commissioner for Refugees (UNHCR) with the Kenyan government established Dadaab Refugee Camp (for 90,000) in 1992 at the host township of Dadaab, Kenya, near the Somali border. No one knew how much time would pass, coinciding with civil war, the instability of Somalia and the collapse of its infrastructure. At that time, the UN estimated that a million people sought refuge in Kenya, Ethiopia, and countries outside Africa, and 300,000 more Somali people died from war-triggered famine (Lewis 2002, p. 265). Schools, training facilities, and universities became casualties in the mass destruction of Somalia's infrastructure, which left a bleak future for its children (Abdi 1998). By 2007, the Kenyan-Somali border was officially closed since the conflict in Somalia showed no evidence of decreasing. However, the influx of refugees into Kenya continued in large numbers at times, categorized as "emergency" conditions (including drought). The UNHCR built more adjacent camps at the site.

112 K. MEYER ET AL.

Today, over 235,000 people are registered in the five camps that now comprise Dadaab Refugee Camp, which covers 50 square kilometers (UNHCR 2018). After 26 years, some say Dadaab Refugee Camp is more a city than a camp; others say more a prison than a city. Although the Kenyan government provides land, it maintains the policy of encampment and strict borders, allowing no opportunity for the people in the camp to locally integrate or have national status in Kenya. A third generation has been born within the camp without a national identity, without a confident answer to "where are you from?"

School in Dadaab

Initially, the expectation that people will return to their homeland in a short time underlies decisions around education. Hence, education remains ancillary to other emergency aid. In long-term situations, the establishment of schools in refugee camps meets rugged obstacles, such as untrained teachers, scarce resources, culture and language diversity, curriculum debates, and a lack of physical structures. Given such obstacles and priorities, the story of formal education in Dadaab offers hope in its accomplishment. Young adults who came to the camp as children are its teachers.

In 1993, CARE-Kenya organized children in classes to provide primary education, using UNESCO material written in Somali language. Three years later, with no end to the conflict in Somalia, debate and discussion formed around a formal curriculum, opened to the Parent–Teacher Association, parents, CARE, and UNHCR. In 1997, discussion led to agreement on the Kenyan National Curriculum, which became formalized with the Kenyan Ministry of Education. While not all parents agreed, the decision ensured students had opportunity to receive a recognized certification. The Kenyan education system consists of eight years of primary education and four years of secondary education, taught in English. At the end of primary school, students sit for the Kenyan Certificate of Primary Education (KCPE), an examination to determine transition into secondary school.

As a beginning step toward formal education, the children needed to be assessed as to grade levels, a huge task concluding with only ten students qualified to be in class eight and sit for the KCPE (although there was no secondary schools in Dadaab at that time). By the year 2000, the number of students passing the KCPE grew to about 200, and the

7 CROSSING BORDERS: A STORY OF REFUGEE EDUCATION   113

UNHCR funded one secondary school with one class in each primary school location and eventually two more schools (one in each of three camps). Given this disparity in numbers between primary and secondary school accessibility, in 2008 the refugee community established three additional community secondary schools, housed initially in a few primary school classrooms. Parents "contributed their money by selling their [food] rations" (Dr. Marangu Njogu, Executive Director Windle Trust Kenya, personal interview, November 2015).

At the end of secondary school, students register and sit for seven examinable subjects for the Kenyan Certificate of Secondary Education (KCSE), the "National Exam." The first KCSE in Dadaab occurred in 2003. As of 2015, about 90,000 learners attended 23 primary schools and seven secondary schools (UNHCR 2015). Still thousands of children do not attend school. Attendance drops after primary school, given KCPE results and other factors, such as working to subsidize family incomes (Dagane 2013).

STORIES AND DIALOGUES

I was a six-year-old boy…

The bond between my father and grandmother, Batulo,[1] meant I was assigned to be by her side and help her, such as bringing her pots of water for *Weyso*[2] before prayer. Batulo loved me more than any of her other grandchildren.

After armed men looted our livestock and belongings, my family decided to move to a nearby town. Batulo declined and instead demanded to be taken to my aunt. I had no choice but to follow her. Upon reaching my aunt's home, Batulo gave my uncle, Aden, and I permission to go and seek refuge in Kenya, as it would be safer and less encumbering than staying with my aunt's family.

One sunny morning, my uncle said he was ready for the long journey. I was six years old. I loved Batulo deeply because I had always been with her. I kept hoping she would let me stay with her. I managed to hide for some hours, refusing to go until Batulo became angry. She hugged me for the very last time. Soon it was time for me to gather my almost

---

[1] Pseudonym names given.

[2] Cleansing in preparation for prayer.

"nothing" belongings. I kept looking back, waving a sorrowful good-bye to my grandmother. My uncle packed rice and twenty liters of water. Our journey was 208 kilometers, all by foot.

On our way to the border, we met other refugees: youth, elders, children, and people with disabilities, walking and hopeful of completing this journey. Aden and I walked, jogged, and ran to cover more ground. When I grew tired, he gave me a short rest. This journey was not only tiresome and tough, but also we encountered militiamen who would interrogate refugee travelers. Numerous times they killed men. To avoid such challenges, my uncle and I travelled at night, which was also precarious because of wild animals.

Sometimes, I couldn't walk and Aden carried me on his shoulders. After a rest, he asked me to walk and encouraged me to stride "otherwise we would either die of hunger on the way or the wild animals would eat us." This tactic worked because, as a young boy, I was scared of hyenas and lions. Toward the end of our journey, a generous Kenyan driver recognized our hardship and gave us a ride part of the way.

Research Team Dialogue: Losses in Leaving

"We were all young when our families decided to cross the border to Kenya."

"My family was looking for security, food and shelter and somewhere to get away from the violence in Somalia."

"Most of the people in rural areas were pastoralists. Gunmen looted their animals, leaving people with nothing. Parents didn't have anything to give to their children, didn't have anything to sustain their lives. The only way out for them was to come to the camps in Kenya."

"We lost everything. For parents leaving meant sacrificing everything; everything they invested in Somalia was lost—property, education, income..."

"From a parent's view, when their children cross that border, they gain access to education. They move forward. But when families don't cross they stay in the same situation. The border is physical in that way."

"So by saying there is a border, we're essentially saying that some will cross it and some won't. Everyone can't cross. We already accept that some will stay behind."

"Initially there is the physical crossing. When you get to the camps, what do you have to overcome, adjust to? You are crossing into a new culture. You are still Somali and you become a refugee, which is traumatizing. So it's a different border. Now *who* you are is being called refugee."

"In the camps, the Kenyan curriculum is used and doesn't teach about Somali history and culture."

"In schools, we were taught about Kenyan history, people and culture and not our own heritage. When we go back, it'll be very hard to identify ourselves with the people in Somalia, and we do not have Kenyan citizenship."

The "Magical" Malaria Tablet

Malaria is a mosquito-borne infectious disease. In Dadaab, mosquitos multiply commonly during rainy seasons and the aftermath when grasses grow near the homesteads. The humanitarian organizations in the camp distribute mosquito nets to us on a yearly basis, so we can protect ourselves from mosquito biting. Malaria attacks indiscriminately and becomes disastrous for those of us students waiting to sit for the Kenyan National Examination. Malaria makes a student too sick to study, go to school, or attend that final examination—the worst nightmare of all time. The examination is administered only once a year to students in the last year of secondary school and takes place over twenty days. Any of us who miss a single paper of the examination, even for a genuine reason, such as a documented, severe heath condition, will have to wait for another year to take it. This time becomes extremely stressful!

At the end of secondary school, Farhan used to take many irregular and unprescribed doses of malaria tablets. He felt the drug was no longer giving him its magical power over malaria. The health implications of taking too many tablets did not deter him as long as he believed the tablets were able to keep him fit for the examination. Many other students faced this issue. When the examination approaches, "perceived" malaria becomes the main worry of many of us, and the tablets seem to be the only way to deal with it. So the same tablet is taken as both prevention and cure of malaria. This situation remains a dilemma in Dadaab between the policy of the secondary curriculum with its examination and the myth surrounding the malaria tablet.

Research Team Dialogue: How Do We Deal with the Risks?

"Taking overdoses of the malaria pills can even have more health risks than the malaria itself, but you get a scary feeling to think of missing the National Exam because then it takes you one more year to wait to sit for the next one."

"Have you all had malaria?" [Heads nod.]

"I had it one time and was supposed to take 24 tables in sets of three. I had the exam in the next few days so I took two more sets at one time. You get dizzy and stuff like that."

"Yea, you have huge side effects. The best time to take the pills is three weeks before the exam."

"So this is about the border of the National Exam."

"The exam is a border to jump over, get a scholarship and out of the camp, or remain in the camp where the opportunity is very much limited."

"The risk is greater on one side of a border. In your mind, if you don't take that exam, that's a bigger long-term risk than taking these malaria pills. You weigh out those risks on either side of that border."

"Most of the students who get malaria are the boys who study in the schools at night. There's grass on school grounds. You have to study at school at night because there are electric lights to study under. You know you will get malaria."

"If you are affected by malaria during the exam, it reduces your thinking ability and your physical strength for this three-week-long exam."

"So we knowingly allowed our life goals to result in health issues."

Learning to Teach: A Male Teacher's Story

In Dadaab camps, it's no surprise to find a teacher teaching in the same secondary school that he or she graduated from a year ago, without having higher education or training. It was 2010 when I graduated from one of the secondary schools in Dadaab. I was immediately hired as an education program instructor for girls. NGOs launched this program in 2008 with the intent of improving and increasing girls' access to quality education. Halima was one of the beneficiaries of this program. She was also a dedicated and goal-oriented student who used to attend all her classes on time. Although Halima was performing well in all other subjects, her score for math was deteriorating after every examination.

As her mathematics teacher, I felt concerned and tried to figure out a solution for her problem. After pondering about it for while, I came to the conclusion that I should adopt the same approach that most of my teachers had used. The approach involved asking her to solve a question on the chalkboard. So, in one of the classes I asked Halima to work out a mathematic question on the board I thought she couldn't answer. Halima tried her best to solve the question, but she failed. As a result, all of her classmates laughed and made fun of her. Although my intention was to motivate Halima to be well prepared in my classes, the consequences turned out negative. Halima stopped attending my classes, which affected her morale in other classes.

Curious to know more about Halima's situation, I met her one day in the school compound. I inquired about her absence. She told me, "I feared that those students would embarrass me again in front of the class if I couldn't answer your questions." I realized that my technique worked in reverse, and I convinced her to come back to class by assuring her that I would not ask any question again unless she was willing.

Research Team Dialogue: How Did We Learn to Teach?

"Teaching at the school you graduated from a year ago without formal teaching training is tough. Earning the respect and trust of the students while maintaining your confidence was the biggest challenge in the first months."

"I learned and taught content in English. If I were to teach in Somalia today, I wouldn't know Somali words for much of the content. What's the Somali word for gravity?"

"We just did what our teachers used to do. The Kenyan curriculum is teacher-centered. It is based on the needs of Kenyans."

"But many Dadaab teachers try their best to come up with new ways of teaching. This leads to crossing the border of restricting oneself to the Kenyan curriculum."

"When the Kenyan curriculum was adopted, we had no strategies to curb the cultural barriers, and girls were more vulnerable than boys."

"What does this story say about gender? For Halima, going out of her comfort zone would be crossing a border. I remember the girls hardly ever standing in front of the rest of the students and expressing themselves. Their involvement doesn't parallel the boys."

118   K. MEYER ET AL.

"The tasks and extra burden performed by girls at home limits their time to focus on learning."
"This has to do with culture."
"Also, approaching a male teacher and saying, 'I can't do this,' would be hard. So, if a girl sees something is wrong, she just keeps silent."
"I wished I would have helped girls far more. It's because of this culture [Canadian] and this exposure that has made me feel that girls can excel at anything they want to."

DISCUSSION: WHAT HAVE WE LEARNED?

The seven of us who grew up in Dadaab Refugee Camp benefitted greatly from the educational system there—enough to once more cross "territories, spaces and contact zones" (Giroux 2005, p. 2) out of the camp to study with scholarships in Canada. What did we "take away" upon leaving the refugee situation and conditions? What have we learned? At the same time, the three of us, who interviewed and taught secondary teachers in the camp within the Canadian-Kenyan university diploma program, ask these same questions. Our responses guide the following discussion around four themes, often contradictions: border, temporality, loss, and choice. As a team of ten, we offer insights and pose further questions related to curriculum and refugee education.

The four interrelated themes appear consistently in our research, reminders of challenges for refugee camp communities living outside the borders of homeland roots and a certain future. Elders are lost to war; families become disconnected. The first story and dialogue in this chapter speak of disruption, trauma, and sacrifice in border crossing, whereby a six-year-old boy will no longer hear his grandmother's stories. The immediate gains for those individuals able to cross are security, food, and shelter. Later for some, there will be access to education in the camp, which initially provides "psychosocial protection" away from danger inside learning spaces with peers and trusted adults (Kirk and Winthrop 2007, p. 715).

However, given that the average length of exile for refugees is seventeen years (Dryden-Peterson 2015), the provision of a temporary curriculum inherited from the host country will not hold the cultural currency of stories and the local language of the homeland. This curriculum will not serve the path to an internalized cultural voice that "critically considers reality," not as "marginals" living "outside" society (Freire 2000,

p. 74). Nor will that established curriculum hold new, inspirational stories vital to building historical and critical consciousness in a diaspora culture (Giroux 2005). Indeed, a primary struggle for refugee students becomes perceiving the reality of encampment not as "closed world," but a "limiting situation which they can transform" (Freire 2000, p. 49). Yet, as the second story and dialogue elaborate, students' motivating force turns into passing the National Examination, wherein they become subjected to a singular choice and the difficult consequences hanging between personal health and an altogether different currency of the examination. "So we knowingly allowed our life goals to result in health issues."

Such an internalized choice relates to the ostensible foreclosure of possibilities inside life as "refugee": *What can I do but take the malaria pills? I am only a refugee.* When students remain unaware of the causes of their reality, they "fatalistically accept" (Freire 2000, p. 64) the conditions. Freire argued that fatalism can be interpreted as "docility," but in fact is the "fruit of an historical and sociological situation" related to the power of destiny rather than an essential behavior characteristic (p. 61). Levinson (2001) argues that students become aware of the weight of their history and ways social positioning attaches to them. The problem is when students see no point or way they can transform "the meaning and implications that attach to their positioning" (p. 15). With "no going back, and an inability to move forward" (p. 15), we argue that living within the over determined status of "refugee," students lose a sense of uniqueness and the capacity (and choice) to act outside these conditions. They adapt.

In the third story, learning to teach in the camp follows the same weight of social positioning. Teachers are immediately hired upon graduation from secondary school without opportunities for higher education or "strategies to curb cultural barriers" and contradictions between culture and curriculum, or between students themselves, i.e., girls and boys. While the teachers play a critical role at the forefront of the community, they rely on their own experiences of school to inform their pedagogy (Kirk and Winthrop 2007).

In closing, we come back to the two questions that guided the intent of this chapter. How might "refugee" be inscribed in curriculum studies and its emphases? What do marginalized narratives of education among displaced peoples offer the conversation on internationalizing curriculum? Firstly, refugee communities deeply value education. As teachers and researchers, we witnessed profound perseverance and persistence among families in Dadaab Refugee Camp, wherein education evolved from primary to secondary school despite severe challenges, such as no light to study at night, a dearth of resources, and health issues. Parents and teachers alongside non-governmental organizations and the UNHCR have kept education alive over two decades.

Secondly, we argue that what critically matters to emergency education for displaced communities appears hidden: the return home. Ironically, the temporary mindset of refugee assistance (refugees will return home) remains one reason such little money is spent on educational development. How can a curriculum, for both the students and teachers, prepare refugee communities to cross physical, social, and cultural borders again, given the fact that most of the children and youth have not lived in their homeland? What are long-term implications of using an inherited system? What changes have occurred in the homeland over time? Conflicts may not have changed significantly. In the case of Somalia, war and destruction of the education system have left two generations of uneducated youth (Abdi 2008). Other options (not necessarily choices) for displaced people are to resettle in a third country or integrate in the country of exile. The question remains: How can emergency education nurture students' capacity to participate, integrate, and make critical choices rather than continually adapting to new conditions?

We pose these explicit questions after listening to narratives of refugee experiences as a "distinct form of discourse" (Chase 2005, p. 656)—interpretive and positioned inside the conditions, challenges, and consequences of emergency education. In our research, narratives have provided an entry point for inquiry into the reality of refugee lives, as well as causes and implications of that reality, particularly in education. The inscription of "refugee" into the larger discourse of education acknowledges the conditions of asylum, "the unhealable rift forced between a human being and a native place" (Said 1994, p. 137). The task of internationalizing curriculum cannot ignore the fact that by the end of 2016, there were 65.6 million displaced people in the world with as many as 17 million under UNHCR care with refugee status (UNHCR 2017). The inside stories reveal a discourse, "polyphonic, partial, and vibrant" (Giroux 2005, p. 104), about filling spaces between homes, "one lost, one not familiar" (Robinson 1994, p. xii).

The relatively small collections of stories in our research disclose the immense urgency for curriculum theorists to rethink emphases and

7 CROSSING BORDERS: A STORY OF REFUGEE EDUCATION   121

create pedagogical possibilities commensurate with: the exigency of time in long-term displacement situations; the implications of crossing physical, social, and cultural borders; the losses endured by marginalized communities; and the problematics of adaptation in lieu of choice in the daily life of displaced people. The task for curriculum to introduce students to the world with critical awareness becomes a formidable task. Of equal importance, students need to acquire an understanding of "who" they are "in relation to the world," which is not fixed, determined, or unchangeable (Levinson 2001, p. 19). We agree with Levinson as she furthers this final point beyond critical understanding and toward imagining the world differently.

> At the same time, we are reminded that the purpose of this introduction to the world is to prepare our students not simply to make their way in the world but to remake the world. (p. 19)

Acknowledgement We thank the newest members on our research team, Abdihakin Muse and Mohamed Halane, who assisted in drafts of this chapter. Our research is supported by a grant from the Social Sciences and Humanities Research Council of Canada. Grant number: 435-2013-7013.

References

Abdi, A. (1998). Education in Somalia: History, destruction, and calls for reconstruction. *Comparative Education, 34*(3), 327–340.

Abdi, A. (2008). From education for all to education for none. In A. Abdi & S. Guo (Eds.), *Education and social development: Global issues and analyses* (pp. 181–194). Rotterdam, the Netherlands: Sense Publications.

Arendt, H. (1994). We refugees. In M. Robinson (Ed.), *Altogether elsewhere* (pp. 110–119). New York: Harcourt Brace.

Chase, S. E. (2005). Narrative inquiry. In N. K. Denzin & Y. S. Lincoln (Eds.), *The Sage handbook of qualitative research* (pp. 651–679). Thousand Oaks, CA: Sage.

Crisp, J. (2003). No solutions in sight: The problem of protracted refugee situations in Africa. *New Issues in Refugee Research.* No. 75. Evaluation and Policy Analysis Unit. Geneva: Switzerland, UNHCR.

Dagane, M. (2013). *Factors influencing refugee learners transition form primary to secondary schools in Dadaab refugee camps, Kenya.* Unpublished MA thesis, University of Nairobi.

Dryden-Peterson, S. (2015). *Building a future for the youngest refugees*. Retrieved from https://www.gse.harvard.edu/uk/blog/building-future-youngest-refugees.

Freire, P. (2000). *Pedagogy of the oppressed*. New York: Bloomsbury.

Gadamer, H. (1975). *Truth and method*. New York: Crossroad.

Giroux, H. (2005). *Border crossings*. New York: Routledge.

IRIN. (2011). *A refugee's story*. Retrieved from http://www.irinnews.org/report/93527/kenya-somalia-refugees-story.

Kirk, J., & Winthrop, R. (2007). Promoting quality education in refugee contexts: Supporting teacher development in northern Ethiopia. *International Review of Education, 53,* 715–723.

Levinson, N. (2001). The paradox of natality: Teaching in the midst of belatedness. In G. Mordechai (Ed.), *Hannah Arendt and education* (pp. 11–36). Boulder, CO: Westview.

Lewis, I. M. (2002). *A modern history of the Somali: Nation and state in the horn of Africa*. Athens: Ohio University Press.

Robinson, M. (1994). Introduction. In M. Robinson (Ed.), *Altogether elsewhere* (pp. xi–xxii). New York: Harcourt Brace.

Said, E. (1994). Reflections on exile. In M. Robinson (Ed.), *Altogether elsewhere* (pp. xi–xxii). New York: Harcourt Brace.

UNESCO. (2015). *Education for all 2000–2015: Achievements and challenges*. Global Monitoring Report, Paris, France: UNESCO Publishing.

UNHCR. (2015). Dadaab refugee camps, Kenya UNHCR by-weekly update March 16, 2015. The United Nations High Commissioner for Refugees. Retrieved from UNHCR data portal http://data.unhcr.org.

UNHCR. (2017). *Global trends forced displacement 2016*. The UN Refugee Agency, The United Nations High Commissioner for Refugees. Retrieved from http://www.unhcr.org/globaltrends2016/.

UNHCR. (2018). *Refugees and asylum seekers in Kenya: Statistical summary* (January 31, 2018). Retrieved from UNHCR data portal http://data.unhcr.org.

Zembylas, M. (2010). Agamben's theory of biopower and immigrants/refugees/asylum seekers. *Journal of Curriculum Theorizing, 26*(2), 31–45.

PART II

Grounding Educational Environments

CHAPTER 8

Curriculum Theorists in the Classroom: Subjectivity, Crises, and Socio-environmental Equity

Avril Aitken and Linda Radford

Through our ongoing work in the field of curriculum studies and with future teachers in the complex world of the classroom, we attempt to draw attention and make space for the inner life and its significance to education. Largely neglected, the inner life and its impact on the social have been well documented by scholars who have written about the ways the unconscious has been marginalized in education (Britzman 1998; Taubman 2012). While the significance of psychic processes emerged with the re-conceptualization of curriculum in the 1970s, this shift was not experienced by the field of teacher education directly. As Pinar explains, "the function of the new scholarship was not to change curriculum practice; it was to understand curriculum as political" (Pinar 2010, p. 736). From the vantage point of this space of tension, shaped

---

A. Aitken (✉)
Bishop's University, Sherbrooke, QC, Canada
e-mail: aaitken@ubishops.ca

L. Radford
University of Ottawa, Ottawa, ON, Canada
e-mail: lradford@uottawa.ca

© The Author(s) 2019
C. Hébert et al. (eds.), *Internationalizing Curriculum Studies*,
https://doi.org/10.1007/978-3-030-01352-3_8

by the affordances of curriculum studies and the competing demands of work with future teachers, we contribute to this volume by taking up socio-environmental equity, an issue of curriculum and pedagogy that has garnered international attention. In keeping with the editors' provocation to "re/direct the familiar into new, toward more hopeful and fresh educational and societal directions" (Hébert et al. 2018, p. 2), we take up the notion of "promises without promise," particularly in light of the question: What is the role of education, globally, in the face of environmental crises and related injustices? We consider this question, by looking at the curricular and pedagogical implications of a project we undertook in our respective teacher education classrooms. Following Taubman (2012), we offer no promise of answers and solutions. Instead we look for the possibility of radical hope (Lear 2006) in the face of widespread vulnerability resulting from escalating global crises.

Following Huebner (1975), who writes of the benefits of attempting to disentangle the activities of the curricularist, we seek, with this chapter, to bring to light the "evolving dialectical relationships among (our) practice, empirical research, and language" (p. 252). While disentangling is not really possible, Huebner notes that efforts at such work are illuminating, given what can be learned about the self, and the conditions in which we attempt to work. Central to our work of untying is the notion of subjectivity, which we define as an individual's sense of self, which is shaped in relation to/with/by others and experiences, as they intersect with issues of power, knowledge, and authority (Britzman 2003; Pinar 2009; Taubman 2012). Indeed, Huebner writes, "practice as human event implies that the curricularist is also a human being with a biography in conflict and harmony with the other emerging biographies being played out in historically evolving institutions" (Huebner 1975, p. 266). Interested in how subjectivity plays out in becoming a teacher and the significance of psychodynamics in relation to education, we draw on a psychoanalytic framework (Britzman 2003; Britzman and Pitt 1996; Brown et al. 2006). In this chapter, we also turn to the work of Mnguni (2010, 2012) as she explores what psychodynamic insights can offer to wider sociocultural phenomena, including institutional efforts for environmental sustainability. These lenses are central to our work as teacher educators and essential in reconsidering the role of the curriculum theorists at this time. Teaching with Lear's (2006) notion of radical hope, we live and work where curriculum intersects with the specter of "megaproblems," such as effects of climate change, poverty, inequality, conflict, and pandemics (Warwick 2012, pp. 132–133).

In what follows, we illustrate the significance of the above lenses by drawing on the story of what unfolded in a capstone course with teacher candidates in the final year of a concurrent education program. We begin with a description of the educative environment we sought to create; we then present an analysis of the findings of our inquiry into the future teachers' perceptions of their professional role in connection with teaching for socio-environmental equity. "We never educate directly, but indirectly by means of the environment" (Huebner 1975, p. 260). Thus, we close with a consideration of our own entanglements and their implications for teacher education and curriculum theorizing, at this point in time.

In our forays into the work of socio-environmental equity, we began by asking students to consider the question, "How do we come to know and think as teachers?" (Robertson 1997, p. 27). We attempted to work against notions of fixed identities and knowledge and rigid imaginations of transformation and outcome-focused models of education by using an inquiry-based approach. In our consideration of socio-environmental equity and sustainability in the capstone course, we took up a holistic understanding of the concepts (Jones et al. 2010; Tillbury 2011; Toh and Cawagas 2010), taking into account "cultural, environmental, health, peace, social justice, scientific and technological dimensions" (Jones et al. 2010, p. 11). Such a perspective does not connect socio-environmental issues uniquely to the teaching of science, geography, or environmental education, as might be the case elsewhere (Esa 2010; Ravindranath 2007; Summers et al. 2005; Sund and Wickman 2008; Yang et al. 2010). Instead, a holistic perspective proposes that economic, environmental, and equity-focused issues are interdependent (Salite and Pipere 2006). From this point of view, we saw a role for all future and practicing teachers in considering socio-environmental sustainability, regardless of the boundaries of their disciplinary backgrounds.

We had, prior to this experience, framed our work through the lens of moral cosmopolitanism, and the possibilities of promoting human rights and dignity through collaborative action (Schattle 2008). However, we turned to the imperative of environmental stewardship as a means to bring future teachers to fuller recognition of the significance of their daily choices and investments. We problematized the use of the terms *sustainability* and *sustainable development* given the ways that

128   A. AITKEN AND L. RADFORD

they can be used without challenging "existing education paradigms" (Jackson 2011; Martusewicz et al. 2011, p. 13). As Hart (2010) writes, "when normative goals of sustainability are left undefined, dominant economics-based rather than social-environmental discourses shape wider socio-political agendas" (pp. 163–164). Within the interdisciplinary capstone course, the integration of the social, natural, political, and economic dimensions served as a means for future teachers to pose problems and design inquiries that they saw as significant to themselves and relevant to their future students (Freire 1990; Salite and Pipere 2006). Interdisciplinarity disrupts the compartmentalization of learning that is prevalent in schools; it also allows for meaning making that might otherwise not have been possible (Ackerson 2007; Boix-Mansilla 2006; Lattuca 2003; Orr 2004; Richards 2007).[1]

The capstone course had three axes with five interrelated assignments, some of which were carried out during an embedded 13-week practicum. Coursework included the individual design and implementation of a socio-environmental service project in the community (public school, university, or wider community). The projects often emerged from the students' analysis of key concepts related to eco-justice, sustainability, education for sustainable development, and environmental, and social equity. Students also carried out collaborative research and the design of informal "educational installations," which we called the "Seats of Knowledge," as the installation had to incorporate a chair, literally, in some way. The unique, eye-catching projects were set up on campus or in local schools to promote increased awareness of socio-environmental practices. This assignment, in particular, was carried out prior to collaborative design of an interdisciplinary unit of study using the theme selected for the installation. Finally, the teacher candidates in the course engaged in a critical examination of subjectivity and the teacher self by working with difficult moments in their teaching practice and producing a related digital film (Aitken and Radford 2012; Radford and Aitken 2014, 2015).

---

[1] The future teachers use the mandated Quebec Education Program to collaboratively design interdisciplinary units around socio-environmental issues and practices that they would attempt to use in practicum placements. The program is flexibly structured and has multiple entry points; two of the program's five main curricular lenses for planning, support sustainability focused teaching, and allow the future teachers to imagine themselves contributing to global change.

By having students work through problems collaboratively and make use of their disciplinary expertise in interdisciplinary ways, we tried to open the space of tension and ambiguity for the teacher candidates, while hoping they would attach themselves to sustainability pedagogies (Cotton and Winter 2010). With these assignments, we had the dual aim of inviting our students to explore the question, "What kind of teacher do you want to be?" and to imagine educative environments (Huebner 1975) that would reflect the type of teacher they imagined they wanted to be. Thus, we asked students to think about their own thinking (Britzman 1998; Britzman and Pitt 1996), their practice, and the language that informed their choices (Huebner 1975).

Disentangling the Language of Practice

What can we learn about the psychological processes underlying responses to the call to take up socio-environmental equity in teacher practice? We turn to the findings of our inquiry into the teacher candidates' perceptions of their professional role in connection with teaching for socio-environmental equity. With and against these findings, we consider the value of attending to psychic dynamics in the classroom, particularly at a time when anxieties around a world in crisis are heightened.

One of the key features to emerge from our inquiry was the overwhelming concern that the pre-service teachers expressed about barriers to such work. This went hand in hand with the common perception that engaging in—or promoting—socio-environmental equity in their teaching would be disruptive in the workplace. This was even the case for those whose lives were explicitly shaped by heightened attention to environmental and justice-focused practices. Despite identifying possible stances, such as helping students build knowledge and critical decision making, the future teachers were very specific in naming features of a school context that would impede them from actively promoting environmental and economic justice in their future work. Particular details include the notion that, "a school might simply have other (more important) priorities," "it might be something that's not done now," and without the interest of other colleagues or their understanding of socio-environmental issues, action would not be possible. This perception of an inability to take action within a school community was further illustrated by these comments: "A new teacher, they would not be the *voice* of reason to go to," (our italics) particularly in the face of "strong

[sic] held opinions by others." Additionally, it was noted that it would be, "difficult for a new teacher to teach for [environmental and social equity] if the other teachers in the school and the school administration are not devoted to [it] and think it is a *waste of time*" (our italics).

Other barriers were connected to feeling responsible for the youth they were teaching. As one teacher candidate indicated, "I want to make sure my students are learning all the content they need to know for the next level." We linked this with the perception that teachers don't have the "freedom" to address issues that seem outside of the prescribed curriculum. On the other hand, some identified the potential problem of the lack of resources and knowledge. This idea of needing plenty of resources matched the idea that such work requires "more" time—which they claimed was unavailable.

While it appears unlikely that the future teachers would take a leadership role in promoting socio-environmental justice through policy, practice, and pedagogy in their schools, they expressed a willingness to contribute, under certain conditions. As one described, they would participate if "the whole staff in the school is devoted" and they "have plenty of resources on the subject." Or as another put it, "If the principal and the other teachers are on board, it won't be a big hassle." Significantly, the inquiry showed that there was an image of school culture as monolithic and possibly impenetrable; this is significant, given that the future teachers also appeared to believe that such work requires participation from the "whole staff", and conceptual knowledge, time, and materials to which they would not have access.

While perceived obstacles such at the need for time, knowledge, and resources have been identified in other studies of pre-service teachers' social-environmental learning (Hasslof et al. 2016), we are particularly interested in thinking about three points that reflect the pre-service teachers' anxiety. These include:

- the perception that the "whole school" must be "devoted" and "onboard" in the work;
- the failure to recognize existing initiatives in schools;
- the idea that taking a position for environmental equity or sustainable living through teaching will be inordinately disruptive and will lead to negative repercussions for them.

8 CURRICULUM THEORISTS IN THE CLASSROOM ...   131

These points are significant and merit further attention because they do not correspond to what we observed nor what was represented by the teacher candidates in relation to their experiences prior to the practicum. That is, their heightened anxiety and characterization of the schools as hostile to teaching with a socio-environmental focus was somewhat incommensurable with their prior school and community-based experiences. These included the interest generated by their installations, the appreciation of community service projects, and their facility with planning sustainability-focused learning situations that made effective use of prescribed program documents.

UNTANGLING PARADOXICAL RELATIONSHIPS BETWEEN PRACTICE AND RESEARCH

In describing the educative environment of the course, we indicated that we began by inviting our students to enter into a dialogue around a world in crisis, the urgency of equitable and sustainable practices, and self-knowledge in teaching and learning. We considered the arguments of those writing about such engagements; for example, Cook et al. (2010) and Jackson (2011) write that individuals need to be equipped to challenge and question their own values, and as McKenzie (2009) suggests, experience "crisis, discomfort [and] difficulty" (p. 218). Correspondingly, we framed the course as part of an vital call for future teachers to not only address what Warwick (2012) calls "megaproblems" with their teaching, but to prepare their own students to "critically and creatively read their world" (p. 143).

In disentangling what became evident, we found that we underestimated the degree to which the candidates found their own beliefs were challenged through the learning experiences; however, this did not appear to be evident at the time as students appeared highly engaged. In thinking about the pedagogical dynamic, we now turn to Mnguni (2010), who writes about anxiety in sustainability. She suggests that such engagements can be understood as a defense against the "complexity and enormity of the task" of saving a world in crisis when wide-scale, massive "long-term behavior changes" in society are required (pp. 132–133). Further illustrating this point, once we had engaged the students in thinking about a world in crisis, our focus turned to what Mnguni refers to as the "creative and restorative intent of sustainability" (p. 118),

132 A. AITKEN AND L. RADFORD

which in the case of the capstone course offered up a relatively simple and straightforward solution for students: build knowledge and take creative action through designs for learning.

READING OUR OWN ENTANGLEMENTS

We have come to understand that in shaping the educative environment, we had not taken into account the significance of our own participation in the frenzy for solutions to the world's "megaproblems." Britzman (1998) writes of the inevitable desire to control the outcomes or manage chaos, in the face of crises. This pull is toward what Britzman terms "curative" practices and what Taubman (2012) calls the "therapeutic project." As Britzman (1998) notes, a "quest for rationality" and scientific certainty is not surprising when problems are faced (p. 32). However, she underlines the importance of disrupting curative approaches, as does Taubman (2012) in this description of an alternate:

> The emancipatory project [in contrast to the therapeutic], works toward deepening and helping us understand and articulate our inner lives without promising the result will be happier, more beautiful, a more just life or better job or a better relationship or a higher test score. The emancipatory project eschews efforts at control and cure, offering questions and an interminable analysis, rather than answers and solutions. (pp. 6–7)

Aided by Taubman's conceptualization of therapeutic and emancipatory stances, we propose that the intensity of our investments was part of our own therapeutic impulse to cure. We provoked students to achieve the idealized ends we had in mind, and consequently they were mirrored by the future teachers' excitement about creating installations, implementing informal learning situations, carrying out community service projects, and developing creative and dynamic plans for student learning. Through this "therapeutic approach" we were defending against "the nature of the anxiety that attends the primary task of trying to restore socio-ecological landscapes" (Mnguni 2010, p. 118).

The future teachers' anxiety was also evident in their comments that a socio-environmental focus in teaching would disrupt or "hassle" others in the school settings. We now propose that this was a projection of the discomfort they experienced while considering the notion of a world in crisis, and in recognizing their isolation and vulnerability (Britzman 2003).

Mnguni (2010) writes, "the problem of sustainability ... involves an intricate web of connectedness among psycho-social and ecological issues. This complexity places sustainability in the inter-organizational domain, making collaboration by multiple stakeholders imperative" (p. 117). In relation to this point, we turn to our other research around teacher candidates' critical moments in teaching, which we have been studying during the last five years. These crises are most likely to erupt around interpersonal relationships within the school setting. The research has revealed the magnitude of the struggles the pre-service teachers face in taking on the identity of teacher, and simply imagining a place for themselves in a school—without also having to imagine changing school culture as well (Aitken and Radford 2012; Radford and Aitken 2014). This furthers our understanding of future teachers' preoccupations with relationships. It also helps us understand why it appears that the pre-service teachers seem unable to imagine themselves as leaders within a school setting around the question of environmental and social equity. This is particularly the case if they imagine such work as being confrontational and involving challenges to others about their beliefs—as they themselves had been challenged through the course design.

Notably, the capstone course is connected to a lengthy placement, preparation for which is marked by the students' heightened desire to be "fully prepared." Significantly, the "creative and restorative" (Mnguni 2010) work on socio-environmental equity and collaborative learning in the teacher education classroom (through the problem-posing designs, installation creation, and inquiry projects) appeared to assuage this need. Yet, it is problematically "curative," as Britzman would say. That is, it appears that such work provides a sense of "control and mastery", until, that is, the future teachers enter the school context (Britzman 1998, p. 32). In leaving behind relationships with collaborative peers from within their well-known cohort in the teacher education classroom, "idiosyncratic subjectivities" (others and their own) bring them into new "relationship[s] fraught with unconscious desires and shadows from the past" (Taubman 2012, p. 7). The future teachers' expressions of anxiety and resistance, and their anticipation that they will be seen as disruptive, confrontational, or "hassling" others, are accompanied by their immobilization. Some candidates attempt to explain this powerlessness and voicelessness as a function of being in an early career position. We propose that this is a function of subjectivities at work and being in the grip of overwhelming emotions, compounded by the notion of a world in crisis. This underlines the importance of decentering efforts to build socio-environmental knowledge and capacity, and instead prioritizing the emancipatory project (Taubman 2012), wherein the future teachers learn to better understand and express their inner lives.

We cannot escape the fact that the pull toward the curative is brought into sharp focus in a world facing an ecological crisis: Informed action is needed and our individual and collective choices have the potential to positively or negatively impact human and ecological degradation. Yet, as our inquiry above illustrates, and as Britzman (1998) writes, "rationality ... can [not] settle the trouble that inaugurates thought"— we cannot think our way out of feelings of vulnerability and helplessness, exacerbated by the specter of increasingly complex megaproblems (p. 32). This proposition returns us to Taubman's (2012) broader conceptualizations of the therapeutic and the emancipatory, which seem in opposition, but cannot be neatly separated. We experienced the pull toward a therapeutic response of trying to smooth over and find solutions for situations instead of dwelling in the emancipatory work of questions and analysis. Taubman (2012) makes the point that anxieties are provoked as we attempt to resist fixed protocols while at the same time desiring some sort of direction. He explains that the therapeutic and emancipatory projects "are related, often in undisclosed ways" and "blur in the hurly-burly world of the classroom," as was the case for us (p. 7).

Our inquiry into our work as curriculum theorists in the classroom underlines the need to focus more explicitly and in prolonged ways with future teachers (and our own selves) around the significance of psychic dynamics in learning and teaching, and in learning to teach. To those who might ask how attention to the inner life would equip becoming teachers to work with youth in such a way that they collectively pursue common goals of living ethically and ecologically mindfully, locally, and globally, we turn to Lear (2006) and Finch et al. (2014). The latter propose that educators' experiences of working with their unconscious states of mind more explicitly helps them "to recognise and rationalise these [states], thus supporting confidence" in decision making (p. 139). So while there may be no promise of "answers and solutions" (Taubman 2012), a change in thinking about the self may take place, and radical hope (Lear 2006) may emerge. Drawing on Lear (2006), Smits and Naqvi (2015) write that, "to understand and confront precariousness requires a sense of oneself as a person who is indelibly linked with others through bonds of caring and responsibility" (p. xiii). These are fitting words for a global manifesto for curriculum theorists bonded to the work of education.

CLOSING PROVOCATION

In our ongoing work in the field of curriculum studies, we draw inspiration from those who have made powerful cases to advance the notion of education as a psychic crisis, and to counter the disavowal of the unconscious in education (Britzman 1998, 2003, 2006; Taubman 2012). We acknowledge that the significance of a psychoanalytic perspective has been purposefully articulated by its advocates for some time (Britzman and Pitt 1996; Brown et al. 2006; Pinar and Grumet 1976; Pitt 2003; Robertson 2001). With this chapter, illustrated by the untangling of our research and practice, we underline fruitfulness of bringing "the radical push of curriculum theorizing" into teacher education classrooms (Hébert et al. 2018, p. 2). Equally, we make a call to curriculum theorists to renew attention to the significance of psychic dynamics in education, particularly in the teacher education classroom where subjectivities are faced with so many competing demands—not the least of which is the challenge to solve the problems of a world in the midst of a socio-environmental crisis.

REFERENCES

Ackerson, V. (2007). *Interdisciplinary language arts and science instruction in elementary classrooms.* New York, NY: Routledge.

Aitken, A., & Radford, L. (2012). Aesthetic archives: Pre-service teachers symbolizing experiences through digital storytelling. *Journal of the Canadian Association of Curriculum Studies, 10*(2), 92–119.

Boix-Mansilla, V. (2006). *Interdisciplinary work at the frontier: An empirical examination of expert interdisciplinary epistemologies.* Harvard Graduate School of Education Interdisciplinary Studies Project. Retrieved from http://www.pz.harvard.edu/interdisciplinary/pubone.html.

Britzman, D. P. (1998). *Lost subjects contested objects: Toward a psychoanalytic inquiry of learning.* Albany, NY: State University of New York Press.

Britzman, D. P. (2003). *Practice makes practice: A critical study of learning to teach* (rev. ed.). New York: State University of New York Press.

Britzman, D. P. (2006). *Novel education: Psychoanalytic studies of learning and not learning.* New York: Peter Lang Publishing.

136 A. AITKEN AND L. RADFORD

Britzman, D. P., & Pitt, A. J. (1996). Pedagogy and transference: Casting the past of learning into the presence of teaching. *Theory into Practice, 35*(2), 117–123.

Brown, T., Atkinson, D., & England, J. (2006). *Regulatory discourses in education: A Lacanian perspective.* Bern, Switzerland: Peter Lang.

Cook, R., Cutting, R., & Summers, D. (2010). If sustainability needs new values, whose values? Initial teacher training and the transition to sustainability. In P. Jones, D. Selby, & S. Sterling (Eds.), *Sustainability education: Perspectives and practice across higher education* (pp. 313–327). London: Earthscan.

Cotton, D. R. E., & Winter, J. (2010). It's not just bits of paper and light bulbs: A review of sustainability pedagogies and their potential for use in higher education. In P. Jones, D. Selby, & S. Sterling (Eds.), *Sustainability education: Perspectives and practice across higher education* (pp. 39–54). London: Earthscan.

Esa, N. (2010). Environmental knowledge, attitude and practices of student teachers. *International Research in Geographical and Environmental Education, 19*(1), 39–50.

Finch, J., Schaub, J., & Dalrymple, R. (2014). Projective identification and the fear of failing: Making sense of practice educators experiences of failing social work students in practice learning sessions. *Journal of Social Work Practice, 28*(2), 139–154.

Freire, P. (1990). *Pedagogy of the oppressed* (M. Bergman Ramos, Trans.). New York: Continuum.

Hart, P. (2010). No longer a "little added frill": The transformative potential of Environmental Education for educational change. *Teacher Education Quarterly, 37*(4), 155–177.

Hasslof, H., Lundegard, I., & Malmberg, C. (2016). Students' qualification in environmental and sustainability education—Epistemic gaps or composites of critical thinking? *International Journal of Science Education, 38*(2), 259–275. https://doi.org/10.1080/09500693.2016.1139756.

Hébert, C., Ibrahim, A., Ng-A-Fook, N., & Smith, B. (Eds.). (2018). *Internationalizing curriculum studies: Histories, environments, and critiques* (pp. 1–11). London, UK: Palgrave.

Huebner, D. (1975). The tasks of the curriculum theorist. In W. Pinar (Ed.), *Curriculum theorizing: The Reconceptualists* (pp. 250–270). Berkeley, CA: McCutchan.

Jackson, M. J. (2011). The real challenge of ESD. *Journal of Education for Sustainable Development, 5*(1), 27–37.

Jones, P., Selby, D., & Sterling, S. (2010). More than the sum of their parts: Interdisciplinarity and sustainability. In P. Jones, D. Selby, & S. Sterling

(Eds.), *Sustainability education: Perspectives and practice across higher education* (pp. 17–37). London: Earthscan.

Lattuca, L. R. (2003). Creating interdisciplinarity: Grounded definitions from college and university faculty. *History of Intellectual Culture, 3*(1), 1–20.

Lear, J. (2006). *Radical hope: Ethics in the face of cultural devastation.* Cambridge, MA: Harvard University Press.

Martusewicz, R. A., Edmondson, J., & Lupinacci, J. (2011). *EcoJustice education: Toward diverse, democratic and sustainable communities.* New York, NY: Routledge.

McKenzie, M. (2009). Pedagogical transgressions: Towards intersubjective agency and action. In M. McKenzie, P. Hart, H. Bai, & B. Jickling (Eds.), *Fields of green: Restorying culture, environment, and education.* Cresskill, NJ: Hampton Press.

Mnguni, P. P. (2010). Anxiety and defense in sustainability. *Psychoanalysis, Culture & Society, 15*(2), 117–135.

Mnguni, P. P. (2012). Deploying culture as a defence against incompetence: The unconscious dynamics of public service work. *SA Journal of Industrial Psychology/SA Tydskrif vir Bedryfsielkunde, 38*(2), 1–9. https://doi.org/10.4102/sajip.v38i2.1000.

Orr, D. W. (2004). *Earth in mind* (2nd ed., rev. ed.). Washington, DC: Island Press.

Pinar, W. (2009). The unaddressed 'I' of ideology critique. *Power and Education, 1*(2), 189–200.

Pinar, W. F. (2010). Currere. In C. Kridel (Ed.), *Encyclopedia of curriculum studies* (pp. 177–178). Thousand Oaks, CA: Sage.

Pinar, W. F., & Grumet, M. R. (1976). *Toward a poor curriculum.* Dubuque, IA: Kendall/Hunt mPub. Co.

Pitt, A. J. (2003). *The play of the personal: Psychoanalytic narratives of feminist education.* New York: Peter Lang.

Radford, L., & Aitken, A. (2014). Becoming teachers' little epics and cultural myths—Writ large in digital stories. *McGill Journal of Education—Special Issue: "Multimedia in/as Scholarship", 49*(3), 641–660.

Radford, L., & Aitken, A. (2015). Digital dreamwork: Becoming teachers' stories of trauma. In N. Ng-A-Fook, A. Ibrahim, & G. Reis (Eds.), *Provoking curriculum studies: Strong poetry and the arts of the possible* (pp. 15–160). New York: Routledge.

Ravindranath, M. J. (2007). Environmental education in teacher education in India: Experiences and challenges in the United Nation's decade of education for sustainable development. *Journal of Education for Teaching, 33*(2), 191–206.

138 A. AITKEN AND L. RADFORD

Richards, J. (2007). Interdisciplinary teaching: History, theory, and interpretations. In V. Ackerson (Ed.), *Interdisciplinary language arts and science instruction in elementary classrooms* (pp. 13–28). New York, NY: Routledge.

Robertson, J. P. (1997). Screenplay pedagogy and the interpretation of unexamined knowledge in preservice primary teaching. *TABOO: A Journal of Culture & Education, 1*(Spring), 25–60.

Robertson, J. P. (2001). 'Art made tongue-tied by authority': A literary psychoanalysis of obstacles in teacher learning. *Journal of Curriculum Theorizing, 17*(1), 27–45.

Salite, I., & Pipere, A. (2006). Aspects of sustainable development from the perspective of teachers. *Journal of Teacher Education and Training, 6,* 15–32.

Schattle, H. (2008). Education for global citizenship: Illustrations of ideological pluralism and adaptation. *Journal of Political Ideologies, 13*(1), 73–94.

Smits, H., & Naqvi, R. (2015). *Framing peace: Thinking about and enacting curriculum as "radical hope".* New York: Peter Lang.

Summers, M., Childs, A., & Corney, G. (2005). Education for sustainable development in initial teacher training: issues for interdisciplinary collaboration. *Environmental Education Research, 11*(5), 623–647.

Sund, P., & Wickman, P. O. (2008). Teachers' objects of responsibility: Something to care about in education for sustainable development? *Environmental Education Research, 14*(2), 145–163.

Taubman, P. (2012). *Disavowed knowledge: Psychoanalysis, education and teaching.* Studies in Curriculum Theory Series. New York, NY: Routledge, Taylor & Francis Group.

Tillbury, D. (2011). *Education for sustainable development: An expert review of processes and learning.* Paris, France: UNESCO.

Toh, S. H., & Cawagas, V. F. (2010). Peace education, ESD and the earth charter: Interconnections and synergies. *Journal of Education for Sustainable Development, 4*(2), 167–180. https://doi.org/10.1177/097340821000400203.

Warwick, P. (2012). Climate change and sustainable citizenship education. In J. Arthur & H. Cremin (Eds.), *Debates in citizenship education* (pp. 132–145). New York: Routledge.

Yang, G., Lam, C. C., & Wong, N. Y. (2010). Developing an instrument for identifying secondary teachers' beliefs about education for sustainable development in China. *The Journal of Environmental Education, 41*(4), 195–207.

CHAPTER 9

Curriculum for Identity: Narrative Negotiations in Autobiography, Learning and Education

Eero Ropo

We human beings are born without identities or any kind of conceptions about what there is around us. Who we are, where we are, and what is around us has to be learned along the course of life. Learning is thus the key process affecting our understanding of the world and also of ourselves. In this chapter, I will describe learning as a continuous holistic process in which the person constructs meanings discursively, through negotiations with and between him/herself, other people and different life contexts. The concept of identity, and particularly identity positioning, is helpful in understanding the nature of this process. It may also help in understanding the difficulties in complex conversations of internationalizing curriculum studies.

Identity is an easy concept as used in everyday language. However, there is not a single definition for the concept in research and theoretical literature (e.g. Brubaker and Cooper 2000). The literature on identity can be divided roughly into philosophical, sociological, and

E. Ropo (✉)
Faculty of Education, University of Tampere, Tampere, Finland
e-mail: Eero.Ropo@staff.uta.fi

© The Author(s) 2019　　　　　　　　　　　　　　　　139
C. Hébert et al. (eds.), *Internationalizing Curriculum Studies,*
https://doi.org/10.1007/978-3-030-01352-3_9

psychological perspectives (see Alcoff and Mendieta 2003; Bruner 1986; Côté and Levine 2002; Giddens 1991; Erikson 1959; Marcia 1994; McAdams et al. 2006; Leary and Tangney 2011; Ricoeur 1987, 1991; Taylor 1989). In psychological discourse on identity, the concept is usually used synonymously with the concept of self. The ontology of identity in psychological discourse refers to the development of self or personal identity as a characteristic developing from childhood to adult age. From an empirical standpoint, identity is a research question. For instance, researchers may ask what kind of identities people have and how those identities develop during the life course. Sociological literature on identity uses the concept in the context of membership to social institutes and structures. This work has a long history from Mead's (1934) seminal book *Mind, Self and Society* to later developments of Giddens (1991) and Weigert et al. (1986) to mention just a few.

Philosophical literature on self and identity has been crucial for understanding the origins and nature of identity. I only refer to Taylor's (1989) and Ricoeur's (1991) contributions to understanding the genesis of modern identity. Taylor relates this discussion to moral issues, and Ricoeur theorizes the narrative nature of identity.

Taking a sociological tack, Côté (2006) has divided literature on identity into eight categories depending on the epistemology (objectivist, subjectivist) and whether the focus is individual or social. Both the individual and social focus are divided into two approaches, namely status quo and critical/contextual. The life historic and narrative approach I am referring to in this article belongs in Côté's categorization to subjectivist and individual focus (status quo).

In the context of school education, identity has been long neglected (Lannegrand-Willems and Bosma 2006; Limberg et al. 2008). For instance, in the 2004 Finnish National Curriculum Framework for school-based curricula, identity has been mentioned only a few times in the context of a need to enhance students' cultural identity (Finnish National Agency 2004).

Whether or not the information age has changed our basic assumptions concerning education can be disputed. Nevertheless, it is evident that in the age of modernity, society has provided a more collective identity and moral basis through different institutions, traditions and faiths. Current ideological changes call for questioning the formerly taken-for-granted knowledge and moral bases. This applies at least to Western societies in which the so-called postmodern order has changed the role

9 CURRICULUM FOR IDENTITY: NARRATIVE NEGOTIATIONS ... 141

of institutions. Such changes in social conditions (i.e. away from collectivity) bring a movement to increasing individuality and demand for individual identities. These processes have also changed the role of education and teachers (Ropo and Värri 2003, p. 305). The societal, cultural and environmental discourses, to mention just a few, make teachers' roles more complicated than ever as facilitators of students' identity negotiations. What should teachers learn in teacher education and what positions should they take in respect to many controversial global, societal or moral conversations? The role of subject-specific expertise cannot be denied as the basis for being a teacher. Like we wrote over ten years ago:

> Modern teachership, the present teacher education, and the present school institution have been constructed on the basis of scientific education and curriculum design (see Hargreaves, 1994). Teachers have consciously aimed at a professional position by emphasizing their educational and subject specific expertise. (Ropo and Värri 2003, p. 306)

Knowledge is important but may not be sufficient anymore. My main argument here is that the construction of identity is more important than ever before. There are several reasons for this. The first is identity's roots in the Enlightenment and the early history of education (see Giddens 1991). According to its main message, people could be emancipated from their wild nature by education. Education became a common interest for nation-building because it was soon understood that educated people were useful for the cohesion of the nation and increasing the welfare of society (Ropo and Värri 2003).

The second reason is the current trend from collective to individual identities. Education as a provider of competences or qualifications is no longer the only capital for good life. Like Côté (2005) has suggested, identity can be regarded increasingly as capital needed in life (see also Goodson 2006). Identity is capital to be used in individual decision-making in the turbulence of work and private lives.

Third, identity is negotiated and expressed in relationships, and from this point of view, recognizing one's identity has become a necessity. If the nature and context of the relation changes identity has to be reconstructed. Like many researchers argue, we do not have a single identity, but many. Some parts of our identities are always under reconstruction, while some may be more stable over time.

142   E. ROPO

The fourth reason refers to the relations between learning and identity processes. Like learning, identity should not be regarded as a fixed construct, or a characteristic of a person that is reached at some point of age or life, but a process. To understand the nature of a process, we need the concept of identity positioning (e.g. van Langenhove and Harré 1999). Positioning and repositioning are important ways to influence the perspective that we have in the relations to people, problema or phenomena. Repositioning changes the meanings constructed during the negotiations, and the new meanings affect our identity. Temporal and embodied positioning are also important phenomena in our meaning making. Like Merleau-Ponty (1986) has pointed, identity is composed in the processes of interpreting and synthesizing our experiences in the flow of temporality.

In summary, we may argue that for education to survive in the turmoil of information age and the new order, it is necessary to first understand and then react. Schools need to be provided with tools and concepts to guarantee its success. We need to educate productive, healthy citizens for the future despite the lack of descriptions of either the future world or its requirements. Continuous reconstruction of one's identity is not only an individual question. It is also the necessity of the schools and teachers to provide required support for this process.

After arguing for the importance of and potential for which identity may have in education, I will discuss the implications of identity theorizing for the design of curricula and processes related to understanding identity negotiations as the main processes of learning and human development.

AUTOBIOGRAPHY, NARRATIVES AND IDENTITIES

How does the concept of identity make education different from what it is now? The question for a researcher studying life history and autobiographical identity is "Who I am and where do I come from?" There are also many why questions that might be reflected on when creating and reconstructing your own narratives of life. Understanding these "whys" is crucial for understanding your learning, interests, decisions, and motivation.

I will start with a narrative of myself to illustrate the importance of the reflection of life history in the construction of identities and positioning to life. This reflective negotiation is crucial to surviving crises, but it is also important in many other respects such as creating dreams and aspirations to become, the will to achieve, or values in conducting one's life.

I was born to Karelian parents in post-war Finland. My mother was a so-called evacuee, born in 1918 in a small village close to the city of Vyborg. Evacuees were people who had to leave their homes (in 1940 and 1944) after the wars and who moved to other regions in Finland because the border between Finland and the Soviet Union was changed. In the peace treaties (1940 and 1944), areas of Eastern Finland and one part of the region of Karelia including Vyborg and the vicinity were merged with the Soviet Union. Life conditions in the early years of Finnish independence (1917) were hard in many respects. My mother had lost her own mother when she was eight weeks old because of the 1918 influenza pandemic (Spanish Flu), which also took other lives all over the Europe and the world. Later on, my grandfather remarried a local lady, and they had four other children. School legislation from 1921 guaranteed a few years of basic education to all. However, it was impossible for poor rural families to send their children to secondary education in towns like Vyborg. My mother skipped the first grade because of already being able to read and write. She went to school for five years. Work in a small family farm and on relatives' farms was the expectation for a countryside teenage girl.

War ruined young people's dreams like it does now. In the Winter War (1939–1940), my mother worked as a dairy worker in her Karelian home village with two teenage girls to provide soldiers with milk and butter. All other people were already evacuated, and life close to the front was full of fears for these young ladies. In the so-called Continuation War in 1941–1944, my mother lost her younger brother during the last months of the war in July 1944. He was just a young 20-year-old soldier.

My father was also a south Karelian, the oldest son in the family of 10 children. His three older brothers had died during their first five years of life. He was the first to survive. Five younger brothers and a sister, who all lived long, were born between 1918 and 1938.

Reflecting on the story of my parents, it is very hard to imagine what inspired their imaginations and dreams for life. Building positive identities as children and young people in such conditions must have been hard, but still they had no other option. Diseases had taken lives of family members, access to education was very limited, and the war had destroyed the dreams of the entire generation. More than 90,000 soldiers were killed, and almost every family lost one or more of their family members. How can anyone construct a healthy identity in those conditions?

I think the melancholic atmosphere in my childhood was mostly due to the emotional suffering of my parents and their whole generation. Those feelings and emotions were not shared with children. Men talked about war experiences only with each other, sometimes only after drinking alcohol. In public, the message was to forget and continue life. Church and religion were ways to overcome bad feelings. A positive outcome was that the country remained independent.

After the war, people tried to take back what the war had postponed in their personal lives. Record numbers of children were born during the first three years of war. The country was rebuilt and the war debts paid. My parents' perspective on life was focused on work and education. They felt that children should be given an opportunity to go to school to have a better life than themselves, although they went to school only for a few years.

School indeed made a change for the expectations and future thoughts of my sisters and me. Since there was not a "script" from our parents, such as farming or a family business, it was evident that education was the only route to independent adulthood.

Finnish education in the 1960s was based on a dual system in which so-called folk school comprised seven years of education leading to vocational schools and worker careers. From grades 4 to 8, it was possible to apply to eight years of secondary education leading to a matriculation examination and university studies. My sisters and I were all admitted to secondary education.

Autobiographical narratives such as the one given here work at their best as tools for repositioning. In my current understanding, it was the prospect of a different future offered by the school that changed the identity of an evacuee's son to thinking of something bigger. The school made it possible to reposition myself with respect to my future dreams of work and career.

School progressed rather well Knowledge, skills, and understanding increased, and there were suddenly many more options to choose from than my parents had ever had in their lives. Identity as a capital to be used in selecting between optional futures seemed to work. Capital meant courage to take risks and trust in the positive future of offering something good. It is also necessary to reposition when your plans get ruined for one reason or another. This kind of identity capital comes from several sources. Some of it originated in my case from acknowledged strengths, knowledge and performance in school. This is hard to separate from the encouragement received from teachers who in some immeasurable ways could create positive prospects for life.

As a result of reflecting on my narrative, I have realized that I benefited a lot from the secondary teachers who were all educated at universities. They had adopted a collegial and supportive position towards their students. In my childhood, there was also a family friend, an evacuee and an older "uncle," who had been working as a forestry foreman. While playing chess together, we talked a lot about my future. He encouraged me to study as far as a master's degree, which for his generation was a sign of belonging to societal upper class. Reflecting on my childhood, it was evident that this kind of support from outside the nuclear family made me ponder different options for the future and also for my initial and most desired career plan of becoming a military pilot.

To understand and verbalize who I am, where I come from, and where I belong, I need to create and understand my story. I have realized that life stories cannot just be adopted from someone else. The story is not personal unless it becomes associated with your autobiographical memory, your own experiences and the meanings you have created by reflection (see Kihlstrom et al. 2003). These stories are never ready or fixed. They are temporally and historically rooted in times and places but also in times and contexts of creation and reflection. The stories are connected to complex social networks of people, institutions and events. They all come alive when we create a plot and meaning that connects the history to our own experiences. These stories describe me and my positioning. However, I am not only the stories. As Ivor Goodson (1998) points out:

> It is important to view the self as an emergent and changing 'project' not a stable and fixed entity. Over time our view of our self changes and so, therefore, do the stories we tell about ourselves. In this sense, it is useful to view self-definition as an ongoing narrative project. (p. 11)

Autobiographical narratives work as anchors to place one's life course in chronological time and contexts, geographical places and environments, and the conditions of everyday lives. Interpretations of these narratives contextualize them into your own story allowing the construction of personally relevant meanings. These meanings are then used in further reflections as part of your own identity narratives. The reflected narratives comprise the capital for identity repositioning as a resource in future life contexts. Reflecting can make a difference in one's life, like it did in my own case. However, storying one's life in such a detail and reflecting it by positioning oneself as an outsider may be, for growing children and young people, a different and sometimes more difficult problem than for adults.

NARRATIVE NATURE OF EXISTENCE

So far I have described identity development as a narrative process in which we construct stories of our own lives to understand through reflection of who we are and our relation to the world outside of us. Those stories are then reconstructed, reinterpreted and reflected upon during the turns and experiences of life. The result of such narrative processes can typically be described as feelings of knowing and understanding but also as emotional states such as belonging, love, joy, anger or frustration. This being a personal experience, can we relate this to the theory of narrativity?

Hanna Meretoja (2014) has suggested, in her recent book *The Narrative Turn in Fiction and Theory*, that the narrative turn in literature,

> is characterized by acknowledging not only the cognitive, but also the complex existential relevance of narrative for our being in the world. From this perspective I suggest conceptualizing it as a shift towards a hermeneutically oriented understanding of the ontological significance of storytelling for human existence. (p. 6)

According to this theory, stories or narratives are crucial to understanding existence. Understanding is a complex process but for the current purpose we say, for instance, that in the understanding process, the elements of a story are connected with personal memories or autobiographically meaningful associations to temporally, situationally, and contextually relevant plots. This is the connection to the concept of learning. Autobiography influences what we learn and what we are able to construct into stories. This process is never complete.

An important ontological question concerns the role of narratives for human existence. For instance, to what extent do people make sense and understand their existence and whole reality in terms of narratives (Meretoja 2014)? An important question related to this is how true and realistic are the narratives of existence that we create through our perceptions and construction processes? For a narrative researcher, however, these questions are in a way irrelevant. Narratives or stories are always constructed from a certain perspective or, to be more exact, an identity position. Subsequently, they are always personal, social and cultural interpretations of existence. Those different layers in our positioning are all evident and relevant. Narratives connect the events and experiences with timelines, contexts, meanings, and plots.

In the literature on narrative, there is no total agreement about terminology. Should we speak of meanings, or experiences, or both? I have referred to reflection as a process to construct personally meaningful narratives. According to Meretoja (2014), meaningful connections between experiences are important but there is no agreement in what ways. Those who refer to the phenomenological-hermeneutic tradition and narrative psychology typically prefer the concept of experience. They are typically interested in narratives as a practice through which subjects make sense of their experiences and exchange them with others (see Ricoeur 1984).

In the narratological tradition, narratives are typically approached in terms of events, or representations to create the links and causal chains of events. For narratological researchers, therefore, experience is not an interpretation or meaning of events, but rather a mental representation of an event.

In an earlier article, we referred to human information processing as aiming at constructing a representation of the acquired information (Yrjänäinen and Ropo 2013). The result of this process can be a verbalized story or something that can be verbalized as a story. However, this story is often partial and incomplete from the point of understanding. Understanding or creating meanings is a process of elaboration or a reflection of the representation and its associations to earlier memories, experiences, narratives and knowledge that the person may already have. This can also be illustrated with a metaphor of negotiation. We can also negotiate with our representation or narrative. Sometimes this negotiation is a kind of inner speech, sometimes it is enhanced by reflections with others. Writing, drawing or some other creative ways of expression can also enhance the construction and reflection of our narratives.

An important question among those who see narratives as important in organizing and interpreting experience is whether narratives are fundamentally ontological (what is) or epistemological (meanings). Do we actually perceive the world as narrative through the narratives, or do we use narratives to make sense of our experiences and create only the meanings related to our perceptions? Like Meretoja (2014), we can ask if the narratives are a kind of cognitive device, or rather are instruments with which we recognize and make sense of reality, create meanings, and make our experiences and the realities around us more meaningful.

I prefer the view that narratives are important both from ontological and epistemological points of view. We do not seem to have direct access to reality, and we do not seem to construct knowledge in any other way than through representations that have similar properties than verbalized narratives, these being realistic to our perspective or positioning during the information acquisition stage and incomplete at the same time, filled with details but concurrently also having open slots of the aspects unknown to us. This is the process of constructing narratives of identities. Identities exist ontologically in the narratives that are under a process. Whether they are based on something other than narratives is a question that we can now leave as open. Epistemologically, sense-making is a process in which we create and negotiate, reconstruct and struggle for better understanding between description and causality (Goodson et al. 2010). The crucial point here is not only learning from stories but also through the reconstruction of stories. This kind of learning becomes possible if, first, the person feels willing to change his/her narrative identity, and second, the change in the identity becomes real through the reconstruction of a new story in which the details support the renewed interpretations of oneself (Ropo and Värri 2003).

The same kind of narrative process can be assumed to apply to children, as well. When thinking of identity negotiations in childhood, the family typically offers the basic family narratives. An individual's positions in those narratives are usually offered, for instance, in terms of age, gender or order of birth. Those narratives are supported by real-life perceptions of parents, siblings, extended family and so on. Narratives become ontologically realistic when people exist both in the real and in the stories; however, epistemologically the child has to interpret and understand who these people are and what kind of meanings to attach to them in his/her own narratives. All human knowledge is like this, narratives constructed out of perceptions, and acquired information. Those narratives have empirically and phenomenologically proven elements, concurrently being vague and open in some respects (Yrjänäinen and Ropo 2013).

Paul Ricoeur's (1987) three-stage Mimesis process is an excellent description of the narrative construction and negotiation. The first phase in the narrative formation is the level of perception, actions and experiences (Mimesis[1]). In the second phase (Mimesis[2]), those experiences serve as raw material on which the narrator takes a stand for the creation of initial narratives. The third level (Mimesis[3]) relates to how the created narratives are applied and returned to the level of perceptions, actions and experiences (Mimesis[1]), as the basis for interpreting new information.

This model can also be applied to school learning. Particularly in the domains of subject-specific learning, the narrative learning model seems very appealing (Yrjänäinen and Ropo 2013). The first phase (Mimesis[1]) is the pre-knowledge and perception stage. We perceive, interpret and experience phenomena on the basis of our previous knowledge of the phenomena. Typically, these kinds of perceptions and predictions are based on naïve theories learned in everyday life. The second stage (Mimesis[2]) concerns the group processes and classroom discourses in which the previous knowledge is challenged, experiments made, new information and concepts offered, and rules and theories developed. Teachers' goals in this stage are typically to enhance the creation and construction of scientifically correct and socially accepted, shared meanings. The third stage (Mimesis[3]) deals with the process of applying the new narratives of the phenomena in the new perceptions to come. In this kind of learning, we typically construct narratives based on personal (or autobiographical) meanings, socially shared meanings (community, class), and culturally shared (scientific) meanings. These are negotiated to a narrative with a plot to understand the different aspects of the phenomenon. The teacher's task, defined in the curriculum, is to ensure that scientific meanings dominate in the students' narratives concerning the topic, phenomenon, or domain, such as gravity, force or electricity.

To summarize, I have hypothesized that the narrative turn in understanding human ontology and epistemology pertains also to understanding learning. In this sense, learning about me, others and the world are similar narrative negotiation processes in which we create stories, reconstruct them through reflection, thinking and problem-solving, and apply them to perception and acquisition to refine the narratives towards personally, socially and culturally accepted and shared narratives and understanding of the phenomena and us as part of them.

Identity Negotiation and Curriculum

If we argue that learning is a narrative process in which we negotiate meanings by positioning ourselves in terms of autobiographical, social and cultural perspectives, the question is how to apply this theorizing in rethinking about curricula. For example, in Latin the word *curriculum* denotes: (1) racing (men or horses), (2) one round in a racing course, and (3) a racing course. However, the most current way of understanding the concept of curriculum has not involved a process of proceeding on a life course. According to the ideas of the German *Lehrplan*, curriculum denotes a description of a given course of a given subject at school or other educational institution. This curriculum is a plan for learning. The current Finnish model of curriculum includes descriptions of aims, contents, teaching methods and descriptions of assessment following the so-called Tylerian model (see Tyler 1949). The Tylerian curriculum model is problematic, and to mention just one problem, it is difficult if not impossible to specify exact instructional methods to achieve particular goals, aims or objectives. The more prescriptive the curriculum is, the less it gives teachers options for teaching in a way that allows students to benefit from teachers' own situational intuitions, knowledge of individual students, and narratives of phenomena. If the required performance is described as achievement standards, it is in this respect even more harmful for teachers' work as facilitators of learning.

Without going into more detail about the problems of the current curricular models, I argue that a curriculum can be viewed as an imaginary space or microcosm within which the teachers and students should explore, process and negotiate, in continuous discourses about the inputs, materials and challenges (see Ropo 1992). This microcosm is a space not just for a learning purposes, but living, growing and learning to know what there is to know (ontology) and understanding (epistemology) in terms of personal, social and cultural and historical identity perspectives. This kind of understanding of curriculum is close to the classical definition of the term *curriculum*.

Naturally, there is a lot of theorizing in the history of curriculum. Such concepts as experience, autobiography or life history are familiar from this literature. For instance, Bobbitt (1918/1972) defines the curriculum as a series of, or a continuum of, matters that children must perform or live through. Bobbitt (1972) gives a two-way definition of curriculum. First, a curriculum can be a series of experiences whose

9 CURRICULUM FOR IDENTITY: NARRATIVE NEGOTIATIONS ... 151

purpose is to unfold the children's talents. These experiences can be intentional and directed, or without a teacher's support. Second, Bobbitt (1972) defines curriculum as the entire range of intentionally planned and directed experiences from teaching at school with a view to unfolding and perfecting the child's abilities.[1] To Bobbitt, the purpose of education is to open up the future for children by helping them to find their strengths and sources of interests.

William Pinar (1994) emphasizes the close similarity between autobiographical processes and curriculum. Pinar developed an autobiographical method which he named the "*currere* method" and in turn is based on a reflective examination of school subjects and personal life histories for the purpose of gaining a better understanding of one's self and reconstructing one's identity. The *currere* method comprises four phases: a regressive phase (return to the past: what has been), a progressive phase (a step into the future: what is going to follow, what is the future going to be like), an analytical phase (simultaneous reflection on the past and the future) and a synthetic phase (return to the present). The phases are related to the ways in which individuals in different phases process or reflect on their personal experiences and life histories.

Although Pinar never recommends the method as such for school teaching, it provides an interesting view on increasing the narrative quality of teaching. The result of this kind of reflection can be expressed in the form of narratives, if the user of the method so wishes. To think of school as a pedagogical microcosm is rather an enchanting metaphor, albeit with certain reservations. A microcosm as such is no guarantee of discursive processes in which personal autobiographical narratives can be reconstructed. What narratives come out of it in the minds of the participants depend on the extent of negotiations and individual reflections. Very often all of this remains unknown to the teachers.

---

[1] "The curriculum may, therefore, be defined in two ways: (1) it is the entire range of experiences, both undirected and directed, concerned in unfolding the abilities of the individual; or (2) it is the series of consciously directed training experiences that the schools use for completing and perfecting the unfoldment. Our profession uses the term usually in the latter sense" (Bobbitt 1918/1972, p. 43).

152   E. ROPO

CURRICULUM FOR ENHANCING NARRATIVE NEGOTIATION

Curricula typically contain subject- or domain-specific descriptions of aims, goals and objectives. They may also specify the materials, teaching methods, and assessment criteria for teachers to follow. The purpose of the specificity is, for instance, to increase the transparency of education and its results, to reduce differences and to guide teachers' and educators' work. Still, the problem of relevance and meaningfulness of goals, objectives and applied methods for the students remains. I suggest that in enhancing the narrative negotiation, not only in schools but also generally in education, we have to consider individuality from totally different points of view than we are used to. Individuality does not as much relate to differences in intelligence or talents, but more to student experiences of meaningfulness. To open up discourses related to meaningfulness, I suggest more explicit application of autobiographical, social and cultural positioning in enhancing narrative negotiations in education. Those positionings can be applied to, for instance, locally and globally important issues. The positionings are described in the Table 9.1 separately, although we can assume that they are closely connected and intertwined.

This kind of curriculum does not prescribe teachers' autonomy in deciding the best methods for reaching the goals. However, the thinking is increasingly based on recognizing the importance of students' identity positioning in processing of meanings and meaningfulness towards the topics and phenomena dealt with in instruction. We may infer that all three perspectives of positioning need active decision-making from a student. Autobiographical positioning searches for meanings from personal resources, life experiences, life contexts, bodily experiences, dreams and hopes, beliefs of efficacy, confidence and so on. This search can be contextualized to both local and global perspectives. I may ask what my resources are in the local context and what they are globally. Social positioning relates to membership, belongingness and ways of strengthening the membership by adopting and accepting common values, habits and knowledge bases (see Wenger and Lave 1991). Looking at the issues from the member position, or the local or global perspective leads to different types of meanings. Cultural and global positioning involves seeing one's own life, the lives of others, history, culture and future from a more abstract, "birds eye view" perspective. Ideologies, religions,

Table 9.1 Identity positioning and instructional aims from local and global perspectives

Identity positioning	Instructional aims, locally and globally
Autobiographical	Local: Construction of narratives in different domains in the position of one's own life history and perceptions of local needs and perspectives
	Global: Construction of narratives in different domains in the position of one's own life history and perceptions of global needs and perspectives
Member of a social community	Local: Construction of socially shared narratives in different domains in the position of a social community and its perceptions of local needs and perspectives
	Global: Construction of narratives in different domains in the position of a social community and its perceptions of global needs and perspectives
Cultural, societal and planetary	Local: Construction of narratives in different domains in position of being a citizen and a member of culture and common perceptions of local needs and perspectives
	Global: Construction of narratives in different domains in position of being a citizen and a member of culture and common perceptions of global needs and perspectives

political and environmental values and positioning are good examples of this kind of positioning perspective.

The model I am suggesting here indicates the importance of identity positioning as a concept. Meanings are created in complex contexts through discourses and conversations in which perspectives and contexts are important.

In this chapter, I do not suggest or introduce methods for this kind narrative negotiation. I do believe that methods are not the biggest problem in adopting the idea. Turning the mindsets from learning and learning results to a new paradigm of seeing schools and educational institutions, and curricula, as spaces and places for narrative negotiation is the biggest challenge. There are promising signs from teacher education, professional education and even in public basic education showing that some teachers are actually implicitly applying this type of method. In foreign language education, for instance, the autobiographical approach has expanded into a popular method (Kohonen et al. 2014). Teacher education has also been shown to benefit by applying the ideas

154   E. ROPO

presented in pre-service teacher education (Yrjänäinen 2011) and pilot studies in basic education of enhancing narrative negotiations show that students' acquirements and willingness to position-taking expands from autobiographical towards social and cultural during the school years (Kinossalo 2015). Hopefully, this kind of theorizing I suggested will help to understand better the complexity of internationalizing curriculum conversations.

CONCLUDING REMARKS

Education is a complex system and changing it is a slow process. Political demands for the transparency of measured results have increased leading to increased standardized testing in schools. Autonomy of schools and teachers has in practice been reduced in many countries. Before we educators lose the political battle of the nature of education, it is time to challenge the simplistic views of the results of education being only competences or skills measurable with tests and exams. Curriculum as a societally accepted, intellectual space for narrative negotiations may not be a new idea among researchers. I believe that seeing learning as a process of complex identity negotiation in differing contextual spaces that I have suggested is at least one of the directions to proceed.

REFERENCES

Alcoff, L. M., & Mendieta, E. (2003). *Identities: Race, class, gender, and nationality.* Oxford: Blackwell.

Bobbitt, J. F. (1918/1972). *The curriculum.* Boston, MA: Houghton Mifflin.

Brubaker, R., & Cooper, F. (2000). Beyond "identity". *Theory and Society, 29*(1), 1–47.

Bruner, J. S. (1986). *Actual minds, possible worlds.* Cambridge, MA: Harvard University Press.

Côté, J. (2005). Identity capital, social capital and the wider benefits of learning: Generating resources facilitative of social cohesion. *London Review of Education, 3*(3), 221–237.

Côté, J. (2006). Identity studies: How close are we to developing a social science of identity?—An appraisal of the field. *Identity: An International Journal of Theory and Research, 6*(1), 3–25.

Côté, J. E., & Levine, C. G. (2002). *Identity, formation, agency, and culture: A social psychological synthesis.* New York, NY: Psychology Press.

9 CURRICULUM FOR IDENTITY: NARRATIVE NEGOTIATIONS ... 155

Erikson, E. H. (1959). *Identity and the life cycle.* New York, NY: W.W. Norton & Company. Reprinted in 1994.

Finnish National Agency for Education. (2004). *National core curriculum 2004.* Retrieved from http://www.oph.fi/english/curricula_and_qualifications/basic_education/curricula_2004.

Giddens, A. (1991). *Modernity and self-identity: Self and society in the late modern age.* Stanford, CA: Stanford University Press.

Goodson, I. F. (1998). Storying the self: Life politics and the study of the teacher's life and work. In W. F. Pinar (Ed.), *Curriculum, toward new identities* (pp. 3–20). New York: Garland Publishing.

Goodson, I. (2006). The rise of the life narrative. *Teacher Education Quarterly, 33*(4), 7–21.

Goodson, I. F., Biesta, G., Tedder, M., & Adair, N. (2010). *Narrative learning.* New York: Routledge.

Kihlstrom, J. F., Beer, J. S., & Klein, S. B. (2003). Self and identity as memory. In M. R. Leary & J. P. Tangney (Eds.), *Handbook of self and identity* (pp. 68–90). New York: Guilford Press.

Kinossalo, M. (2015). Oppilaan narratiivisen identiteetin rakentumisen tukeminen perusopetuksessa [Enhancing narrative negotiations of identity in basic education]. In E. Ropo, E. Sormunen, & J. Heinström (Eds.), *Identiteetistä informaatiolukutaitoon: tavoitteena itsenäinen ja yhteisöllinen oppija* [From identity to information literacy: Towards independent and social learner] (pp. 48–82). Tampere: Tampere University Press.

Kohonen, V., Jaatinen, R., Kaikkonen, P., & Lehtovaara, J. (2014). *Experiential learning in foreign language education.* New York: Routledge.

Lannegrand-Willems, L., & Bosma, H. (2006). Identity development-in-context: The school as an important context for identity development. *Identity, 6*(1), 85–113.

Leary, M. R., & Tangney, J. P. (Eds.). (2011). *Handbook of self and identity.* New York, NY: Guildford Press.

Limberg, L., Alexandersson, M., Lantz-Andersson, A., & Folkesson, L. (2008). What matters? Shaping meaningful learning through teaching information literacy. *Libri, 58*(2), 82–91.

Marcia, J. E. (1994). The empirical study of ego identity. In H. A. Bosma, T. L. G. Graasfma, H. D. Grotevant, & D. J. De Levita (Eds.), *Identity and development: An interdisciplinary approach* (pp. 67–80). Thousand Oaks, CA: Sage.

McAdams, D. P., Josselson, R., & Lieblich, A. (Eds.). (2006). *Identity and story: Creating self in narrative.* Washington, DC: APA.

Mead, G. H. (1934). *Mind, self and society* (Vol. 111). Chicago: University of Chicago Press.

156　E. ROPO

Meretoja, H. (2014). *The narrative turn in fiction and theory: The crisis and return of storytelling from Robbe-Grillet to Tournier*. Basingstoke, UK: Palgrave Macmillan.

Merleau-Ponty, M. (1986). *Phénoménologie de la perception* [Phenomenology of perception]. London: Routledge (Original publication, 1945).

Pinar, W. F. (1994). *Autobiography, politics, and sexuality*. New York: Peter Lang.

Ricoeur, P. (1984). *Time and narrative* (K. McLaughlin & D. Pellauer, Trans.). Chicago: University of Chicago Press.

Ricoeur, P. (1987). *Time and Narrative III*. Chicago: The University of Chicago Press.

Ricoeur, P. (1991). Narrative identity. In D. Wood (Ed.), *On Paul Ricoeur: Narrative and interpretation*. London: Routledge.

Ropo, E. (1992). Opetussuunnitelmastrategiat elinikäisen oppimisen kehittämisessä [Curriculum strategies for developing lifelong learning]. *Kasvatus, 23*(2), 99–110.

Ropo, E., & Värri, V.-M. (2003). Teacher identity and the ideologies of teaching: Some remarks on the interplay. In D. Trueit, W. E. Doll, H. Wang, & W. E. Pinar (Eds.), *The internationalization of curriculum studies* (pp. 261–270). Selected Proceedings from the LSU Conference 2000. Peter Lang. ISBN 0-8204-5590-3.

Taylor, C. (1989). *Sources of the self*. Cambridge: Cambridge University Press.

Tyler, R. W. (1949). *Basic principles of curriculum and instruction*. Chicago: University of Chicago Press.

Van Langenhove, L., & Harré, R. (1999). Introducing positioning theory. In R. Harré & L. van Langenhove (Eds.), *Positioning theory* (pp. 14–31). Malden, MA: Blackwell.

Weigert, A. J., Teitge, J. S., & Teitge, D. W. (1986). *Society and identity: Toward a sociological psychology*. Cambridge: Cambridge University Press.

Wenger, E., & Lave, J. (1991). *Situated learning: Legitimate peripheral participation (Learning in doing: Social, cognitive and computational perspectives)*. Cambridge, UK: Cambridge University Press.

Yrjänäinen, S. (2011). *'Onks meistä tähän?' Aineenopettajakoulutus ja opettajaopiskelijan toiminnallisen osaamisen palapeli* ['But really, are we the right sort of people for this?' The puzzle of subject teacher education and the teacher student professional practical capabilities]. Acta Universitatis Tamperensis 1586. Tampere: Tampere University Press.

Yrjänäinen, S., & Ropo, E. (2013). Narratiivisesta opetuksesta narratiiviseen oppimiseen [From narrative teaching to narrative learning]. In E. Ropo & M. Huttunen (Eds.), *Puheenvuoroja narratiivisuudesta opetuksessa ja oppimisessa* [Conversations on narrativity in teaching and learning]. Tampere: Tampere University Press.

CHAPTER 10

High Passions: Affect and Curriculum Theorizing in the Present

Alyssa D. Niccolini, Bessie Dernikos, Nancy Lesko and Stephanie D. McCall

Passions are high in education. In the USA, anxieties over the educational system rival panics around terrorism and Ebola in national imaginaries. "The fate of our country won't be decided on a battlefield, it will be determined in a classroom," warns the tagline on the book accompanying the film, *Waiting for "Superman"* (Weber 2010). Helle Bjerg and Dorothe Staunæs (2011) explore how business management techniques have infiltrated classrooms whereby "affects and affectivity are not simply

A. D. Niccolini (✉)
Neckargemuend, Germany

B. Dernikos
Florida Atlantic University, Boca Raton, FL, USA

N. Lesko
Columbia University, New York, NY, USA

S. D. McCall
University of Pennsylvania, Stroudsburg, PA, USA

© The Author(s) 2019   157
C. Hébert et al. (eds.), *Internationalizing Curriculum Studies*,
https://doi.org/10.1007/978-3-030-01352-3_10

by-products or something to be overcome, but the core matter to be managed by and through" (p. 139). In an age of accountability (Boldt et al. 2009; Taubman 2009) or what William Pinar (2004) deems the "nightmare of the present," we see the recent turn to affect as a robust interpretative community for contemporary curriculum theorists navigating an educational present marked by intensities. An attention to affect offers a means of feeling out and making sense of the historical present (Berlant 2011; Shaviro 2010). Affect, as Brian Massumi (2015b) argues, "provides the invitational opening for a rationality to get its hooks into the flesh. Affect is the domain of "mere" feeling. It represents the vulnerability of the individual to larger societal forces" (p. 85). As we move within a hypermodernity marked by transnational flows of bodies and capital (Miller 2013; Whitlock 2006), where terror and displacement mark the everyday, and where swift relays of information and bodily affective responses are increasingly honed for traction, power, and profit, Massumi (2015c) sees new forms of thinking-feeling, or *ontopower*, taking hold. Ontopower works through channeling affectivity and collective attunement, stoking fleshly reactivity, and engendering an "ontological reworking of ecologies of sensation" (Rai 2015, n.p. citing Massumi 2015b). As Amit Rai (2015) offers:

> Affect is not the site of social struggle in the sense health care, benefits, wages, and capitalist value are. Affect concerns complex, multi-causal states of affairs that have taken form through non-linear histories involving flows of biomass ... forms of habituation, sensory feedback loops, mutations in machinic perception and other such circuits of actualized potentiality. (n.p.)

Within such a context, Nigel Thrift (2004) decrees it "criminal neglect" (p. 58) to ignore affect today.

This chapter introduces affect studies' potential to contribute to curriculum research and theory. One specific contribution is affect's attention to emergence, or becoming, that is, to how thinking-feeling comes into being. This focus on emergence is well suited to the heightened passions around, for example, becoming good readers and preparing for college as measures of academic success. We explore such emergences below after a brief introduction to affect theory.

The Affective Turn

What's been deemed the "affective turn" (Clough and Haley 2007) has greatly influenced work in cultural studies, the humanities, and the social sciences, and is increasingly influencing educational research. Affect theorists, largely energized by the Spinozist-inspired philosophy of Gilles Deleuze and Félix Guattari, have embraced conceptions of affect to put pressure on humanist legacies of subjectivity, telos-driven narratives of temporality, and Cartesian devaluations of the body's experiences and intelligences. Aligned with curriculum theorizing and post-qualitative work challenging notions of the conventional humanist subject (Lather and St. Pierre 2013; St. Pierre 2013), affect theorists work with impetuses from feminist and queer poststructuralist thought to explore the immaterial forces that *move* and are *moved by* bodies writ large.

Bodies, embodiment, and corporeality have had considerable importance within curriculum theorizing (see, among others, Grumet 1988; Irwin 1999; Pillow 2007; Springgay and Freedman 2007; Springgay 2008); affect theory continues this attention by figuring bodies as intensely permeable, interconnected assemblages of both material and immaterial, human and non-human forces (Bennett 2010; Blackman 2013; Brennan 2004; Deleuze and Guattari 1987). A body then is a processual "event" constantly being remodulated through affects, rather than a static and contained entity being acted on from without; a body is defined not by what it is, but what it *does* and *can do* (Clough 2008; Massumi 2015a; Puar 2012). Some theorists of affect have sought to dissolve traditional disciplinary boundaries to rethink how bodies and materialities encounter affect and co-constitute each other (Barad 2007; Bennett 2010; Blackman 2013; Damasio 2000; Massumi 2015a; Sedgwick 2003; Sedgwick and Frank 1995). Other scholars have joined historical and discursive analyses to attend to *moods* (Flatley 2008), *atmospheres* (Anderson 2014; Brennan 2004), *feelings* (Cvetkovich 2012; Muñoz 2000; Ngai 2005), *phenomenologies of emotions* (Ahmed 2011), and *vibrations* (Henriques 2010).

Affect theory has also provided methodological tools and aesthetic interventions foregrounding the ordinary alongside heightened affective states such as wonder, enchantment, and surprise as alternatives to the hermeneutics of suspicion that beset poststructuralist thought and ideological critique (Bennett 2001; Berlant 2011; Coleman and Ringrose 2013; MacLure 2013; Hickey-Moody 2013; Jackson and Mazzei 2012; Lesko and Talburt 2012; Sedgwick 2003; Springgay et al. 2008; Springgay and Truman 2016; Springgay and Zaliwska 2016; Stewart 2007; Vannini 2015).

Commensurate with long-standing work within curriculum theorizing whereby curriculum is understood as a *doing* rather than a stable and bound body of knowledge or set of content (Miller 2014; Pinar and Grumet 1976; Pinar 2004; Pinar et al. 1995), affect offers an attention to "relations of motion and becoming" (Rai 2015, n.p.). This chapter explores how affect theory offers important conceptual tools for understanding and navigating the educational historical present by attending to emergent encounters of bodies, desires, and things.

FACING OFF: FEELING AGAINST THOUGHT

Affect has been deemed particularly potent for offering what Eve Sedgwick (2003) deems "promising tools and techniques for nondualistic thought and pedagogy" (p. 1). Part of the legacy of such dualistic thinking in curriculum theory and practice is to view affect as opposed to cognition. The second handbook of the widely influential *Taxonomy of Educational Objectives, Handbook II: Affective Domain* (Krathwohl et al. 1956) concludes that "society fluctuates in permitting affective objectives … Pressing the school for some affective objectives … and restricting others" and that this "has made teachers and administrators wary." Consequently, schools often "retreat to [the] less dangerous cognitive domain" (cited in Weinstein and Fantini 1970, p. 25).

In *The Affective Domain in Education*, T. A. Ringness (1975) similarly argues that where affect and cognition are concerned, "*one domain tends to drive out the other*" (p. 25, emphasis added). For Ringness, only the "the highly skilled teacher" is capable of effectively producing both cognitive and affective learning without doing violence to one or the other. For the majority, "the affective domain usually loses out" (p. 25). This perceived incommensurability of affect and cognition has persisted with affect being positioned as at odds, even at war, with cognition. This is aptly captured by Fig. 10.1.

Fig. 10.1 A "face-off" image of affect and cognition. Retrieved from http://serc.carleton.edu/NAGTWorkshops/affective/index.html

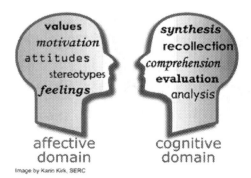

This "face-off" logic continues to shape conceptions of curriculum today. For example, Common Core proponents argue that the US educational system has been too touchy-feely for too long, which has compromised its competitive edge in a global economy. Take, for example, this statement for *evidence-based writing* from the Common Core Web site:

> Frequently, forms of writing in K–12 have drawn heavily from student experience and opinion, which alone will not prepare students for the demands of college, career, and life. Though the standards still expect narrative writing throughout the grades, they also expect a command of sequence and detail that are essential for effective argumentative and informative writing. The standards' focus on evidence-based writing along with the ability to inform and persuade is a significant shift from current practice. (http://www.corestandards.org/other-resources/key-shifts-in-english-language-arts/)

In this statement, the Common Core is a "significant shift" from a perceived over-emphasis on the affective domain that has jeopardized students' futures ("college, career, and life" itself) and is charged with weakening the vitality of the American educational system. Many critics of the Common Core bemoan that ever-increasing accountability measures sap students and teachers of vital creative energy (see e.g., Greene 2014). Affect in both instances has the capacity to animate (Chen 2012), or if wasted on investment in the wrong objects (like standardized tests or opinion-driven writing), enervate teachers and learners perpetuating a view that affect works against thought. For conservatives and progressives alike, affect and cognition are deemed incompatible in teaching and learning.

THINKING-MOVEMENT

In contrast, many affect theorists offer a non-dualistic conception of affect and thought, seeing affect as a vital form of intelligence and resistance. Raymond Williams' (1977) notion of "structures of feeling" emphasizes "not feeling against thought, but *thought as felt* and *feeling as thought*" (p. 132, emphasis added). Massumi (2015a) calls this simply *thinking-feeling* while others deem it an "affective intelligence" (Berlant 2011; Marcus et al. 2000; Thrift 2007). As Massumi (2015a) submits "affect is thinking, bodily—consciously but vaguely, in the sense that is not yet a fully formed thought. It's a movement of thought, or a thinking movement" (p. 10). According to this line of thought, affect is a creative, unpredictable, and vital force that offers means of interrupting and remodulating dominant modes of power and rigid normativities (Berlant 2011; Cvetkovich 2012; Marcus et al. 2000; Massumi 2015a, b; Sedgwick 2003; Staiger et al. 2010; Thrift 2007) but simultaneously bears the risk of reentrenching racism, classism, and other exclusions (Saldahna 2005). We explore these capacities of affect to both push against and reentrench dominant configurations of power in schools in the following two vignettes.

AFFECTIVE ENCOUNTERS AND DESIRING BODIES

As Massumi (2015a) submits "[o]ur bodies and our lives are almost a kind of resonating chamber for media-borne perturbations that strike us and run through us, that strike us and strike beyond us simultaneously" (p. 114). In the USA, headlines such as "The Failure of American Schools" (Klein 2011), "Why Schools Are Failing Our Boys" (Fink 2015), and "The Kids Can't Read" (Biddle 2010) are ubiquitous, reifying troubling images of failing schools, failing boys, and literacy crises (Ringrose 2013). These media-generated words and images "strike" by pulling at us in very bodily ways. That is, before we can even grasp the overall complexities of the situation and all that is happening, we are immediately disturbed, *affected*.

In what follows, we hone in on the affective intensities moving through a New York City first grade classroom where such "literacy letdown" (Harris 2015) is addressed via mandated literacy practices. We explore the way affects flow from the macro (e.g., the affective circulation of a national literacy "epidemic") into the micro (here, the impulse to control and measure literacy, students, and textual practices) levels of Ms. Rizzo's first grade classroom, inviting both wonder (MacLure 2013) and an attention to the processes that make, unmake, and remake "literate bodies."

LEVELED READING PRACTICES[1]

According to Tim Shanahan (2011), scant empirical evidence exists to support instructional leveling practices within literacy and, yet, leveled reading systems promoting "just right" books actively shape K-8 curricula

---

[1] This excerpt is drawn from a larger study of first grade literacy practices (Dernikos 2015).

across the USA. In such systems, students independently read self-selected, instructional leveled texts with the aim of systematically progressing from a hierarchized reading system marked A–Z. Though these practices seem innocent enough, we see them as inextricably entangled within a media-driven panic logic that has affectively spread throughout American public schools (Masny 2012; Ringrose 2013), where (in one way or another) intense fear, worry, and shame feed off each other as a full-blown "crisis in literacy" actualizes. These unwanted affects (Brennan 2004) cling to our educational policies and practices, re/creating knowledges, norms, and interventions that fuel the reconfiguration of literacy as rational, normative, and standardized (e.g., Common Core) (Dernikos 2015). And, just like that, climbing up the leveling hierarchy becomes something other than temporal, spatial, and sequential movement. This encounter (more than anything) involves wishing and willing—lingering desires that have the potential to do some real harm or good (Ahmed 2014; Wiegman 2012). So, while leveling systems optimistically draw upon meritocratic discourses of social mobility/success in order to position "movin' on up" as desirable and attainable (Jones and Vagle 2013), we cannot ignore the social investments of desire that serve to regulate bodies. Desire, as a productive force, materializes on bodies and impacts a subject's becomings by creating connections that enable possibility, expression, and movement, and/or constrain a body's capacity to act (Zembylas 2007). Within the following vignette, we offer up desire as a possible pedagogic or "interpretive" tool (Zembylas 2007), exploring the ways its affective flows dynamically intra-act (Barad 2007) with human and non-human bodies to organize, intensify, and *produce*—rather than reveal—literate identities.

'I'M GONNA KEEP DOING IT'

Throughout the day (and perhaps longer), students in Ms. Rizzo's first grade classroom remained alert to an expected future goal (e.g., reading at a G level by March) that could be achieved by moving up text levels—a goal that, if unmet, may have impacted their status as a "successful" literacy learner. Yet, some students, such as Dylan, actively resisted normative reading expectations by choosing texts *above* their reading levels:

164   A. D. NICCOLINI ET AL.

Dylan: Sh! Don't tell but I love Biscuit. He's my favorite.
Miss Bessie: Why is that a secret?
Dylan: I took Biscuit by accident. I'm not supposed to take from G. I'm an E, but those books are fake. Who wants to read them? Nobody! No story! Look, this one's real. (shows Miss Bessie the cover of the Biscuit book) Cool, right? I like him, so I'm gonna keep doing it.

Since early reading levels tend to focus less on story development and more on basic print concepts and simple story lines, Dylan seems to form the idea that lower-level texts are *fake* books with *no [real] story*. He, thus, positions lower-level texts as unappealing (something *nobody* wants to read) and higher-level texts, such as *Biscuit*, as desirable (or *cool*). Here, worries swirl around Dylan's body (*Sh! Don't tell*), investing it/him with the capacity to take furtive action. Instead of returning the Biscuit book to the G-level basket, Dylan reads it secretly and soon proclaims he will continue to take Biscuit books (*I'm gonna keep doing it*). Dylan's desire, in effect, moves him to disregard classroom reading expectations (i.e., reading "appropriate" leveled texts) in order to connect with a book above his current reading level: a *real* book that has characters he *like(s)*.

While some of Dylan's actions work to deterritorialize the leveling system (e.g., choosing a G, not E, level book), others, such as not writing in his Reader Response notebook, reterritorialize the normative and impact his becomings:

Ms. Rizzo: (pointing) Dylan, get busy … Let me see your Reader Response. (Dylan is silent)
Ms. Rizzo: You don't have one? (Dylan moves his head from left to right, signaling no) What have you been doing this whole time?

At this point in the school year (March), students are expected to read at or above level G. Because Dylan is still reading E-level texts, he is not yet meeting standards or "benchmarks." As such, Ms. Rizzo tended to pay more attention to what Dylan was (or was not) doing ("What have you been doing this whole time?"). Unable (or-willing) to offer Ms. Rizzo a rationale for his behavior, Dylan seems to get lost in his desires, resulting in his failure to read any E-level texts and complete any Reader Responses for E or G texts. Even though Dylan *was* reading and even desired to read more challenging G-level texts, his actions are ultimately read as off-task, irrational, and inefficient (for not using his time wisely). Not only do these actions serve to potentially reinscribe him as a "struggling reader," but they also problematically forward the idea that boys, especially boys of color, are somehow "failing." Thus, affective encounters, as an entanglement of mixed forces, desires, and things, have the capacity to mark a body's belonging *or non-belonging* to a social world (Seigworth and Gregg 2010).

While this scene may indeed offer other possibilities and/or threats (Stewart 2007), we have tried to highlight how affective encounters are "never defined by a [human] body alone" (Seigworth and Gregg 2010, p. 13) and how a *thing*, as part of a complex assemblage, functions to *affectively conduct* (Puar 2012) and intensify reading experiences and identities. To make our point stick: The leveling system in Ms. Rizzo's class, while seemingly neutral, draws its power, its "meaning," not from language alone (Stewart 2007), but from an assemblage of *sounds* (e.g., Sh!), *affects* (e.g., Dylan's willfulness), *texts* (e.g., *Biscuit*), *bodies* (e.g., Dylan's Black, male body), *spaces* (e.g., Dylan's table is near Ms. Rizzo's physical body), and *sociopolitical forces* (e.g., meritocratic discourses and national panics about literacy). Ordinary things, then, even though they seem dead and lifeless, actively work to orient *desiring bodies* (Grosz 1993) in molar and/or molecular ways (Deleuze and Guattari 1987), thereby impacting the making of successful literacy learners.

The Cruelty of Happy Futures

In this next section, we further explore *affective conductors* (Puar 2012) that orient bodies toward what Sara Ahmed (2011) calls "happy objects" as they circulate around notions of educational "success," in this instance for young women in an urban public all-girls' high school in the USA. Ahmed (2011) writes, "If we think of instrumental goods as objects of happiness then important consequences follow. Things become good, or acquire their value as goods insofar as they point toward happiness. Objects become 'happiness means'" (p. 34). Here, postfeminist scenes of unambiguous female success (Harris 2004; Ringrose 2013), the failure to "choose" particular objects of future success by the girls was thought to be a failed project of self-invention, not a critique of promises and happy endings. Fear, uncertainty, and disappointment were left out of college-going processes in the discussions below, often leaving girls to feel as failed female subjects should they desire a different post-secondary school path or to not attend college. We attend to the dualist thought process of success/failure, right/wrong, good/bad in circulation in this vignette and analyze the affective intensities to do so.

COLLEGES AND KITCHENS[2]

The futures of the girls in this focus group were talked about as a choice between going to college and staying in the kitchen.

> *Fatima*: We do talk about femininity because sometimes there are kids that do not go to college. Teachers—not force them, but urge—encourage them to go to college so they get better jobs and not stay in the kitchen the whole day taking care of family, but going outside and earning some money.
>
> *Nadia*: The teachers don't say "you belong in the kitchen" … I think what they mean is to encourage you to go to college because of the economy and the society we are in now.

College and kitchen are "right" and "wrong" objects. Domesticity, signified as femininity, was how girls referenced their futures in relation to college. Students reported that teachers invoked their concerns about the cultural histories of domesticity and lack of educational choice for this group of girls from many different South Asian countries. In the current postfeminist era of girl power choices of freedom, flexibility, and reflexivity (Ringrose 2013), it seemed anachronistic to suggest that college and the kitchen were the only post-school options, or *objects of desire* (Berlant 2011), today. Students cited some of the reasons their teachers had given them for going to college: better jobs, financial independence, and social mobility. These are the "important consequences" (Ahmed 2011) that follow objects of happiness. The list of investments in college (going outside of the home and earning money) appeals to girls' vulnerability, or even fears, for failure in the political context of *girlpower* that media, teachers, and school curricula sell.

The promises of college were unlike the promises associated with the kitchen. "Femininity," or the term they used interchangeably with domesticity, was what girls learned about when they did not go to college. The idea of staying in the kitchen revived a historical trope of the

---

[2] This excerpt is drawn from a larger study of single-sex schools for girls (McCall 2014).

kitchen as the feminine future. In this discussion, 11th grade girls were moved toward some happy objects (like college) and away from unhappy objects (like kitchens and domesticity). Ahmed (2011) argues that not all objects carry the same status and those objects that accrue the most valued promises, like financial security and market participation, have the highest status. In this case, the kitchen is the wrong object while college is the more valued object or the *happy object*. Ahmed (2011) writes, "If objects provide a means for making us happy, then in directing ourselves toward this or that object we are aiming somewhere else: toward a happiness that is presumed to follow" (p. 34). Teacher discourse in classrooms at this school transported dualist and overly simplistic messages to the girls about the promises of happiness by going to college and, thus, that of being trapped in the kitchen should they not attend college.

The kitchen and college were the objects used to evaluate the girls' potential for future happiness in their becoming and as they planned their post-secondary school futures. Ahmed (2011) writes that "happiness puts us into contact with things" and "to be affected by something is to evaluate that thing. Evaluations are expressed in how bodies turn toward things" (p. 23). In this scene, college is "passed around, accumulating positive affective value as social goods" (p. 21).

As an object of happiness, college was talked about speculatively by one student, Sasha, an 11th grade student.

> *Maia*: Most girls in this school say they're going to college.
> *Nadia*: Some people in our group don't want to go to college.
> *Fatima*: It's not that they don't want to go to college, but it's their culture that influences them ... leading her away.
> *Sasha*: I disagree. I don't want to go to college myself. I'm just too lazy. You graduate high school and then you have to go to school again.

Sasha goes on to say later in the discussion, "I'm just not sure what I want to do with my life." Sasha refused to blame her culture as a constraint or effect. In refusing normative conditions of educational success, she also made her choice about herself, her own desire and internal resources (calling herself lazy). She took herself out of the game by saying she was lazy, when what she may also be thinking-feeling (Massumi 2015a) is uncertainty and skepticism about the promises and guarantees of college, as this social good that is to be "accumulating positive affective value" (Ahmed 2011, p. 15). Unfortunately, in the eyes of Sasha's teachers and parents she would not be read as wondering or enchantment with a darker side of futurity; she would be read as taking up a failed position. By the utterance, "I'm just too lazy" she may have been trying to free herself from the affects brought on by futurity and what she saw as a more speculative endeavor of college-going.

The cruelty of happy futures can be understood as what girls do not learn in *school curriculum* about how to "identify, manage, and maintain the hazy luminosity of their attachment to being x and having x" (Berlant 2011, p. 112). Notions about female success and failure are readily available but narrow in school knowledge (McCall 2014). Understanding the presences of this duality of success/failure and good/bad objects has meaning for the selection and organization of curricular knowledge, which is thought to be the knowledge that these girls *needed* for educational success defined for them, in part, by the school. This functional approach to future success and failure can be analyzed as what Berlant (2011) calls *cruel optimisms*:

> a cruel optimistic relation exists when the objects of optimism are blockages to the achievement of desire for which they stand in. They come to represent not only things and promises about life by which one wants to be structured but the possibility of attachment to the world itself, so that their potential loss is a double loss: of a particular attachment, and of the fantasy as such. (p. 182)

Analyzing the objects that carry promises to bring happiness, and therefore, are the "good" objects to which girls should attach, shows the limits of a curriculum that privileges certain affects, attachments, and objects over others.

Margins of Maneuverability

The Dylan vignette examines becoming literate as an affective encounter of standardized curriculum, leveled reading materials, an individual student's desires for interesting, real books, and a teacher's sticking to standardized accountability measures. This irreducible set of material and immaterial forces produces literate students; neither discourse nor human intentionality nor structural context alone suffices. This thrown-togetherness animates and makes meaningful the concept of a *struggling reader*, and affect theory helps us consider the histories, intensities, materialities, and feelings involved in early literacy.

In a similar way, interrogating college as the ubiquitous standard of educational success leads to a nuanced appreciation of young women's veiled ambivalences. How could young women "choose" the kitchen over college? The emergence of thinking-feelings laden with uncertainty about economic options, wariness of pushy teachers, and gendered longings for "happiness" clouded college as the sole guarantor of success. This affective interpretation refuses dualistic orientations of success/failure and thinking/feeling. Both vignettes push against static configurations of power—whether local, national, or transnational—by emphasizing emergence.

In concluding, we ask if curriculum theorists can find an alternative stance to "cynical resignation on the one hand and naïve optimism on the other hand" (Halberstam 2011, p. xiii). In transnational landscapes marked by intensities, "the nightmare of the present" (Pinar 2004) may indeed offer up multiple forms of "radical hope" (Smits and Naqvi 2015). For Massumi (2015a) affect *is* precisely hope:

> I use the concept of 'affect' as a way of talking about that margin of maneuverability, the 'where we might be able to go and what we might be able to do' in every present situation. I guess 'affect' is the word I use for 'hope.' (p. 3)

According to Anderson (2006), hope anticipates becomings:

> Hope, and hoping, are taken-for-granted parts of the affective fabric of contemporary Western life. The circulation, and distribution, of hope animates and dampens social-cultural life across numerous scales: from the minutiae of hopes that pleat together everyday life to the larger scale flows of hope that enact various collectivities. ... Frequently likened to the immaterial-matter of air, or sensed in the prophetic figure of the horizon, hope anticipates that something indeterminate has not-yet become. (p. 733)

We join Smits and Naqvi (2015) to propose that a crucial task of the contemporary curriculum theorist is to think with and through hope. Though seemingly lifeless, an encounter with hope cannot help but impact our bodies, as its after-affects (Niccolini 2016)—a simultaneous defeat and openness—wash over us again and again. A hopeful body must, in some way, understand that defeat is always already present;

170 A. D. NICCOLINI ET AL.

otherwise there would be no reason to hope at all (Anderson 2006). At the same time, hope opens us up to the possibility of something new to come: bodies (of knowledge, literacy, etc.) maneuvering within stratified territories in order to move on, live, experiment (Deleuze and Guattari 1983; Rajchman 2000). "To experiment is to try new actions, methods, techniques and combinations, 'without aim or end'" (Deleuze and Guattari 1983, p. 371). We experiment when "we do not know what the result will be and have no preconceptions concerning what it should be" (Baugh 2010, p. 91). And when we experiment with interpretive tools, such as affect, our explorations move away from hierarchical classification or judgment. Rather, they are filled with hope; encounters that are both absent and present, here and there, past/present/future.

Affect is also hopeful in how it always connects us to other bodies. Massumi (2015a) argues:

> In affect, we are never alone. That's because affects in Spinoza's definition are basically ways of connecting, to others and to other situations. They are our angle of participation in processes larger than ourselves. With intensified affect comes a stronger sense of embeddedness in a larger field of life–a heightened sense of belonging, with other people and to other places. (p. 6)

If affect is always a form of relationality, what happens if we ask not just what bodies can do, but "what can bod[ies] do when [they] become hopeful" (Anderson 2006, p. 734)? For example, how might Dylan's low level of literacy offer collective spaces of maneuvering within the politics of leveling systems or Common Core and, in turn, tune us into them? How might Sarah's described "laziness" resist the ways school curriculum functions as an "affective straightening device" (Ahmed 2014, p. 7), opening more orientations for bodies beyond a limited set of right choices? How might curriculum theorists use these questions and others in order to approach curriculum as a hopeful doing that reanimates bodies, spaces, and "things": a doing that opens us up to the current moment, with all its horror and joy, while acknowledging that the current is always "on the go" (Bennett 2010), rife for experimentation and surprise? After all, "the current is not what we are but rather what we become, what we are in the process of becoming, in other words the Other, our becoming-other" (Deleuze 1992, p. 164).

References

Ahmed, S. (2011). *Promise of happiness*. Durham, NC: Duke University Press.

Ahmed, S. (2014). *Willful subjects*. Durham, NC: Duke University Press.

Anderson, B. (2006). Becoming and being hopeful: Towards a theory of affect. *Environment and Planning D: Society and Space, 24*(5), 733–752.

Anderson, B. (2014). *Encountering affect: Capacities, apparatuses, conditions*. Farnham: Ashgate.

Barad, K. (2007). *Meeting the universe halfway: Quantum physics and the entanglement of matter and meaning*. Durham, NC: Duke University Press.

Baugh, B. (2010). Experimentation. In A. Parr (Ed.), *The Deleuze dictionary* (pp. 93–95). Edinburgh: Edinburgh University Press.

Bennett, J. (2001). *The enchantment of modern life: Attachments, crossings, and ethics*. Princeton, NJ: Princeton University Press.

Bennett, J. (2010). *Vibrant matter: A political ecology of things*. Durham, NC: Duke University Press.

Berlant, L. (2011). *Cruel optimism*. Durham, NC: Duke University Press.

Biddle, R. (2010). *The kids can't read*. Retrieved from http://spectator.org/39390_kids-cant-read/.

Bjerg, H., & Staunæs, D. (2011). Self-management through shame – Uniting governmentality studies and the 'affective turn.' *Ephemera: Theory & Politics in Organization, 11*(2), 138–156.

Blackman, L. (2013). *Immaterial bodies: Affect, embodiment, mediation*. Los Angeles, CA: Sage.

Boldt, G., Salvio, P., & Taubman, P. (Eds.) (2009). *Classroom lives in the age of accountability*. Bank Street College of Education Occasional Papers Series 22, 3–7.

Brennan, T. (2004). *The transmission of affect*. Ithaca, NY: Cornell University Press.

Chen, M. (2012). *Animacies: Biopolitics, racial matters, and queer affect*. Durham, NC: Duke University Press.

Clough, P. T. (2008). The affective turn: Political economy, biomedia, bodies. *Theory, Culture and Society, 25*(1), 1–22.

Clough, P., & Haley, J. (2007). *The affective turn: Theorizing the social*. Durham, NC: Duke University Press.

Coleman, R., & Ringrose, J. (2013). *Deleuze and research methodologies*. Edinburgh: Edinburgh University Press.

Cvetkovich, A. (2012). *Depression: A public feeling*. Durham, NC: Duke University Press.

Damasio, A. (2000). *The feeling of what happens: Body, emotion and the making of consciousness*. London: Vintage.

172 A. D. NICCOLINI ET AL.

Deleuze, G. (1992). What is a dispositif? In J. Armostrong (Ed.), *Michel Foucault philosopher*. New York: Routledge.

Deleuze, G., & Guattari, F. (1983). What is a minor literature? (R. Brinkley, Trans.). *Mississippi Review, 11*(3), 13–33.

Deleuze, G., & Guattari, F. (1987). *A thousand plateaus: Capitalism and schizophrenia*. Minneapolis: University of Minnesota Press.

Dernikos, B. (2015). *A gender gap in literacy? De/territorialing literacy, gender, and the humanist subject*. Doctoral dissertation, ProQuest LLC (3704464).

Fink, J. (2015). *Why schools are failing our boys*. https://www.washingtonpost.com/news/parenting/wp/2015/02/19/why-schools-are-failing-our-boys/.

Flatley, J. (2008). *Affective mapping*. Cambridge, MA: Harvard University Press.

Greene, D. (2014). *How common core standards kill creative teaching*. http://www.usnews.com/opinion/articles/2014/03/17/how-common-core-standards-kill-creative-teaching.

Grosz, E. (1993). Bodies and knowledges: Feminism and the crisis of reason. In L. Alcoff & E. Potter (Eds.), *Feminist epistemologies* (pp. 187–215). New York, NY: Routledge.

Grumet, M. (1988). *Bitter milk: Women and teaching*. Amherst, MA: University of Massachusetts Press.

Halberstam, J. (2011). *The queer art of failure*. Durham, NC: Duke University Press.

Harris, A. (2004). *Future girl: Young women in the twenty-first century*. London and New York, NY: Routledge.

Harris, S. (2015). *Literacy letdown in primary schools*. http://www.dailymail.co.uk/news/article-81287/Literacy-letdown-primary-schools.html.

Henriques, J. (2010). The vibration of affect and their propagation on a night out on Kingston's dancehall scene. *Body & Society, 16*(1), 57–89.

Hickey-Moody, A. (2013). *Youth, arts and education: Reassembling subjectivity through affect*. London: Routledge.

Irwin, R. (1999). Facing oneself: An embodied pedagogy. *Arts and Learning Research, 16*(1), 82–86.

Jackson, A. Y., & Mazzei, L. (2012). *Thinking with theory in qualitative research*. New York, NY: Routledge.

Jones, S., & Vagle, M. (2013). Living contradictions and working for change: Toward a theory of social class-sensitive pedagogy. *Educational Researcher, 42*(3), 129–141.

Klein, J. (2011). *The failure of American schools*. http://www.theatlantic.com/magazine/archive/2011/06/the-failure-of-american-schools/308497/.

Krathwohl, D., Bloom, B., & Bertram, M. (1956). *Taxonomy of educational objectives: Handbook II: Affective domain*. New York, NY: David McKay Company.

Lather, P., & St. Pierre, E. (2013). Post-qualitative research. *International Journal of Qualitative Studies in Education, 26*(6), 629–633.

10 HIGH PASSIONS: AFFECT AND CURRICULUM THEORIZING ... 173

Lesko, N., & Talburt, S. (2012). Enchantment. In N. Lesko & S. Talburt (Eds.), *Keywords in youth studies: Tracing affects, movements, knowledges* (pp. 279–289). New York: RoutledgeFalmer.

MacLure, M. (2013). Coding as an analytic practice in qualitative research. In R. Colemand & J. Ringrose (Eds.), *Deleuze and research methodologies* (pp. 164–183). Edinburgh: Edinburgh University Press.

Marcus, G., Neuman, R., & Mackuen, M. (2000). *Affective intelligence and political judgment.* Chicago, IL: University of Chicago Press.

Masny, D. (2012). Cartographies of multiple literacies. In D. Masny & D. Cole (Eds.), *Mapping multiple literacies: An introduction to Deleuzian literacy studies* (pp. 15–42). New York: Continuum.

Massumi, B. (2015a). *Politics of affect.* Malden, MA: Polity.

Massumi, B. (2015b). *Q & A with Brian Massumi.* Retrieved March 13, 2018, from https://dukeupress.wordpress.com/2015/08/19/qa-with-brian-massumi/.

Massumi, B. (2015c). *Ontopower: War, powers, and the state of perception.* Durham, NC: Duke University Press.

McCall, S. (2014). *What kind of girl?: Curricular knowledge and the making of girls in two all-girls schools.* Doctoral dissertation, ProQuest LLC (3622268).

Miller, J. (2013). *Traveling auto/biography.* Paper presented to the American Educational Research Association annual meeting, San Francisco.

Miller, J. (2014). Curriculum theorizing in the throes of audit culture. *Curriculum and Teaching Dialogue, 16*(1), 13–30.

Muñoz, J. (2000). Feeling brown: Ethnicity and affect in Ricardo Bracho's *The sweetest hangover (and other STDs). Theater Journal, 52*(1), 67–79.

Ngai, S. (2005). *Ugly feelings.* Cambridge, MA: Harvard University Press.

Niccolini, A. D. (2016). Animate affects: Censorship, reckless pedagogies, and beautiful feelings. *Gender and Education, 28*(2), 230–249.

Pillow, W. (2007). 'Bodies are dangerous': Using feminist genealogy as policy studies methodology. In S. Ball, I. Goodson, & M. Maguire (Eds.), *Education, globalisation, and new times: 21 years of the Journal of Education Policy* (pp. 139–147). London: Routledge.

Pinar, W. (2004). *What is curriculum theory?* Mahwah, NJ: Lawrence Erlbaum.

Pinar, W., & Grumet, M. (1976). *Toward a poor curriculum.* Dubuque: Kendall/Hunt.

Pinar, W., Reynolds, W., Slattery, P., & Taubman, P. (1995). *Understanding curriculum: An introduction to the study of historical and contemporary curriculum discourses.* New York, NY: Peter Lang.

Puar, J. (2012). 'I would rather be a cyborg than a goddess': Becoming intersectional in assemblage theory. *PhiloSOPHIA, 2*(1), 49–66.

Rai, A. S. (2015). *The politics of affect: Berlant on affect and austerity.* Retrieved from:https://mediaecologiesresonate.wordpress.com/2010/12/27/politics-of-affect/.

174   A. D. NICCOLINI ET AL.

Rajchman, J. (2000). *The Deleuze connections.* Cambridge, MA: MIT Press.

Ringness, T. (1975). *The affective domain in education.* Boston, MA: Little, Brown.

Ringrose, J. (2013). *Postfeminist education? Girls and the sexual politics of schooling.* London: Routledge.

Saldahna, A. (2005). Vision and viscosity in Goa's psychedelic trance scene. *ACME: An International e-Journal for Critical Geographies, 4*(2), 172–193.

Sedgwick, E. (2003). *Touching feeling: Affect, pedagogy, performativity.* Durham, NC: Duke University Press.

Sedgwick, E. K., & Frank, A. (Eds.). (1995). *Shame and its sisters: A Silvan Tomkins reader.* Durham, NC: Duke University Press.

Seigworth, G., & Gregg, M. (2010). An inventory of shimmers. In M. Gregg & G. Seigworth (Eds.), *The affect theory reader* (pp. 1–25). Durham, NC: Duke University Press.

Shanahan, T. (2011). *Common Core vs. guided reading: Rejecting instructional level theory.* Retrieved March 13, 2018, from http://www.cdl.org/articles/common-core-vs-guided-reading/.

Shaviro, S. (2010). *Post-cinematic affect.* New York, NY: Zero Books.

Smits, H., & Naqvi, R. (2015). *Framing peace: Thinking about & enacting curriculum as 'radical hope'.* New York, NY: Peter Lang.

Springgay, S. (2008). *Body knowledge and curriculum: Pedagogies of touch in youth and visual culture.* New York, NY: Peter Lang.

Springgay, S., & Freedman, D. (2007). *Curriculum and the cultural body.* New York, NY: Peter Lang.

Springgay, S., & Truman, S. E. (2016). Stone walks: Inhuman animacies and queer archives of feeling. *Discourse: Studies in the Cultural Politics of Education, 38*(6), 851–863.

Springgay, S., Irwin, R., Leggo, C., & Gouzouasis, P. (Eds.). (2008). *Being with a/r/tography.* Rotterdam: Sense.

Springgay, S., & Zaliwska, Z. (2016). Learning to be affected: Matters of pedagogy in the artists' soup kitchen. *Educational Philosophy and Theory, 49*(3), 273–283.

Staiger, J., Cvetkovich, A., & Reynolds, A. (Eds.). (2010). *Political emotions.* New York: Routledge.

Stewart, K. (2007). *Ordinary affects.* Durham, NC: Duke University Press.

St. Pierre, E. (2013). The posts continue: Becoming. *International Journal of Qualitative Studies in Education, 26*(6), 646–657.

Taubman, P. (2009). *Teaching by numbers: Deconstructing the discourse of standards and accountability in education.* New York, NY: Routledge.

Thrift, N. (2004). Intensities of feeling: Towards a spatial politics of affect. *Geografiska Annaler: Series B, Human Geography, 86*(1), 57–78.

Thrift, N. (2007). *Nonrepresentational theory: Space/politics/affect.* London and New York, NY: Routledge.

Vannini, P. (2015). *Nonrepresentational methodologies: Reenvisioning research.* New York, NY: Routledge.

Weber, K. (Ed.). (2010). *Waiting for "Superman": How can we save America's failing public schools?* New York, NY: PublicAffairs Perseus.

Weinstein, G., & Fantini, M. (1970). *Toward humanistic education: A curriculum of affect.* New York, NY: Praeger.

Whitlock, G. (2006). *Soft weapons: Autobiography in transit.* Chicago, IL: University of Chicago Press.

Wiegman, R. (2012). *Object lessons.* Durham, NC: Duke University Press.

Williams, R. (1977). *Marxism and literature.* Oxford: Oxford University Press.

Zembylas, M. (2007). Risks and pleasures: A Deleuzo-Guattarian pedagogy of desire in education. *British Educational Research Journal, 33*(3), 331–347.

CHAPTER 11

The Power of Curriculum as Autobiographical Text: Insights from Utilizing Narrative Inquiry Self-Study in Research, Teaching, and Living

Carmen Shields

INTRODUCTION

In this chapter, I consider aspects of curriculum as autobiographical text that support my view that at the heart of our work as curriculum scholars lies the important and sometimes difficult work of addressing our own autobiographical experience. In my teaching and research practices, narrative inquiry self-study provides a research and teaching venue that supports the unpacking of seminal experiences that inform and guide our definitions of curriculum.

In the various sections of this chapter, I describe how I use the frameworks provided by Pinar (1994, 1995, 2012) and Connelly and Clandinin (1988, 1990, 1995, 2000) that focus curriculum on autobiographical texts. Underlying these frameworks are definitions of curriculum that

C. Shields (✉)
Nipissing University, North Bay, ON, Canada
e-mail: carmens@nipissingu.ca

© The Author(s) 2019
C. Hébert et al. (eds.), *Internationalizing Curriculum Studies*,
https://doi.org/10.1007/978-3-030-01352-3_11

177

move far beyond the "course of study" thinking that is focused on subject matter alone. Connelly and Clandinin (1988) write:

> Curriculum can become one's life course of action. It can mean the paths we have followed and the paths we intend to follow. In this broad sense, curriculum can be viewed as a person's life experience. (p. 1)

Pinar's (1994) method of *currere* supports the exploration of personal experience, which,

> discloses experience so that we may see more of it and see more clearly. With such seeing can come deepened understanding of the running [of the course] and with this can come deepened agency. (Pinar and Grumet 1976, p. vii, quoted in Pinar et al. 1995)

Underlying my curricular thinking throughout this chapter is the position that our past experiences direct and guide our interpretation of curriculum in the present and thus, as scholars, it is imperative that we come to know the roots of our own perceptions about what is important to promote in our curriculum theorizing and teaching. The goal of making present-day meaning of past experiences is to continue to deepen and extend our understanding of what we thought we knew, and to welcome new interpretations that enlarge the vision of curriculum that we can share with others.

Autobiographical Text as a Basis for Understanding Curriculum

Adopting the definitions of curriculum noted above during my years of doctoral study transformed my way of thinking about my students, my research and myself. Prior to those years, I taught in the field of special education, yet never made the important connection to my own life experience of growing up with a handicapped sibling. My focus was on amassing the "expert texts," which I then shared with my students in education building theory and practice that was distant from myself. In coming to understand the significance of my own life experience on my teaching and learning, my move to thinking narratively as a primary source of knowledge has supported and sustained my adopting of curriculum as autobiographical text over the last twenty years.

In curricular terms, the methods outlined by Connelly and Clandinin (1994, 2000) and Pinar (1994, 1995, 2012) have provided the necessary frameworks for thinking and writing narratives of experience that I draw on as I inquire into the events and situations that inform my theorizing and practice as a teacher and researcher. Clandinin and Connelly (2000) write that there are,

> four directions in any inquiry: inward and outward, backward and forward. By inward, we mean toward the internal conditions, such as feelings, hopes, aesthetic reactions, and moral dispositions. By outward, we mean toward the existential conditions, that is, the environment. By backward and forward, we refer to temporality – past, present, and future. [In 1994], we wrote that to experience an experience is to experience it simultaneously in these four ways and to ask questions pointing each way. (p. 50)

In recounting a story, it is clear that we move in these directions quite naturally as we share events and situations with others.

Pinar's (1994, 1995, 2011, 2012) framework for inquiring into personal experience is comprised of four stages: regression, progression, analysis, and synthesis. Pinar (1994) writes that, "the method is the self-conscious conceptualization of the temporal ... the viewing of what is conceptualized through time" (p. 19). As in the four-step process of narrative inquiry described by Clandinin and Connelly (2000), one crosses backward and forward through time in the first two stages, and one inquires into and analyses past experiences, synthesizing them in order to bring them forward to re-conceptualize them in the present in the last two stages. Pinar (1994) notes that this method "attends explicitly to the experience of knowledge creation, from the point of view of the subjectively-existing individual" (p. 61).

In both of these autobiographical frameworks, which are meant to be fluid in nature, re-interpretation of stories again at a later date is always a possibility. Individuals engage in their own process of re-writing life scripts and are empowered to think in new ways about past experience in the present. It then becomes possible to move forward with new vision with its inherent possibilities for action. In this way, curriculum is never static, but like life itself, is situated in the experiences we live across time and situations.

Autobiographical Text as a Place for Inquiry

Clandinin and Connelly (1995) have noted that, "stories are not icons to be learned but inquiries on which further inquiry takes place through their telling and through response to them. In this way, thinking again, relationship, and storytelling are interrelated" (p. 156). Adding to this perspective Ben Okri (1998, cited in King 2003) writes, "If we change the stories we live by, quite possibly we change our lives" (p. 153).

As a narrative inquirer focused on autobiographical research, my work is centered on asking students to "think again"; to revisit and reconstruct stories from past experiences in present-day terms in order to inquire into the meanings held there—meanings that can help enlarge or change present-day thinking. Very often, I find that as individuals delve into past events and situations, they encounter iconic tales, often family stories or stories framed by those with cultural power like teachers that are so engrained into consciousness that they have not even been thought of as possibilities for inquiry.

I am not surprised at this perspective as I experienced this same revelation more than twenty years ago in a doctoral seminar when I shared with fellow graduate students some of the trauma held in my family story of life at home with my handicapped sister. This story was bigger than I was as most mythic family stories are, because family stories represent the collective story that subsumes and often silences each individual member's tale. My sense of increased personal power upon shedding the unconscious weight of that family version of the story was equally mythic, as through that sharing of experience, I took my first big step toward reconstructing my own story of my sister and her impact on my personal and professional development across the years. I use the word "mythic" here following Eliade (1963), to mean "a story ... that is a most precious possession because it is sacred, exemplary, [and] significant" (p. 1). In my family story, my sister's life was a sacred story, too significant to share with outside others. We had the account of her birth, and we lived with her numerous difficulties. In her difference, she was a precious possession to my parents. This story though was not my story.

In the stories of many of the individuals that I have worked with over the years, the sacredness of some stories waiting to be told is similarly of epic proportions and, too often, can hold the power to keep at bay a connection to a personally and professionally meaningful path to the future. It is at such a juncture that narrative inquiry self-study methods can offer an opening for inquiry into past situations and events that both support and challenge the stories that have been left unexamined in our lives. In my experience, the result is a gradual awakening to the fact that the more we share our stories with listening others, the less fearful our stories become and the less power they hold over us in our present-day thinking. We learn that our voice holds the power to not only find new meaning in our own story, but also some of the views that others who listen to our story hold as well.

AUTOBIOGRAPHICAL TEXT AS A PLACE FOR RECOVERING AND RECONSTRUCTING MEANING

Connelly and Clandinin (1988) write:

> When we tell [write] a story as descriptively as we can, we are recovering an important event [or situation] in our experience. It is when we ask ourselves the meaning of a story [in the present] and tell [write] it in a narrative, that we reconstruct the meaning recovered in the story. (p. 81)

In my teaching and graduate supervision practice, I apply this concept of inquiring into the meaning held in stories of experience to self-study or autobiographical exploration using the two-step process of recovering meaning from the past and reconstructing that meaning in present day. To do so, I use multiple genres in writing and arts-based narratives that highlight new self-understanding that is uncovered in the act of re-interpreting the past.

First, the recovery of meaning step provides a vehicle for transporting us to stories remembered. It seems obvious to say that we must remember an event or situation before we can engage in any reconstruction, but memory is a crucial ingredient in this process. Timelines that place specific events and situations in an orderly fashion can be used as a first step for the purposes of recovering meaning. Dates and the events or situations that accompany them can be noted in point form along the timeline that can then be added to as other experiences are remembered. Depending on the focus being studied, seminal experiences can be made visible across time and can then be written in story form. I find that in the remembering process, "way leads unto way" and events and situations we have forgotten or tucked away in the back of our minds unfold

182 C. SHIELDS

before us in secondary and tertiary fashion attached in some way to our initial memory.

Second, the reconstruction of meaning process provides new perspectives on present and future living. It is not enough to remember the stories alone because then they remain as they were in the past. It is in the reconstruction process that we bring stories from the past forward in time, inquiring into the meaning we find there in the present—meaning we can then use to reinterpret past events and situations, using all the experience we have lived in the intervening years. And in that move across time and situation lies the power of curriculum as autobiographical text.

One example from my own writing during my doctoral studies that illustrates this two-step process was writing a story under the heading *Lessons from a Teacher*. I chose to write about a high school teacher who was belittling to students, who had little interest in the subject matter, and had favorites among my classmates. Her true stripes were revealed one day when, trying to get a better mark, I had copied an assignment from one of the favorite students word for word, and she received a perfect mark and I failed. Bringing this to her attention in class by asking how this could be, I was thoroughly chastised and told I was stupid, but the overall result was shock and distrust by the class. As I reconstructed this story so many years later, I thought about myself as the teacher I was and how important being caring and just was to me in relationships with my adult students. I realized the influence that teacher's behavior had had on my impressionable teenage self all those years ago. I could see and name the teacher and person I never wanted to be in her actions.

Personal Methods for Supporting New Insights Through Storying Experience

There are many methods for awakening the self to new meaning inherent in stories of past experience. For many years, qualitative researchers have utilized methods such as keeping a personal journal to gather data, and using letters, photos, stories, poems, and interviews. Increasingly, new research is adding fiction, art installation, music, blogs, and a number of arts-based and arts-informed methods to share data in qualitative research (Knowles and Cole 2008). All of these methods are available for autobiographical researchers. Over the years, I have used many of these

11 THE POWER OF CURRICULUM AS AUTOBIOGRAPHICAL TEXT ... 183

techniques in my graduate classes, modified them and made up new ones to help myself and my students connect personal and professional experience. In doing so, I keep in mind Dewey's (1938) notion that we learn from "the particular"—singular events and situations, rather than from an array of experiences that cross time. I premise the methods I use on this theorizing and have found them invaluable for the reconstruction of the experience process that helps build new pedagogical understanding.

As a doctoral student, I was introduced to specific narrative writing activities such as the *Lesson from a Teacher* used in the previous section as an example of the recovery of meaning and reconstruction of meaning process. I have used them as methods consistently for many years now with students to help them construct and reconstruct their own stories of experience. I ask students to focus on one particular event, situation, and experience at a time and to write them using enough thick description (Glesne 2011) so that readers or listeners can place themselves inside the stories. They can be written in story or poetic form, illustrated, or in another form of their choice. We share these stories in class and I find they are often powerful and educative for individuals in tangible ways that they can name, and that open a door to new understanding and direction forward in their studies, work, and lives. I have captured these autobiographical methods using some of the following titles: *A Childhood Story, Revelations Held in a Memory Box, A Lesson from a Teacher* (who can be anyone who has taught a life lesson), *A Personal Metaphor, Letter to a Mentor, Principles and Rules to Live By* and a *Letter Unsent.*

I also introduce techniques from other authors and sometimes use them for assignment purposes. For example, Jack Maguire (1998) has added *Family Storytelling, Lifelines and Storylines, Meeting Your Inner Storyteller, The Voice of Your Being,* to my repertoire. Sabrina Ward Harrison (2004, 2005) models ways of representing experience utilizing arts-based techniques such as collage, mixed media, and illustration, and Carey et al. (2002) display an approach to keeping an artful journal using words, poems, and drawings. I use all of these techniques as methods in my graduate classes as a means of uncovering past experience. Clara Pickola Estes (1992) has provided two techniques that I have adapted for assignment purposes: one is called an *Ofrenda,* which I use as a way of constructing a tribute to the self in the past in words, objects, and artifacts. The other is called *Descansos,* which is a way of formally acknowledging and honoring past experiences that have been

184 C. SHIELDS

left unexamined where parts of us have been left behind and not yet mourned or reconstructed.

One assignment that students find powerful is one I tried by chance following a classroom discussion about finding ways to represent experience other than through language. I call it *Representing the Self Without Words*. Many art pieces, dioramas, and actual puzzles have been shared in classes where metaphors abound, helping to provide new insights and pathways for present and future direction in curricular learning.

All these methods focus on shifting the scripts of our lives, building awareness in the meta-cognitive realm so that skills such as self-reflection, self-questioning, self-awareness, self-consciousness are brought to the fore as we search through specific events and situations that mark places of importance in our pasts where our self-perception was impacted. All of these methods are open to various ways of representing experience— textual accounts, drawings, poetry, illustrations—and utilizing artifacts.

AUTOBIOGRAPHICAL TEXT AS A PRIMARY TEACHING TOOL

In my role as instructor or supervisor, I set the milieu in which my students and I dwell as inquirers. I help students frame techniques for their inquiry and provide some examples, which I usually do by sharing my own work. I alert them to the three-dimensional inquiry space we enter as we engage with others in a re-storying process where the new meaning we construct emerges from attending to the voices of others as well as our own. Clandinin and Connelly (2000) name the three dimensions:

> personal and social (interaction); past, present, future (continuity); combined with the notion of place (situation). This set of terms creates a metaphorical three-dimensional inquiry space, with temporality along one dimension, the personal and social along a second dimension, and place along a third. Using this set of terms, any particular inquiry is defined by this three dimensional space. (p. 50)

I also illustrate the fluid movement that the backward, forward, inward, outward motion of storytelling provides so that we naturally move in all of these directions when we share a story. Students quickly see this theorizing come to life in their work.

Along with everyone else, I listen attentively as narratives are shared, let silence settle over the group for thoughtful response and then, before the following class or meeting, provide written feedback, offering any questions, thoughts or insights I might have into situations or events being explored, and sharing experiences of my own to try to help extend or broaden re-interpretation of meaning on the part of students.

Each of the methods noted in the section above offers a broad canvas such that everyone can choose personal and/or professional experiences they are ready to share with others. I find that as individuals become comfortable sharing their stories, narratives chosen evolve to a deeper level and connections between personal and professional development become evident, much in the way that my own did when I shared my story of life with my sister in class so long ago.

In a professional life, the writing of stories remembered provides an opportunity to turn our gaze inward to re-connect with knowledge we have learned through experience. Such knowledge is often forgotten in our haste to engage in professional degrees and formal development and activities that focus us outward. The addition of speaking our stories opens us to the emotional dimension of experience, both our own and others': We feel and express the impact that life has had on our choices and our direction, and listening to others translate our story to aspects of their own experience can join us in our particular journey.

Autobiographical Text Connects Self with Self and Self with Others

All these actions are premised on individuals sharing stories that as Bullough and Pinnegar (2001) note, "ring true and enable connection" (p. 16). That connection is focused on enabling individuals to understand that the roots of their professional lives are emotionally and experientially interwoven with their personal experience, and their actions and choices as professionals are often premised on their whole-life experience, not just their professional ones. Bullough and Pinnegar note:

> As self-narrative, autobiography has a great deal in common with fiction. But as Graham argues, for autobiography to be powerful it must contain and articulate "nodal moment(s)." For self-study researchers these moments are central to teaching and learning to teach. Autobiography, like fiction, reveals to the reader a "pattern in experience" and allows a reinterpretation of the lives and experience of both the writer [speaker]

186   C. SHIELDS

and the reader [listener]. To be powerful, this pattern must be portrayed in a way that engages readers [listeners] in a genuine act of seeing the essential wholeness of life, the connections of nodal moments. In seeing, the reader [listener] is enabled to see self and other more fully. (p. 66)

It is very hard to make meaning of the rich world of ideas and beliefs espoused by others if they remain disconnected from our own lived experience. As John Dewey (1938) noted, it is our own experience that forms the actual basis of our understanding about the world. Self-study, woven into the fabric of thoughts and ideas put forward by others, allows us in Bruner's (1996) terms, agency and reflection that help us make what we learn our own. I look back on my years working in special education, while I was busy amassing degrees, working with students, parents, and school communities, becoming the "expert" I thought I wanted to be and I know my actions were grounded in an acquired knowledge base without connection to my own experience. While I knew in my heart and bones what some of those families were experiencing in their home lives because they so closely replicated my own, growing up with a handicapped sibling, my conscious self relied entirely on knowledge from courses and experts to offer support and solutions to problems with living and learning. Looking back now, I hope my deeds were good ones but I know my professional self did not include my personal, heartfelt self as it does now. My theorizing and practice did not include my own experiential knowledge and so did not align with who I was. Missing my own subjectivity in curricular decision-making, I was unaware that my sense of personal power was diminished.

AUTOBIOGRAPHICAL TEXT AS A PLACE FOR BUILDING PERSONAL POWER

Engaging in narrative methodology and methods, I have understood that autobiographical inquiry provides a curricular space for understanding that through rethinking, retelling, and rewriting our life stories, we gain personal power. We become open to the understanding that our story, like each person's story, is of value and can add a new dimension to our thinking about curriculum. Over the years, I have seen many instances where through the sharing of personal stories, individual students have understood that their stories are educative and can be used

11 THE POWER OF CURRICULUM AS AUTOBIOGRAPHICAL TEXT ... 187

to awaken new thought; that their stories have the capacity to heighten awareness and add to the "complicated conversation" (Pinar 2012) that curriculum can be when it is based in inquiry.

Castaneda (1974) writes in *Tales of Power*:

> Everything we do, everything we are, rests on our own personal power ... if you have enough power, my words alone would serve as a means for you to round up the totality of yourself and to get the crucial part of it out of the boundaries in which it is contained. (p. 17)

I consistently see that for those engaging in self-study research, issues, and aspects of personal power emerge and are addressed as part of story writing and sharing, even if at first they have not been visible or thought to be central to personal or professional development. I often think of a few lines from Sarton's (1993) poem *Now I Become Myself* as I see individuals begin to embrace their own history and sense the power in their own voice which they can use to build their own expert text to add to their previous versions of curriculum development.

When I was a doctoral student just beginning to understand the power held in autobiographical inquiry, I read a chapter by Pinar (1994) entitled *Working From Within* that changed the way I had understood curriculum previously and opened the way for me to approach my students with the intent of hearing their voices and my own as a foundation for curricular learning. Pinar wrote:

> I have knowledge of my discipline, some knowledge of my students, and some self-knowledge ... I come ready to respond, not only as a student and teacher ... but as a person. In fact I must be willing to disclose my thoughts and feelings if I am to hope for similar disclosures from students. (p. 9)

Returning to the quote by Castaneda above, these words helped me to "round up the totality of myself" and break through the boundaries that I had contained me as a teacher and person. Engaging in curriculum through a mutuality of sharing stories of experience provided me with a place to understand the power held in my own and others' experiences.

FINAL THOUGHTS

The process of revising our life scripts to ascertain what Bruner (1996) calls "the past, the present and the possible" clearly situates curriculum in Connelly and Clandinin's (1988, 1994, 2000) definition of curriculum as all of life's experience, and in Pinar's (1994, 1995, 2012) *currere*, where the point of curriculum scholarship is to participate in the ongoing and complicated conversation that springs from engaging in existential experience. If one accepts these definitions, then curriculum as autobiographical text can be embraced as it provides a way to place our whole selves in our research and teaching.

Atkinson (1995) writes: "Story is a tool for self-discovery; stories tell us new things about ourselves that we wouldn't have been as aware of without having told the story" (p. 3). In this vision of curricular thought, self-study narrative inquiry as a personal and professional journey and a research genre makes perfect sense. My work remains teaching and supporting others who want to inquire into the tensions and complications they have lived, interrogate the relationships and contradictions they find there and use that data to illuminate their way forward in their personal and professional lives.

REFERENCES

Atkinson, R. (1995). *The gift of stories: Practical and spiritual applications of autobiography, life stories, and personal mythmaking.* Westport, CO: Bergin & Garvey.

Bruner, J. (1996). *The culture of education.* Cambridge, MA: Harvard University Press.

Bullough, R. V., Jr., & Pinnegar, S. (2001). Guidelines for quality in autobiographical forms of self-study research. *Educational Researcher, 30*(2), 13–21.

Carey, M., Fox, R., & Penney, J. (2002). *The artful journal.* New York: Watson-Guptill.

Castaneda, C. (1974). *Tales of power.* New York: Simon & Schuster.

Clandinin, D. J., & Connelly, F. M. (1994). Personal experience methods. In N. K. Denzin & Y. S. Lincoln (Eds.), *Handbook of qualitative research* (pp. 413–427). Thousand Oaks, CA: Sage.

Clandinin, D. J., & Connelly, F. M. (1995). *Teachers' professional knowledge landscapes.* New York: Teachers College Press.

Clandinin, D. J., & Connelly, F. M. (2000). *Narrative inquiry: Experience and story in qualitative research.* San Francisco: Jossey-Bass.

11 THE POWER OF CURRICULUM AS AUTOBIOGRAPHICAL TEXT ... 189

Connelly, F. M., & Clandinin, D. J. (1988). *Teachers as curriculum planners: Narratives of experience.* New York: Teachers College Press.

Connelly, F. M., & Clandinin, D. J. (1990). Stories of experience and narrative inquiry. *Educational Researcher, 19*(5), 2–14.

Dewey, J. (1938). *Experience & education.* New York: Collier.

Eliade, M. (1963). *The sacred & the profane.* New York: Harcourt Brace Jovanovich.

Estes, C. P. (1992). *Women who run with the wolves.* New York: Ballantine Books.

Glesne, C. (2011). *Becoming qualitative researchers* (3rd ed.). New York: Pearson.

Harrison, S. W. (2004). *Messy thrilling life: The art of figuring out how to live.* New York: Villard Books.

Harrison, S. W. (2005). *Spilling open: The art of becoming yourself.* New York: Villard Books.

King, T. (2003). *The truth about stories.* Scarborough, ON: HarperCollins.

Knowles, J. G., & Cole, A. L. (2008). *Handbook of the arts in qualitative research.* Thousand Oaks: Sage.

Maguire, J. (1998). *The power of personal storytelling.* New York: Penguin.

Okri, B. (1998). *A way of being free.* London, UK: Orion Publishing Group Ltd.

Pinar, W. F. (1994). *Autobiography, politics and sexuality: Essays in curriculum theory 1972–1992.* New York: Peter Lang.

Pinar, W. F. (2011). *The character of curriculum studies: Bildung, currere, and the recurring question of the subject.* New York: Palgrave Macmillan.

Pinar, W. F. (2012). *What is curriculum theory?* (2nd ed.). New York: Routledge.

Pinar, W. F., & Grumet, M. (1976). *Toward a poor curriculum.* Dubuque, IA: Kendall/Hunt.

Pinar, W. F., Reynolds, W. M., Slattery, P., & Taubman, P. M. (1995). *Understanding curriculum.* New York: Peter Lang.

Sarton, M. (1993). Now I become myself. From *Collected Poems 1930–1993.* New York: W. W. Norton.

PART III

Grounding Curricular Critique

CHAPTER 12

Nonviolence as a Daily Practice in Education: A Curriculum Vision

Hongyu Wang

What is the task of the curriculum theorist in the local, national, and international world? For me, an international person who traveled from China to the USA and who currently lives in Oklahoma, at this historical moment and in this particular location, the task is to practice nonviolence in daily educational life.[1] While my autobiographical account is narrated in my previous books (2004, 2014a) and cannot be detailed in this essay, it is important to mention that my cross-cultural journey of learning from different places has given birth to the vision of nonviolence as an educational project in daily practice in the context of internationalizing curriculum studies, a vision obscured by the noises of modernization worldwide, the standardization in American educational reform, and the dominance of technical reason.

---

[1] This paper is a revision of a keynote presentation at the 5th triennial meeting of the International Association for the Advancement of Curriculum Studies (IAACS) at the University of Ottawa, Canada, in May 2015. My thanks go to conference organizers especially Dr. Nicholas Ng-A-Fook for inviting me to speak to an international audience. I also thank the Association of Canadian Deans of Education for sponsoring my visit.

H. Wang (✉)
Jenks, OK, USA
e-mail: hongyu.wang@okstate.edu

© The Author(s) 2019
C. Hébert et al. (eds.), *Internationalizing Curriculum Studies*,
https://doi.org/10.1007/978-3-030-01352-3_12

193

194   H. WANG

Furthermore, my intellectual history in bridging different interpretative traditions from both East and West—not as a binary but as a marker of difference—has taken me onto less- traveled pathways. Engaging with psychoanalysis, Eastern philosophy, international wisdom traditions, feminist theory, post-structuralism, peace education, and their contested intersections for the past two decades has enabled me to study and teach about, for, and through nonviolence. Practice lies at the heart of bringing the purpose, content, and means of education together toward nonviolence. In this paper, I first discuss the concept of nonviolence and then explore three important aspects of engaging nonviolence in education as a vision for internationalizing curriculum studies: nonviolent engagement with the self, nonviolent relationships with difference, and practicing nonviolence as an essential task of the curriculum theorist. In so doing, I also explore different international intellectual traditions and their contributions to this vision.

WHAT IS NONVIOLENCE?

Nonviolence in modern human history is, by and large, a political concept developed through political movements led by Mohandas K. Gandhi and Martin Luther King Jr. However, in the popular imagination, many people tend to link nonviolence with passivity or "playing nice" even though action is an essential part of nonviolent resistance. For me, most importantly, nonviolence is an educational project, centering on cultivating the integration of the body and the mind within the individual person and promoting compassionate relationships between the self and the other. In achieving the integration of the self and cultivating humane relationality, practicing nonviolence also involves converting negative psychic energies internally and fighting against social injustice externally. It is a practice that every teacher and student can engage in and has already engaged to a certain extent without speaking its name, yet somehow nonviolence is almost a muted voice in education. It is not difficult to discern that the nature of compulsory schooling in many nations, with its structural, social, and cultural impositions, is not conducive to spreading the message of nonviolence, but I think it is time for us to claim the site of nonviolence in education.

Michael Nagler (2004) traces the word *nonviolence* to the Sanskrit word *Ahimsa,* which basically means doing no harm and being kind to all living beings because life is an interconnected whole. Nagler points out that after it is translated into English as "non-violence," rather than "nonviolence," it conveys a negative sense of responding to violence, but loses the positive quality of nonviolence as an integrative way of life. Nonviolence as *Ahimsa* is cultivated daily, integrating body/mind and self/other. Nagler (2004) further explains, "unlike the English translation, in Sanskrit abstract nouns often name a fundamental positive quality indirectly, by negating its opposite" (p. 44). Similarly, the English translation of the Chinese Daoist definition of *wuwei* as non-action also obscures the positive quality of *wuwei* in its capacity to enable appropriate action without imposition. *Wuwei* is both receptive and creative. The African notion of *ubuntu* passed down through orality and tradition is also difficult to translate into English without losing its original meanings. As Tutu (1999) points out, *ubuntu* refers to a different worldview in which one becomes a person through other persons and the self-other relationship is mutually enhancing (see Lesley Le Grange's chapter in this volume). Without reifying these international wisdom traditions—and the indigenous tradition of restorative justice—I argue that the interconnected world view they share provides a solid foundation for nonviolence education.

I have discussed the concept of nonviolence in the context of education in my previous work (Wang 2013, 2014a, b). Organic relationality that transcends dualism, non-instrumental engagement that engages students' growth without trying to control the outcome, playfulness that decenters fixity and allows emergence in teaching and learning, the necessity of the inner work simultaneous with the outer work, a radical denouncement of violence in all forms, and the feminist advocacy of peace are all important aspects of nonviolence. I believe that the fundamental task of education is personal cultivation and self-transformation that enables social transformation, unlike a political task that aims at mobilizing mass action (Wang 2014b). Education is necessarily a long-term project, not seeking immediate effects as the current standardization movement demands. Nonviolence is a positive energy that permeates the shared fabric of life, in which passion rather than passivity and sustainability rather than submission mark its existence. With non-duality (within the self and between the self and the other) as the central thread, the educational practice of nonviolence is a process of seeking individuation in the Jungian sense while simultaneously learning from the differences of the other.

There is an inherent mechanism in nonviolence against all forms of violence, not only physical, but also intellectual, emotional, and spiritual. In today's world in which intellectual imposition is common at schools, democracy is used as a vehicle to impose the will of the powerful on others, and peace is manipulated as a weapon for warfare rather than the welfare of humanity, it is imperative to speak about nonviolence that does not condone any form of violence. In this sense, nonviolence education is intimately related to social justice education, including eco-justice education. Nonviolence has two intertwined aspects indicating "no" to any system or action of violence with one hand and with the other hand stretching out to build productive, integrative, and sustainable relationships. These two gestures cannot be separated.

In formulating nonviolence education, I have studied peace education literature. While being enlightened by educators' work in dealing with intense conflicts and finding peaceful solutions, my work does not fit into this camp very well. First, many curriculum and pedagogical innovations in peace education deal with international conflicts or inter-racial/ethnic tensions, but I perceive nonviolence as a daily practice that is fundamental to individual growth. What is missing in the focus on the inter-group work is the daily educational work on integrating body and mind to cultivate generative and generous aspects of nonviolence that can prevent violence from happening in the first place. Second, the role of difference is usually downplayed in peace education. Difference, as the phrase "conflict resolution" suggests, needs to be smoothed out or negotiated toward the middle ground. Influenced by psychoanalysis and post-structuralism, I believe difference must not be erased but be put into use to generate new possibilities.

However, nonviolence based on the notion of nonduality and interdependence is also in conflict with both psychoanalysis and post-structuralism. In my own intellectual trajectory, the move to nonviolence has been enabled through both psychoanalytic insights, particularly those of Julia Kristeva and Carl Jung, and the post-structural affirmation of the alterity of the other, particularly of Michel Foucault, Emmanuel Levinas, and Jacques Derrida. Jane Addams' notion of positive peace as dynamic and nurturing (Addams 1906/2007) and the post-structuralist feminist notion of "working difference" (Miller 2005) at the site of creativity have also been influential. At the same time, with the further studies of Chinese intellectual and cultural history, my vision of nonviolence is a recursive return to Taoist and Buddhist insights. These strands of thought are not all necessarily in harmony, and I discuss specific contestations among them later.

Living with this contested site of multiple intellectual traditions, I tease out several threads important for engaging nonviolence as a daily educational practice. First, engaging nonviolence within the self goes hand in hand with engaging nonviolence with others. Here is where nonviolence and psychoanalytic tasks both support and contest each other. From them, I affirm the necessity of not only transforming negative energies but also connecting to the inherent interconnectedness in nonviolence education. Second, nonviolent engagement with difference welcomes and hosts the unknown as potentiality, not as a threat to the ego. Here is where the poststructuralist effort not to colonize the Other and the Buddhist nonduality both inform and question each other. From both, I affirm the positive role of difference without radicalizing it. The implications of nonviolence for the internationalization of curriculum studies are also briefly discussed. Third, nonviolence is a daily practice of each individual person and a vision to be embodied and lived every day. It is not a utopian ideal to pursue but rather grows through committed practice. Drawing inspiration from different strands of thought—in both resonance and dissonance—I illuminate nonviolence as a curriculum vision through its daily practice.

WORKING FROM WITHIN

"Working from within" was a call from William F. Pinar (1972/1994) during the 1970s in the American field of curriculum studies (p. 7). This call was informed by psychoanalysis, phenomenology, aesthetics, and Buddhism. It is a call we in education still need to attend to, especially now when public education is in crisis. External turbulence may trigger the projection of our internal negativity onto others, so the inner work becomes more important in a difficult time for integrating diverse elements within the self. In owning the problematic aspects of ourselves and not repressing them into the shadow or projecting them onto the other, we can sustain our capacity to relate to others and transformatively participate in social action (Shim 2012, 2014; Taylor 2009). Jeremy Taylor (2009) names such a psychic working through as "nonviolence." His use of Jungian dream analysis in his first group work in the 1970s was proved helpful to social activists in understanding their subconscious racial biases, and in turn, in forming better relationships with local communities. The inner work toward nonviolence can also be triggered by external events. As Naomi Poindexter (2015) relates, a student's

198   H. WANG

engagement with Holocaust Education caused her to look inside and find constructive ways of working through difficulty rather than resorting to self-harming practices.

Nonviolence work contributes to the process of working through by using aesthetic, imaginative, literary, mindful, and meditative modes of practice that can transform difficult emotions such as anger and fear, contain and sublimate psychic aggression into productive activities, and put us in touch with the interconnected energy of life. Ashwani Kumar (2013) theorizes curriculum as meditative inquiry that supports "playful, imaginative, meditative (of thoughts, emotions, and body) and artful" (p. 110) learning. Lindsey Bolliger (Bolliger and Wang 2013) discusses how she uses yoga in the classroom with young children to enact a pedagogy of nonviolence. Yoga has helped her students center themselves, engage in meaningful learning, and create a classroom culture of peace. Stillness and quietude is inside of us, a source of vitality and peace, and despite children's endless action, they also have access to this inner source. There are reports of introducing mindfulness into school and college classrooms with success in the USA and Canada, and I have practiced it in my teaching. Most of my students have responded positively to the calming and integrative effects of mindful activities. Some also introduce them into their own teaching at school while there are some other students who are skeptical. Without romanticizing the effect of mindfulness practices, I think it is important to incorporate nonviolence in various forms into daily educational practices.

However, there is contestation between psychoanalytic theory and nonviolence studies: Psychoanalysis assumes the repressive mechanism of civilization and the existence of psychic violence in becoming oneself while nonviolence acknowledges the existential interconnectedness of life. For example, Sharon Todd (2001) argues that learning is ontologically violent, as it is implicated in the pedagogical demand that students change themselves, a demand serving civilization.[2] She further suggests

---

[2] Organic relationality lies at the heart of nonviolence but it necessarily contains the difficulty of growth and life in general. Refusing to grow up and staying in one's comfort zone is, arguably, doing violence to oneself. In this sense, the loss, pain, and anxiety of growing up cannot be avoided, but can be sustained by compassionate relationships. Moreover, Freudian psychoanalysis is embedded in modern Western discourses that set individuality and sociality at odds with each other. As much as sociality can repress individual desire, individuality relies on sociality to enable its own independence. In this sense, the relationship between the two cannot be only subversive but must be dialectic.

the necessity of ethical nonviolent relationships as pedagogical responses: "[It is] precisely because violence is inherent to 'learning to become' and because teachers and students are continually vulnerable to each other in the face of this violence, that the question of nonviolence can even be raised" (p. 439). In this way, violence is perceived as primary, nonviolence as secondary, and the possibility of compassion as compensational for the vulnerability under violence. However, if learning is ontologically violent and nonviolence is only a counteracting response, upon what basis can nonviolent teaching be developed? Only when the basis of nonviolence connects with its original possibility can it accumulate an equal force to counteract negative energy. Here the difference between the terms *nonviolence* and *non-violence* is not trivial, as the use of nonviolence affirms itself primarily as a positive and compassionate life force rather than a negation of violence.

On the other hand, in nonviolence studies, as Michael Nagler (2004) argues, violence is socially and heavily media-constructed and aggression is a learned behavior. He suggests that nonviolence is a primary force driving humanity toward a better future. The different emphases of psychoanalysis on individuality and of nonviolence on relationality are also at work. I try to contain their contestation in my own vision. I believe both aggression and compassion exist in the human psyche and society and that humanity has an inherent capacity for containing destructive impulses and establishing nonviolent relationships. I don't perceive pain or loss in the process of growth as necessarily violent, but psychoanalytic insights can help nonviolence work to acknowledge and work through difficulty. Individuality and sociality are not dualistic opposites but mutually embedded in the human life. Engaging nonviolence from within is closely connected with engaging nonviolence with others in an ongoing process of individual and social transformation.

Nonviolent Relationships with Difference

My formulation of nonviolence is not based on seeking commonality or consensus but on cultivating nonviolent relationships with difference. Difference, whether it is psychic difference or social difference, cannot be erased into perceived commonality because such an erasure itself can become a form of violence. The psychoanalytic notion of the unconscious is that it can never be mastered although it can provide a source for learning from the otherness of the psyche. The Levinasian alterity

(Todd 2003) and the Derridian difference (1992) as the basis for ethical relationships in the postmodern condition emphasize the necessity of not colonizing or assimilating difference into sameness. To preserve the creative and generative potential of difference, post-structural thinkers radicalize the alterity of the other toward the unknown.

Drawing upon Buddhism, Peter Hershock (2013) argues that the interconnectedness of shared life is enabled by the contribution of difference and diversity. A healthy ecosystem, for example, requires diversity, not sameness. He also argues for difference not as an entity but as a process of differentiation in which the relational dynamics of education can lead to a mutually flourishing community. Valuing difference is for the welfare of the whole community without the mark of separateness. Here is where I depart from post-structuralism and soften its radical edge of alterity—while recognizing difference as generative—with the wisdom of Buddhism, Taoism, and other Indigenous traditions that highlight an interdependent viewpoint. When the other is positioned so distantly in the unknown, the threads of connection with the self become too fragile to sustain relationality. The self and the other are already organically connected prior to their first encounter in a specific time and place.

With the increasing diversity in society, the issue of how to live with difference has been under discussion for several decades in Western education. There are many approaches, including pushing away difference to pursue equality, positioning differences as separate entities, essentializing difference into social identities opposed to one another, and radicalizing difference as unknowable otherness, among others. Not necessarily opposed to these approaches that can be useful in certain contexts, a nonviolent approach to engaging difference does not suppress, separate, essentialize, or radicalize difference but considers it an organic part of interconnected life. Depending on the situation, sometimes difference needs to be highlighted in order to contest the authoritarianism of a system, while at other times it needs to be dissolved in order to reach a higher level of integration for a more inclusive communal life. In a nonviolent orientation, we recognize and respect difference's positive role but do not elevate it above the web of life. Furthermore, this organic approach to difference is also connected to the necessity of working from within to integrate different elements in the self. Nonviolent relationships with difference are not only between the self and others but also within the self.

Such an engagement with difference is particularly important for transnational and intercultural relationships in the internationalization of curriculum studies (Pinar 2014). The Accord on the Internationalization of Education by the Association of Canadian Deans of Education (2014) emphasizes the principle of economic and social justice, reciprocity, sustainability, intercultural awareness, and equity in the internationalization of education. All these principles are important for engaging difference, and the practice of nonviolence supports them as long as they are inclusive and restorative of human interconnectedness. Not intending to set nonviolence above other principles, I see it as an underlying thread for shared educational commitment to personal growth, community building, and humanity/nature harmony through engaging differences in organic relationality.

In the nonviolent dynamics of international and transnational relationships, difference and multiplicity are neither excluded nor self-contained, but are transformed through interactive, dynamic interplay. This emphasis on dynamic interaction within a bigger picture necessarily challenges the self-closed nationalism and the economically motivated uniformity in globalization. The nation can become a site of differentiation to contest the totalizing power of globalization as Julia Kristeva's (1993) vision of "nation without nationalism" indicates, but close-minded nationalism does not allow differences within the nation to play a positive role. Although globalization increases connections through the Internet and economic and cultural exchanges, globalization is centered by a sweeping force that pushes away different indigenous and local heritages. Neither a fixation on a separate entity in nationalism nor a pursuit of one path for the whole planet, the internationalization of curriculum studies takes difference as a positive site for transforming the relational dynamics between and among the local, the national, and the global. Nonviolent relationality lies at the heart of such internationalization (Wang 2014b).

As I have become committed to nonviolence education, I remind myself of the necessity of not reifying it into a fixed ideal. In Derrida's deconstruction practices, he questions the essentialistic Western discourses of metaphysics, democracy, and justice, along with other concepts, but he does not propose any definite alternative to replacing these central notions. Rather, he envisions democracy as yet to come (Derrida 1992). Tracing the social, cultural, and political impact and historical evolution of these notions in Western society, Derrida exposes and denaturalizes their dominance. While embracing nonviolence as an educational project, I am not proposing another metanarrative that is exclusive and suppressive but perceive it as compatible with other principles such as democracy, social justice, and ecological sustainability as long as they serve to promote integrative relationships (Wang 2010). Certainly nonviolence can be deconstructed if it becomes a reified concept. Here I approach nonviolence as both a vision and a practice based on the perception of "violence-nonviolence as a continuum" (Weigert 1999, p. 16) rather than a binary, in which violence must be continually worked through to enable nonviolence in daily practice. It is a vision because nonviolence must be evoked in order to illuminate less-traveled pathways that lead us to a more compassionate world. As an almost muted voice in education, it has hardly achieved a dominant status to be deconstructed. It is a practice because it is a daily struggle to transform psychic and social constraints and form nonviolent relationships with both the self and the other. It is a disciplined practice in word, thought, and deed that must be consistently cultivated.

Practicing Nonviolence in Daily Educational Work

Nonviolence is a practice that has existed throughout human history (Harris 2008; Lynd and Lynd 2006). I don't position education about, for, and through nonviolence as something new but see it as already practiced in some educators' daily work. It is not the newness that I claim, but that we must do more by shifting our lens to foreground nonviolence work in education and spread the message of nonviolence as a viable vision.

Molly Quinn (2014) approaches peace as "*an experience*, in which *the senses are engaged* ... and an experience one ... must *actually choose to pursue*, actively, intentionally, consciously" (p. 51; emphasis in the original). I also approach nonviolence as an experience that educators can intentionally craft for themselves and for students. Any effort to integrate body/mind, self/other, inner/outer work through choosing materials or designing activities beneficial for students' whole-being experiences contributes to nonviolence work. Essential educational questions about what we teach and learn, why we teach and learn, how we teach and learn can be guided by the principle of nonviolence.

David Jardine (2012) speaks of the everydayness of "cultivating free spaces in teaching and learning" through "a pedagogy left in peace."

In particular, he argues that there are free spaces for play in the midst of difficulty if we can see through the ontological illusion of separateness to deeply experience "the dependent co-arising of things and the dependent co-arising and shaping of our selves" (p. 17). Underneath the scarcity and constraint intensified by standardization and uniformity in education, there is abundance of relationships. There are many different ways of creating nonviolent and nondualistic relationality in education, ranging from the mindful and meditative inner work to the outer work of social action and service learning to engage both subjective and social transformation.

I have been teaching about nonviolence for quite a few years in American teacher education, and I remain amazed by many students' resistant responses. It appears to be more difficult to teach the importance of nonviolence than of social justice. I realize that the very foundation of nondualistic interdependence in nonviolence is not easy to imagine in a strongly individualistically oriented society. While the notion of social justice can be traced back to the concept of the individual in the West (Wang 2013) and the concept of non-violence with a hyphen can be understood along the lines of individual human rights, nonviolence as a holistic concept is based on the ability to go beyond the confinement of separate identities such as self, group, nation, or even humanity itself. It is a further step that is difficult to take. The dualistic mechanism of control (in response to fear), domination (in response to threat), and mastery (in response to failure) is so entrenched in the American psyche that the logic of violence is often taken for granted and that nonviolence can only be imagined as a secondary reaction to violence.

To change such a perspective takes nothing less than nonviolence as a practice for both the teacher and students. Only can a pedagogy of nonviolence (Bolliger and Wang 2013) in its persistent effort in daily work undo the grip of violence. It takes practice to transform a sense of separateness into an experience of interconnectedness. Cultivated practice clears the ground for developing the clarity and stillness that leads to the revelation of human, ecological, and cosmic interrelatedness. Without experiencing interrelatedness, the human attachment to individual reification and aggression (psychic or social) can be difficult to dissolve. The human ability to transcend fragmented self-centeredness, to contain aggression, and to rise above hatred is closely related to the human capacity to share, to connect, and to relate. Critiques of violence do not automatically lead to a better society if the foundations for a better world are not built. It is the persistent practice of nonviolence that enables us to imagine the world otherwise. As an educational project, nonviolence can be practiced through many different ways in a classroom, and the teacher's engagement with nonviolence education cannot be accomplished once for all, but must be renewed on a daily basis.

The rigorous practice of letting go of attachment to separateness not only takes time but also requires intense engagement with what is at hand in curriculum, teaching, and education (Jardine, in press). The notion of the subject in education is necessarily doubled as both the human subject and subject matter (Pinar 2011). Full immersion in an experience can lead to self-transcendence, and students' learning is a site for practicing nonviolence. Here the teacher's task at school is somewhat different from students' task since students are in the process of self-formation and development of a healthy ego is beneficial, but students can develop a sense of interconnectedness that provides the foundation for their balanced personal growth. The teacher, who is in the authority position, must closely examine her or his own teaching self so that "a breathing space for teaching and learning" (Jardine, in press) can be provided for students to explore their relationships with themselves, others, the subjective matter, and the environment. Practicing pedagogical relationships nonviolently, rather than by imposition, the teacher embodies nonviolence in the classroom.

Nonviolence is not a destination or an ideal to reach, but an ongoing process of daily work to unlearn the mechanism of domination internally and relate compassionately externally to others and to the world. Both the inner work and the outer work of nonviolence are filled with struggles, tensions, and the effort of working through internal and external difficulty. In this sense, nonviolence is not a noun but functions as a verb, mobilizing educational experiences along lines of movement toward a higher aspiration. I have been working with a group of teachers, principals, teacher mentors, and activists in the local area to implement nonviolence into educational work. Each of us has at least one specific educational project to work on and we also engage in nonviolence work with the self. Advocating education about, for, and through nonviolence in the worldliness of curriculum studies (Miller 2005), this paper invites individual and collective efforts to enact the principle of nonviolence in daily practices to open up new possibilities. Individually and together, we can make the world a bit more loving and a bit more sustainable each day. What effort can you make in your own sphere of influence to enact the principle of nonviolence? Can we practice nonviolence as a shared educational project for a world yet to come, in our different places, times, and contexts, extending hands across difference?

REFERENCES

Addams, J. (2007). *Newer ideals of peace.* Urbana: University of Illinois Press (Original published in 1906).

The Association of Canadian Deans of Education. (2014). *The accord on the internationalization of education.* Retrieved from: www.csse.ca/ACDE.

Bolliger, L., & Wang, H. (2013). Pedagogy of nonviolence. *Journal of Curriculum and Pedagogy, 10*(2), 112–114.

Derrida, J. (1992). *The other heading* (Trans. from French by P. Brault & M. B. Naas). Bloomington: Indiana University Press.

Harris, I. (2008). History of peace education. In M. Bajaj (Ed.), *Encyclopedia of peace education* (pp. 15–24). Charlotte, NC: Information Age Publishing.

Hershock, P. (2013). *Valuing diversity.* New York: SUNY Press.

Jardine, D. W. (2012). *Pedagogy left in peace.* London: Continuum.

Jardine, D. W. (in press). *In praise of radiant beings.* Charlotte, NC: Information Age Publishing.

Kristeva, J. (1993). *Nation without nationalism* (L. S. Roudiez, Trans.). New York: Columbia University Press.

Kumar, A. (2013). *Curriculum as meditative inquiry.* New York: Palgrave Macmillan.

Lynd, S., & Lynd, A. (Eds.). (2006). *Nonviolence in America.* Maryknoll, NY: Orbis Books.

Miller, J. (2005). *Sounds of silence breaking.* New York: Peter Lang.

Nagler, M. N. (2004). *The search for a nonviolent future.* Makawao, HI: Inner Ocean Publishing.

Pinar, W. F. (1972). Working from within. In W. F. Pinar (1994), *Autobiography, politics and sexuality* (pp. 7–11). New York: Peter Lang.

Pinar, W. F. (2011). *The character of curriculum studies.* New York: Palgrave Macmillan.

Pinar, W. F. (Ed.). (2014). *The international handbook of curriculum research* (2nd ed.). New York: Routledge.

Poindexter, N. K. (2015). *Holocaust education and nonviolence.* Presentation at the 5th triennial meeting of the International Association for the Advancement of Curriculum Studies, May 26–29, University of Ottawa, Canada.

Quinn, M. (2014). *Peace and pedagogy primer.* New York: Peter Lang.

Shim, J. M. (2012). Exploring how teachers' emotions interact with intercultural texts. *Curriculum Inquiry, 42*(4), 472–496.

Shim, J. M. (2014). Multicultural education as an emotional situation. *Journal of Curriculum Studies, 46*(1), 116–137.

Taylor, J. (2009). *The wisdom of your dreams.* New York: Jeremy P. Tarcher/Penguin.

Todd, S. (2001). Bring more than I contain. *Journal of Curriculum Studies, 33*(4), 431–450.

Todd, S. (2003). *Learning from the other.* New York: SUNY press.

Tutu, D. (1999). *No future without forgiveness.* New York: Doubleday.

Wang, H. (2004). *The call from the stranger on a journey home.* New York: Peter Lang.

Wang, H. (2010). A zero space of nonviolence. *Journal of Curriculum Theorizing, 26*(1), 1–8.

Wang, H. (2013). A nonviolent approach to social justice education. *Educational Studies, 49*(6), 485–503.

Wang, H. (2014a). *Nonviolence and education.* New York: Peter Lang.

Wang, H. (2014b). A nonviolent perspective on internationalizing curriculum studies. In W. F. Pinar (Ed.), *The international handbook of curriculum research* (2nd ed., pp. 69–76). New York: Routledge.

Weigert, K. M. (1999). Moral dimensions of peace studies. In K. M. Weigert & R. J. Crews (Eds.), *Teaching for justice* (pp. 9–21). Washington, DC: American Association for Higher Education.

CHAPTER 13

Currere's Active Force and the Concept of *Ubuntu*

Lesley Le Grange

William Pinar avers that the internationalization of Curriculum Studies is about complicated conversations that occur across national boundaries. In this chapter, I open up a conversation that draws on insights from North American scholars including William Pinar and Jason Wallin and the African concept of *Ubuntu* (humanness) in exploring the becoming of pedagogical lives in a post-humanist era. I do not perform this work within a single interpretive community but draw on insights from post-structuralism, indigeneity and post-colonialism.

I borrow the words of Michel Foucault: "Each time I have attempted to do theoretical [academic] work it has been on the basis of elements of my experience – always in relation to processes that I saw taking place around me" (Foucault in Rajchman 1985, p. 36). And so I begin this chapter by referring to recent instances of xenophobia in South Africa. In 2015, we witnessed a second wave of xenophobic attacks in post-apartheid South Africa. Although incidences of xenophobia date back to the Union of South Africa (1910–1948), it has intensified (or has perhaps taken on a new form) in post-apartheid South Africa. In the period from

L. Le Grange (✉)
Stellenbosch University, Stellenbosch, South Africa
e-mail: llg@sun.ac.za

© The Author(s) 2019
C. Hébert et al. (eds.), *Internationalizing Curriculum Studies*,
https://doi.org/10.1007/978-3-030-01352-3_13

2003 to 2008 at least 67 people are reported to have died in xenophobic attacks, with another 62 people dead from xenophobic riots in 2008. In 2015, we saw a nationwide spike of xenophobia in South Africa, which prompted several foreign governments to repatriate their citizens (see South African History Online 2015).

Since 1994, the number of foreign nationals entering South Africa has increased as a consequence of, among other reasons, people fleeing war-torn countries such as Somalia and the Democratic Republic of Congo, and hardships in countries such as Zimbabwe, with others leaving African countries to seek a "better life." The number of foreigners from other countries such as China, Thailand and Pakistan has also increased, but it is Africans in particular that have been the targets of xenophobic attacks. In such attacks local South Africans claim, that "*kwerekwere* are stealing our jobs."[1] The invocation of *kwerekwere* in xenophobic attacks is significant. Boitumelo Magolego (2008) points out that *kwerekwere* is a word that has been in use long before 1994 (so it is not a post-apartheid word) and that his grandparents say that the word has been in use as long as they can remember. He writes: "From what I gather it has undertones which speak of how black Africans are believed to be sub-human, too dark and have a pungent smell."

Since its first democratic elections in 1994, South Africa has achieved much. The Bill of Rights of the South African constitution guarantees the right of every citizen to receive basic services, access to education, freedom of association, protection from harm and so forth. But challenges remain: the gap between rich and poor has widened, and violent crime of all kinds is prevalent, including close to 50 murders per day; environmental degradation is on the increase; youth unemployment is rising; corruption of politicians and public servants is rife, incidences of xenophobia continue and so on (for details see Republic of South Africa 2014).

South Africa is a microcosm of the world. Globally, growing inequalities are evident among and within nations; environmental problems

---

[1] *Kwerekwere* is the common word used by many South Africans to refer to foreign nationals from African countries. Depending on the language spoken, a different prefix is used for the singular and plural forms. In the Nguni languages, the prefix i—is used for the singular being and ama—for the plural, therefore *ikwerekwere* and *amakwerekwere*, respectively. Nguni languages are a group of Bantu languages spoken in southern Africa. Nguni languages include: Xhosa, Zulu, Hlubi, Phuthi and Ndebele.

have reached unprecedented levels (Le Grange 2016); youth employment is prevalent (Cahuc et al. 2013; Azeng and Yogo 2013); in mainstream USA, for example, the life of an African-American is less valued than that of a white American (Edwards and Harris 2016); in Europe racism towards migrant workers is on the increase (Hazekamp and Popple 2013); global violence and terror have reached unparalleled levels (Kaldor 2012). Many more problems/crises could be mentioned, but the point is sufficiently made.

At least some of the challenges named are manifestations of a single crisis, the crisis of humanism. By this I mean, the Enlightenment idea of what is means to be human—that the human being is an "autonomous rational being" captured in Descartes' (2006) *cogito*, "I am thinking therefore I exist" (p. 28). However, Heidegger (1962) points out that humanism's response to the question of what it means to be human focuses on the essence or nature of the human being instead of on the being of this human being, on the existence of the human being. The upshot of focusing on the essence of the human being is that "human" is defined in a particular way that declares others as less human, sub-human or non-human. The holocaust, apartheid and genocides in Bosnia, Rwanda and Cambodia forcefully remind us of the effects of humanism (Biesta 2006). Levinas (in Biesta 2006) goes as far as to argue that the crisis of humanism began with the inhuman events of recent history:

> The 1914 War, the Russian Revolution refuting itself in Stalinism, fascism, Hitlerism, the 1939-45 War, atomic bombings, genocide and uninterrupted war ... a science that calculates the real without thinking it, a liberal politics and administration that suppresses neither exploitation nor war ... socialism that gets entangled in bureaucracy. (p. 5)

The crisis of humanism might be understood as the manifestation of a broader concern, that Nietzsche argued is one of the great errors in Western thought: the problem of transcendence. Transcendence is the idea that there are two ontological substances and that the one transcends the other. It is a notion that underpins Plato's Forms, monotheistic religions' idea of God, Decartes's dualism, Hegel's dialectic, Marx's superstructure that creates ideological relations and so forth (Wallin 2010). I shall return to the problem of transcendence later.

In relation to education, Biesta (2006) avers that central to education is the cultivation of the human person or the individual's humanity but that this idea of education became distorted during the European Enlightenment period. He argues that the idea that education is about cultivating the human person could be traced back to the tradition of *Bildung*—an educational ideal that emerged in Greek society, and through its adoption in Roman culture, humanism, neohumanism, and the Enlightenment, became one of the central notions of the modern Western educational tradition (see Biesta 2006, for a more detailed discussion). The upshot of these developments was that human being became configured in a particular way. For example, when *Bildung* became intertwined with the Enlightenment and the particular influence of Emmanuel Kant, human being came to mean "rational autonomous being"—consequently the purpose of education was to develop rational autonomous beings. Critical pedagogy and its derivatives followed from this understanding of education—that emancipation was a rational process—a process of conscientization in the case of Freireian pedagogy. My use of rationality has reference to a particular kind of rationality that the Enlightenment period gave us. I acknowledge that there might be other kinds of rationality. For example, the Norwegian philosopher Arne Naess (1977) argued that rationality includes emotions and experiences, suggesting that it should be rescued from an erroneous turn (Le Grange 2013). But let me come back to South Africa and discuss humanism in relation to schooling.

In terms of its demographics, South African schools have changed significantly since the late 1980s. Many former white schools have a diverse student population. Although township[2] schools have remained the same with respect to its "racial" composition, its demographics have changed in that these schools now house students who are "foreign nationals." Classrooms in schools are the spaces in which complicated conversations about societal issues/challenges can and should occur—issues such as xenophobia, rape, corruption, HIV and AIDS and environmental degradation. Such conversations should occur in an atmosphere of respect and where the humanity of all present is affirmed, nurtured and cultivated. Moreover, it is in classrooms that teachers (with local communities), who know their students best, should play a key role in deciding what knowledge is of most worth to the students they teach. But, in South African classrooms, complicated conversations on issues such as xenophobia

---

[2] Townships are underdeveloped peri-urban living areas that are mainly inhabited by black South Africans. They are the consequence of apartheid settlement policies.

are unlikely to occur, because teachers have very little say as to what is taught, for how long, and when it gets taught. The reasons for this situation are complex and detailed, but it links to Enlightenment humanism, how the latter became interwoven with colonialism and in South Africa also with apartheid-capitalism, and presently with neoliberal-capitalism—through all these processes, what it means to be human has become distorted. This distortion in education policy of the apartheid government is most illustrative. According to Enslin (1984), the apartheid education philosophy of Christian National Education stated:

> The final point reflects a significant paternalistic element in the policy. This is particularly evident in articles 14 and 15, entitled 'Coloured Teaching and Education' and 'African (Bantu) Teaching and Education' respectively. Black education is the responsibility of 'white South Africa,' or more specifically of 'the Boer nation as the senior white trustee of the native', who is in a state of 'cultural infancy.' A 'subordinate part of the vocation and task of the Afrikaner,' is to 'Christianise the non-white races of our fatherland.' It is the 'sacred obligation' of the Afrikaner to base black education on Christian National principles. Thus, revealingly, 'We believe that only when the coloured man has been Christianised can he and will he be secure against his own heathen and all kinds of foreign ideologies which promise him sham happiness, but in the long run will make him unsatisfied and unhappy.' (p. 140)

In post-apartheid South Africa, racial content has been removed from policies and curricula and we have seen the infusion of environmental concerns, social justice issues, Indigenous knowledge, etc. But, I have argued elsewhere that all versions of post-apartheid curricula are iterations of the same thing (Le Grange 2010, 2014), namely, all variants of the Tylerian rationale. That all curricula versions have been based on an instrumentalist logic that manifests what Wallin (2010) refers to as an a priori image of a pedagogical life. I shall return to this idea of curriculum later. Moreover, the most recent version of the national curriculum, the Curriculum Policy and Assessment Statements (CAPS) prescribes what is to be taught, when and how it should be taught. Standardized tests have become the order of the day in South African schools following their introduction at the national, provincial and school level (in Western Cape province), thwarting the becoming of pedagogical lives and resulting in perverse practices in schools. Concerning the latter, for example,

212   L. LE GRANGE

a few years ago a Stellenbosch[3] school principal kept back 16 children in the reception year[4] because their birthdays were in the second half the year. His argument (supported by an educational psychologist) was that the children might not be mature enough when they reach grade 3, and therefore negatively impact the schools' performance on standardized tests, and consequently threaten the 100% pass rate that the school has maintained.[5]

Moreover, curriculum scholars in South Africa have in their work, reinscribed a transcendent view of the subject and *currere* as a priori image of a pedagogical life, that is, "to run the course" has become "the course to run." Although the field of curriculum studies is divided and in its infancy in South Africa (Le Grange 2014; Pinar 2010), this idea (a course to run) of curriculum underpins research in the field through large- and small-scale quantitative studies, pedagogical research using the work of Basil Bernstein,[6] critical realist curriculum research and so on. Much of the curriculum research in post-apartheid South Africa has focused on matters related to the implementation of national curriculum frameworks in schools and specifically on pedagogy (as a technology) rather than on the becoming of pedagogical lives (Le Grange 2014). It is for this reason that curriculum research in South Africa (perhaps elsewhere) needs rethinking.

The crisis of humanism alluded to manifests in all spheres and dimensions of life, individual political, social, economic, educational, biophysical and so on. Contemporary problems faced by humanity on all scales (global, national and local) are manifestations of the same underlying crisis—the environmental crisis, the global financial crisis, the education crisis are all expressions of the same crisis. So too is curriculum in the Tylerian mould, an approach that continues to dominate how curriculum is viewed across the globe and in South Africa. Transversal thinking helps us to understand the mutual contagion of humanism in all domains of

---

[3] Stellenbosch is South Africa's second oldest town and located approximately 50 km from central Cape Town.

[4] The reception year (Grade R) is a formal year of compulsory pre-schooling before children begin Grade 1.

[5] I was present in a parent-teacher meeting when this was communicated by the school principal.

[6] For detail on Basil Bernstein's influence on Curriculum Studies in South Africa, see Hugo (2010) and Hoadley (2010).

life, and so too such thinking can help us to invigorate vectors of escape so as to generate new connections that open up alternative pathways for becoming. And it here that *currere's* active force holds particular promise in liberating thought from the colonizing fetters of humanism that find expression in *currere's* reactive force.

The Active Force of *Currere*

More than 40 years ago William Pinar first invoked the etymological root of curriculum, the Latin *currere*, which means "to run the course." He did so to refocus curriculum on the significance of individual experience, "whatever the course content or alignment with society or the economy" (Pinar 2011, p. xii). *Currere*, privileges the individual. Pinar (2011) argues that it is a complicated concept because each of us is different, in our genetic makeup, our upbringings, our families, and more broadly our race, gender, class and so on. Because each of us is different, our experiences of the world are different, therefore the running of our course is different. In the running of each of our courses, we interact with others and the conversations that we have with others are not easy or simple ones, but complicated or hard ones; conversations which the dominant approach (Tylerian) to curriculum excludes.

It is against this background that Pinar develops *currere* as an autobiographical method comprised of the following four steps or moments: (1) regressive, (2) progressive, (3) analytical, and (4) synthetical, that depicts both temporal and reflective moments for autobiographical research of educational experience (Pinar et al. 1995). *Currere* has strong phenomenological foundations in common with scholars such as Aoki (1993) and Jardine (1988) who have put forth phenomenological critiques of mainstream social science and in particular quantitative research. In his later work on autobiographical method, Pinar engages post-structuralism in rethinking notions of authenticity, self and autobiography, influenced by the ideas of Nietzsche and Derrida. As Pinar (1988) writes: "We are not the stories we tell as much as we are the modes of relation to others our stories imply, modes of relation implied by what we delete as much as what we include" (p. 28). Few would disagree that Pinar's invocation of *currere* has made a huge contribution to curriculum studies in North America and the rest of the world, and in particular to the reconceptualist curriculum movement in the USA.

214   L. LE GRANGE

However, more recently, Canadian scholar Jason Wallin has revisited the notion of *currere*—he rethinks the idea with Deleuze and Guattari (1994) and their contention that a concept is not a name attached to something but a way of approaching the world. Deleuze and Guattari's (1994) interest is not in what a concept is but what it does. In reviewing Wallin's work, Waterhouse (2012) argues that though inspired by curriculum scholars such as Ted Aoki, Jacques Daignault, William F. Pinar and William M. Reynolds (all interested in the productive potential of Deleuze's ideas for curriculum studies), Wallin does not follow in their footsteps. As Deleuze (1990/1995) writes: "thinkers are always, so to speak, shooting arrows into the air, and other thinkers pick them up and shoot them in a different direction" (as cited by Waterhouse 2012, p. 175).

And so Wallin's work is not autobiographical and does not lean towards reflection. His interest is rather in what *currere* wills to power, in other words, what *currere* does or might do—his mode of analysis might best be considered as a "thought experiment" (Wallin 2010, p. ix). If in its territorialized form *currere* means "the course to run," and in Pinar's invocation, "to run the course," then for Wallin *currere* evokes "a radically different way of thinking the course to be run" (p. 7)—a radically different way of thinking the course of a pedagogical life.

Wallin draws our attention to the paradoxical character of *currere*'s etymology: its active and reactive forces. Firstly, curriculum can be thought of as an active conceptual force. Thinking curriculum as an active conceptual force means that the concept does not have fixity or closeness—that the term does not convey an a priori image of a pedagogical life. It instead relates to the immanent potential of the becoming of a pedagogical life—the multiple coursings of a pedagogical life that exists prior to thought. As Wallin (2010) elaborates:

> [To] *run* implies that the conceptual power of *currere* is intimate to its productive capacity to create flows, offshoots, and multiplicitous movements. For example, the "running" roots of rhizomatic bulbs and tubers extend to create new interfaces with other organic and nonorganic bodies, extending the experience of what a body can become ... Running flows of volcanic magma create new courses along and through the ostensible stability of the Earth's mantle, articulating the immanent geomorphic potential of territories to deterritorialise ... A musical "run" creates lines of

flight potentially incongruous with the codes that structure it, overflowing, extending, and traversing tonal registers in producing new affects. (p. 2)

The conceptual power of *currere* implies newness, creation of things unforeseen, experimentation, expanding of difference and movement.

However, what has occurred in Western education is the territorialization of *currere's* active force into a reactive force whereby "to run" has become an a priori image—the Grecian "chariot track" or literal "course to run" (Wallin 2010, p. 2). In other words, one way of doing has become the way of doing. This reactive force of *currere* has dominated schooling and university education in the twentieth century (and continues to do so in the twenty-first century) evident in instrumentalist approaches to teaching whereby outcomes or aims are predetermined and often derived from existing disciplines. Students are tracked by standardized tests and kept on track by subject disciplines. The territorialization of *currere's* active force has led to the ossification of potential movements, thwarting of experimentation, freezing of living and domestication of self. Wallin (2010) writes about the humanistic character of *currere's* reactive force:

> The territorialisation of the pedagogical course is indicative of another privilege central to its reactive image. That is, the reactive image of currere is distinctly humanistic, reducing life to its human-all-too-human enframement. Potential ways of thinking a life are reduced to the image that the world is "just like us", and following, that the course to run finds full representation in the anthropocentric imaginery. (p. 6)

The dominance of *currere's* reactive force in education needs to be understood in terms of Western society's commitment to transcendence. Deleuze and Guattari (1994) assert that transcendence is the belief in the existence of a substance/thing beyond empirical space, power or existence (ontological being). It is the commitment to transcendence that has separated humans from nature (causing nature's destruction) and that has informed an education system that has reinforced dualisms. Transcendent thinking is not only evident in conservative positivist approaches to education but also in critical pedagogy informed by Marxist thinking. Bowers (1980) points out that proponents of critical pedagogy frame capitalism and socialism in a dualistic logic of right/wrong, truth/illusion and salvation/damnation.

216   L. LE GRANGE

In his work Wallin (2010) experiments on the lines of flight that are created by an active concept of *currere*, which he argues becomes a way of transforming a life and which extends experience beyond knowledge and opinion. Each line of flight escapes from a priori ways of thinking and brings something new into existence. These experimentations are performed across a wide range of genres of film, music, games, visual arts and technology (Wallin 2010).

In this chapter, I wish to experiment with connecting *Ubuntu* and the active force of *currere*, Deleuzo-Guttarian thought, and post-human(ist) theory so as to generate, in Deleuzian terms "circles of convergence" or in Wallin's (2010) terms unlikely fidelities. I am invoking *Ubuntu* as a way of rethinking the inhuman(e) events of our time, of rethinking the post-human condition and also because *Ubuntu* is an idea/practice that is known to rural communities in the Global South for whom some of the genres that Wallin uses might not be part of their life-world. But, before invigorating these lines of connection, let me first discuss *Ubuntu*.

UBUNTU

Ubuntu/Botho[7] is a concept that is derived from proverbial expressions (aphorisms) found in several languages in Africa south of the Sahara. However, it is not only a linguistic concept but a normative connotation embodying how we ought to relate to the other—what our moral obligation is towards the other. Battle (1996) explains the concept *Ubuntu* as originating from the Xhosa[8] expression: *Umuntu ngumuntu ngabanye Bantu*, "Not an easily translatable Xhosa concept, generally, this proverbial expression means that each individual's humanity is ideally expressed in relationship with others and, in turn, individuality is truly expressed" (p. 99).

Metz and Gaie (2010) argue that there are two ways in which sub-Saharan African morality (as embodied in *Ubuntu*) is distinct from Western

---

[7] In this chapter, I shall use the term *Ubuntu* which derives from the aphorism "*Umuntu ngumuntu ngabantu*" found in the Nguni languages of Zulu, Xhosa or Ndebele. However, I wish to point out that a similar concept exists in Sotho-Tswana languages derived from the proverbial expression, "*Motho ke motho ka batho babang*".

[8] The Xhosa people are Bantu language speakers living in the southeast of South Africa. The mains tribes of the Xhosa are: Mpondo; Mpondomise; Bonvana; Xesibe; and Thembu. isiXhosa is one of the official languages of South Africa.

approaches to morality. Firstly, they argue that sub-Saharan morality is essentially relational in the sense that the only way to develop one's humanness is to relate to others in a positive way. In other words, one becomes a person solely through other persons—"one cannot realize one's true self in opposition to others or even in isolation from them" (p. 275). They point out that *Ubuntu* means that our deepest moral obligation is to become more fully human and to achieve this requires one to enter more deeply into community with others. One therefore cannot become more fully human or realize one's true self by exploiting, deceiving or acting in unjust ways towards others. Metz and Gaie argue that the second way in which African morality differs from an Aristotelian or other Western moral philosophy is that it defines positive relationship with others in strictly communal terms. They write:

> One is not to positively relate to others fundamentally by giving them what they deserve, respecting individual human rights grounded on consent, participating in a political sphere or maximizing the general welfare, common themes in Western moral philosophy. Instead the proper way to relate to others, for one large part of sub-Saharan thinking, is to seek out community or to live in harmony with them. (p. 275)

Following from this is that moral obligation concerns: doing things for the good of others; to think of oneself as bound up with others; and to value family (in a broad sense of the term) for its own sake and not for its efficacy.

When reference is made to the other by Metz and Gaie (2010), then they are evidently referring to the human other—that relatedness means connectedness with other human beings. In other words, *Ubuntu* means becoming more fully human through deeper relationships with other human beings. It is because of this understanding that Enslin and Horsthemke (2004) have argued that *Ubuntu* is by definition speciesist and therefore cannot contribute positively towards addressing environmental problems. Through a categorical lens of environmental ethics, we would say that *Ubuntu* is anthropocentric. However, I wish to argue that this is not the case and that *Ubuntu* has very strong ecocentric leanings (if the categorical lens of environmental ethics is used) or that it transcends the binary of anthropocentrism and ecocentrism. To appreciate the ecocentric leanings of the concept *Ubuntu* a broader/similar concept, *Ukama*, of which it forms part, should be understood.

218 L. LE GRANGE

In the Shona[9] language, there is a broader concept *Ukama* which means relatedness—relatedness to the entire cosmos. Murove (2009) argues that *Ubuntu* (humanness) is the concrete form of *Ukama* (relatedness) in the sense that "human interrelationship within society is a microcosm of the relationality within the universe" (p. 316). It is against this backdrop that Murove's (2009) assertion that, "ukama provides the ethical anchorage for human social, spiritual and ecological togetherness," might be understood (p. 317). This idea of ecological togetherness is supported by others such as Bujo (2001) who writes: "The African is convinced that all things in the cosmos are interconnected" (pp. 22–23). Also by Tangwa (2004) who avers: "The precolonial traditional African metaphysical, outlook ... impl[ies] recognition and acceptance of interdependence and peaceful coexistence between earth, plants, animals and humans" (p. 389). Opoku (1993) notes: "There is community with nature since man [sic] is part of nature and is expected to cooperate with it; and this sense of community with nature is often expressed in terms of identity and kinship, friendliness and respect" (p. 77).

Moreover, humanness is not humanism and is in fact antithetical to it. As Ramose (2009) writes:

> Humanness suggests both a condition of being and the state of becoming, of openness or ceaseless unfolding. It is thus opposed to any, '-ism', including humanism, for this tends to suggest a condition of finality, a closedness or a kind of absolute either incapable of, or resistant to, any further movement. (pp. 308–309)

Humanness is therefore inextricably bound up in the human being's connectedness with other human beings and with an ever changing and complex (biophysical) world. The sense of wholeness and interconnectedness of self with the social and natural by implication means that caring for others also involves a duty to care for nature (the more-than-human-world). *Ubuntu*, therefore is not by definition speciesist as Enslin and Horsthemke (2004) suggest, but is rather an ecosophy that connects Guattari's (2001) three ecologies; self, social and nature—self, social and

---

[9]Shona is the collective name for several groups of people in the east of Zimbabwe and southern Mozambique. The Shona speaking people are categorised into five main ethnic groups: Zezuru; Manyika; Karanga and Kalanga; Korekore; and Ndau. There are substantial numbers in South Africa and Botswana.

nature are inextricably bound up with one another. Cultivating *Ubuntu*, by definition therefore involves healing of self, social and nature.

Guattari's notion of transversality helps us to gain a more nuanced sense of the notion of *ukama* when he argues that when suffering is witnessed in one ecological register it will also be witnessed in other ecological registers. Africa's suffering evident in the, "staggering incidence of genocide, patriarchy, dictatorships and autocratic rule, corruption, sexism (and practices of genital excision), heterosexism and homophobia, xenophobia, and environmental degradation (and connected with this, human suffering) on the continent" (Horsthemke and Enslin 2005, p. 67) should be understood as the breaking or erosion of *ukama* through among other influences, years of colonial rule and apartheid-capitalism (manifestations of the crisis of humanism). Healing in one ecological register will therefore effect healing in other ecological registers. If *Ubuntu* means that our deepest moral obligation is to become more fully human, then this means not only fostering a closer and deeper relationship with human communities but also with biotic communities and the entire ecosphere. In other words, the realization of one's true self cannot be achieved if other human beings and nature are exploited or harmed.

Understanding *Ubuntu* as a concrete expression of *Ukama* also problematizes the categories of anthropocentrism and ecocentrism (and those in between) which have come to characterize debates in environmental ethics/philosophy and on those who wish to impose such categories on African values such as *Ubuntu*. Nurturing the self or caring for other human beings is not antagonistic towards caring for the-more-than-human world—*Ubuntu* cannot simply be reduced to a category of anthropocentrism or ecocentrism. The self, community and nature are inextricably bound up with one another—healing/development in one results in healing in all dimensions and so suffering too is transversally witnessed in all three dimensions. Put simply, African spirituality cannot be reduced to a category of anthropocentrism.

Ubuntu and *Currere's* Active Force

Responses to the challenges facing Africa (and elsewhere)—xenophobia, poverty, environmental destruction, etc. do not necessarily lie outside of the concepts known to the communities perpetrating them or who are victims of harm, but in reviving, reinventing, reimagining, rethinking such concepts. And so I wish to rethink *Ubuntu* by generating connections with *currere's* active force and post-human "theory."[10] By the latter, I mean emerging thoughts on the post-human condition that Braidotti (2013) has also described as the "post-human predicament" (p. 1). Here Braidotti views post-human theory as both a genealogical and a navigational process. By the former, she means an approach to rethink the basic unit of reference for the human in a bio-genetic age known as the "anthropocene"—a historical moment where humans are capable of affecting all life. By the latter, she means mapping how the post-human is circulating as a dominant term in our globally interconnected and technologically mediated societies. Post-human theory is a critical response to post-human capitalism (the genetic code that has become capital, robotics and a fourth industrial revolution, etc.) but it also positively draws on new materialist thought that posits that there are material flows that connect everything in the cosmos—an immanent plane from which human, animal and physical forms are actualized. This wider macro context serves as the basis for exploring *Ubuntu* in relation to the following notions: *people-yet-to-come*; *subjectivity that is ecological*; and *transcending the anthropocentric-ecocentric divide*.

Unprecedented levels of destruction in Guattari's (2001) three ecological registers (mental, social and environment) by present generations might suggest that those who could take us beyond the crisis of humanism are not yet with us, that is, that they are a *people-yet-to-come*. However, when Deleuze and Guattari invoke the notion of a *people-yet-to-come* it is not a historical lament on their part but more an expression of an ontological concept. As Hroch (2014) writes:

> Deleuze and Guattari's plea for a 'people-yet-to-come' does not presume that the pedagogical or political process of transformation at work is one through which a pre-existing (though not-yet existing) 'people' will come to adopt a pre-existing 'idea' over time. Rather, they understand the people present *in the present* as *already* the 'people-yet-to come'. That is, for Deleuze and Guattari, we are always already people-in-becoming and thus the concept of a 'people-yet-to-come' expresses the perpetual potentiality of becoming-other inherent to the present. (italics in the original) (p. 50)

Those that are to respond to the crises of humanism (in all its manifestations) and the challenges of the post-human condition are not a

---

[10] I put theory in scare quotation marks because the post-human predicament might also signal a post-theory mood.

people-yet-to-come in the sense of a future people, but a people here and now—it is the people in the present that are in-becoming. This notion connects with *currere* as an active conceptual force which holds that there is no a priori image of a pedagogical life, but multiple coursings for the becoming of a pedagogical life—it concerns the immanent potential for the becoming of a pedagogical life. The notions *people-yet-to-come* and *currere's* active force conveys an anti-humanist stance—if the "human" is always in-becoming then it can't be defined or essentialized. Moreover, the two notions align with post-human theory that draws on new materialism, which is premised on the idea that bodies (including human bodies) are material flows of energy that have become actualized— the materiality of the human being denies it fixity, makes it fleeting and connects it to all of life. It is with the (material) immanent plane that the life force in human beings is connected (or flows from), a term that Braidotti (2013) refers to as *potentia. Potentia* is a positive force that expresses the human's desire to endure, to become and to connect to other human beings and the more-than-human world. Earlier I noted Ramose's (2009) argument that *Ubuntu* is anti-humanism, that it concerns a state of becoming, of openness or ceaseless unfolding. The conceptual connection between *Ubuntu, currere's* active force and the new materialism turn in post-human theory is clearly evident. An education informed by *Ubuntu* therefore makes possible the expression of *potentia*, the expression of the desire to live, to connect and care for other humans and the more-than-human-world. It opens up multiple coursings for the becoming of a pedagogical life. *Ubuntu-currere* is anti-humanist, because it is in contrast to education informed by humanism that is driven by a negative power, *potestas*, which centralizes control, colonizes desire, predetermines the course to run through predefined aims, objectives or outcomes, etc. In other words, *potestas* territorializes *currrere's* active force into a reactive force.

Furthermore, an education informed by *Ubuntu* liberates thought from the fetters of Cartesian duality—from Descartes's *cogito*, I think therefore I am. *Ubuntu*, the active force of *currere* and new materialist post-humanism celebrates the oneness of mind and body and the oneness of humans and the more-than-human-world. Rather than subjectivity being individual, it is ecological. An education informed by *Ubuntu* represents a shift from what Doll (2015) calls the arrogant "I" (of Western individualism) to the humble "I"—to the "I" that is embedded, embodied, extended and enacted. In an ever-changing world, the pathways for becoming of a pedagogical life cannot be known or defined. *Ubuntu-currere* signifies both our movement in the world and how the world moves through us which generates potentially creative ways for us to inhabit the world. The oneness of the self and other humans as a microcosm of the oneness of self and the cosmos provides impetus for becomings that are caring towards other humans and the more-than-human world. An education informed by *Ubuntu-currere* is based on co-operation and not competition.

Ubuntu-currere is post-anthropocentric and in fact overcomes the anthropocentric-ecocentric divide. Braidotti (2006) importantly points out that geo-centric (ecocentric) theories such as deep-ecology and gaianism humanize the more-than-human-world by imposing human attributes on other species and the physical world. *Ubuntu-currere* suggests thinking differently about ecological domains, akin to Guattari's (2001) notion of thinking about the three ecological registers transversely. Education informed by *Ubuntu-currere* suggests moving beyond disciplinary thinking to explore the mutual connections among disciplines, to explore their mutual contagion and to invigorate transdisciplinary trajectories. *Ubuntu/ukama*, *currere*, and Guattari's three ecologies are ideas with different epistemological histories. The experiment here was not to reduce any of the concepts by collapsing them into each other but to expand them, to explore points of resonance among them, to explore their mutual contagion, to enrich each concept so as to open up alternative pathways for the becoming of the young in a world with complex challenges that revolve around the self, social relations and the condition of the environment. Pathways that will enable us to live more "hopefully, radically, ethically, and lovingly" (Hébert et al. 2018, p. 5).

CONCLUSION

In this chapter, I have argued that *Ubuntu-currere* shifts our registers of reference away from the individual human being to an assemblage of human-human-nature. In other words, subjectivity is ecological. Moreover, the subject is always in-becoming and the becoming of a pedagogical life is relational—the subject becomes in relation to other humans and the more-than-human-world. The notion in-becoming ensures that the human cannot be defined nor have fixity and therefore *Ubuntu-currere* is anti-humanist. Put differently, *Ubuntu-currere* negates the construction of a molar identity that is a screen against which anything different is othered in a negative sense. *Ubuntu-currere* has resonance with new materialist post-human theory in that it embraces an ontology of immanence—that there is a material immanent plane that connects everything in the cosmos and from which all actualized forms unfold/become. *Ubuntu-currere* opens up multiple coursings for developing post-human sensibilities driven by the positive power of *potentia* that connects, expresses desire and sustains life. It is this power that connects curriculum scholars across national boundaries and makes possible conversations where we can hear "what people do, how they do it, how they think about things with the hope that we could learn from each other" (Hébert et al. 2018, p. 3). But, it also makes possible conversations with the more-than-human so that we can listen to rhythm and heartbeat of the earth—so that our conversations do not happen on the earth but are bent by the earth (Le Grange 2016). *Potentia* promises to counteract the manifestations of the crisis of humanism such as racism, sexism, homophobia, xenophobia, environmental destruction, centrally controlled and standardized education systems. These crises are manifestations of a negative power, *potestas*, the same form of power that produces *currere's* reactive force. Counteracting *postestas* (criticism of and resistance to it) and the releasing of *potentia* is at the heart of living hopefully and that make possible the internationalization of curriculum studies mooted in this volume.

In Kappeler's (1986) words: "I do not really wish to conclude and sum up, rounding off the arguments so as to dump it in a nutshell for the reader. A lot more could be said about any of the topics I have touched upon … I have meant to ask questions, to break out of the frame … The point is not a set of answers, but making possible a different practice" (p. 30)—a different way of viewing *Ubuntu* and *currere* and the internationalization of curriculum studies.

References

Aoki, T. (1993). Legitimating lived curriculum: Toward a curricular landscape of multiplicity. *Journal of Curriculum and Supervision, 8*(3), 67–76.

Azeng, T. F., & Yogo, T. U. (2013). *Youth unemployment and political instability in selected developing countries* (Working Paper No. 171). Tunis: African Development Bank Group.

Battle, M. (1996). The *Ubuntu* theology of Desmond Tutu. In L. D. Huley & L. Kretzschmar (Eds.), *Archbishop Tutu: Prophetic witness in South Africa* (pp. 99–100). Cape Town: Human & Rousseau.

Biesta, G. (2006). *Beyond learning: Democratic education for a human future.* London: Paradigm Publishers.

Bowers, C. (1980). Curriculum as cultural reproduction: An examination of the metaphor as carrier of ideology. *Teachers College Record, 82*(2), 267–290.

Braidotti, R. (2006). *Transpositions.* Malden, MA: Polity Press.

Braidotti, R. (2013). *The posthuman.* Malden, MA: Polity Press.

Bujo, B. (2001). *Foundations of an African ethic: Beyond the universal claims of Western morality.* New York: The Crossroad Publishing.

Cahuc, P., Carcillo, C., Rinne, U., & Zimmermann, K. (2013). Youth unemployment in old Europe: The polar cases of France and Germany. *IZA Journal of European Labor Studies, 2*(18), 1–23.

Deleuze, G. (1990/1995). *Negotiations, 1972–1990* (M. Joughin, Trans.). New York: Columbia University Press.

Deleuze, G., & Guattari, F. (1994). *What is philosophy?* (H. Tomlinson & G. Burchell, Trans.). New York: Columbia University.

Descartes, R. (2006). *A discourse on the method* (I. Maclean, Trans.). Oxford: Oxford University Press.

Doll, W. (2015). *Seeking method-beyond-method.* Keynote address at the fifth triennial conference of the International Association for the Advancement of Curriculum Studies. University of Ottawa, 26–29 May.

Edwards, S. B., & Harris, D. (2016). *Black lives matter.* North Mankato: Essential Library.

Enslin, P. (1984). The role of fundamental pedagogics in the formulation of education policy in South Africa. In P. Kallaway (Ed.), *Apartheid and education: The education of black South Africans* (pp. 139–147). Johannesburg: Ravan Press.

Enslin, P., & Horsthemke, K. (2004). Can *Ubuntu* provide a model for citizenship education in African democracies? In *Proceedings of the 9th biennial conference of the International Network of Philosophers of Education.* Madrid: Universidad Complutense.

Guattari, F. (2001). *The three ecologies* (I. Pindar & P. Sutton, Trans.). London: The Athlone Press.

Hazekamp, J. L., & Popple, K. (2013). *Racism in Europe: The challenge for youth policy and youth work.* London: Routledge.

Hébert, C., Ibrahim, A., Ng-A-Fook, N., & Smith, B. (Eds.). (2018). *Internationalizing curriculum studies: Histories, environments, and critiques* (pp. 1–11). London, UK: Palgrave.

Heidegger, M. (1962). *Being and time* (J. Macquarrie & E. Robinson, Trans.). New York: Harperperennial.

Hoadley, U. (2010). Tribes and territory: Contestation around curriculum in South Africa. In W. F. Pinar (Ed.), *Curriculum studies in South Africa: Intellectual histories, present circumstances* (pp. 125–176). New York: Palgrave Macmillan.

Horsthemke, K., & Enslin, P. (2005). Is there a distinctively and uniquely African philosophy of education. In Y. Waghid (Ed.), *African(a) philosophy of education: Reconstructions and deconstructions*. Stellenbosch: Department of Education Policy Studies.

Hroch, P. (2014). Deleuze, Guattari, and environmental pedagogy and politics: *Ritournelles* for a planet-yet-to-come. In M. Carlin & J. Wallin (Eds.), *Deleuze & Guattari, politics and education* (pp. 49–76). New York: Bloomsbury.

Hugo, W. (2010). Drawing the line in post-apartheid curriculum studies. In W. F. Pinar (Ed.), *Curriculum studies in South Africa: Intellectual histories, present circumstances* (pp. 51–106). New York: Palgrave Macmillan.

Jardine, D. (1988). Reflections on phenomenology, pedagogy, and *Phenomenology + Pedagogy*. *Phenomenology + Pedagogy, 6*(3), 158–160.

Kaldor, M. (2012). *New and old wars* (3rd ed.). Cambridge: Polity Press.

Kappeler, S. (1986). *The pornography of representation*. Cambridge: Polity Press.

Le Grange, L. (2010). South African curriculum studies: A historical perspective and autobiographical account. In W. F. Pinar (Ed.), *Curriculum studies in South Africa: Intellectual histories, present circumstances* (pp. 177–200). New York: Palgrave Macmillan.

Le Grange, L. (2013). Why we need a language of (environmental) education. In R. Stevenson, M. Brody, J. Dillon, & A. E. J. Wals (Eds.), *International handbook of research on environmental education* (pp. 108–114). New York: Taylor & Francis.

Le Grange, L. (2014). Curriculum research in South Africa. In W. F. Pinar (Ed.), *International handbook of curriculum research* (2nd ed., pp. 466–475). New York: Taylor & Francis.

Le Grange, L. (2016). Sustainability education and (curriculum) improvisation. *Southern African Journal of Environmental Education, 32*, 26–36.

Magolego, B. (2008). On makwerekwere. *Mail & Guardian*. Retrieved from http://www.thoughtleader.co.za/mandelarhodesscholars/2008/05/15/on-makwerekwere/.

Metz, T., & Gaie, J. B. R. (2010). The African ethic of *Ubuntu/Botho*: Implications for research on morality. *Journal of Moral Education, 39*(3), 273–290.

Murove, M. F. (2009). An African environmental ethic based on the concepts of *Ukama* and *Ubuntu*. In M. F. Murove (Ed.), *African ethics: An anthology of*

226 L. LE GRANGE

comparative and applied ethics (pp. 315–331). Pietermaritzburg: University of Kwazulu-Natal Press.

Naess, A. (1977). Spinoza and ecology. In S. Hessing (Ed.), *Speculum Spinozanum 1677–1977* (pp. 418–425). London: Routledge & Kegan Paul.

Opoku, K. (1993). African traditional religion: An enduring heritage. In J. Olupona & S. Nyang (Eds.), *Religious plurality in Africa* (pp. 67–82). Berlin: Mouton de Gruyter.

Pinar, W. (1988). Autobiography and the architecture of self. *Journal of Curriculum Theorizing, 8*(1), 7–36.

Pinar, W. (2010). *Curriculum studies in South Africa: Intellectual histories & present circumstances.* New York: Palgrave Macmillan.

Pinar, W. F. (2011). *The character of curriculum studies: Bildung, currere and the recurring question of the subject.* New York: Palgrave Macmillan.

Pinar, W. F., Reynolds, W. M., Slattery, P., & Taubman, P. M. (1995). *Understanding curriculum: An introduction to historical and contemporary curriculum discourses.* New York: Peter Lang.

Rajchman, J. (1985). *Michel Foucault: The freedom of philosophy.* New York: Columbia University Press.

Ramose, M. B. (2009). Ecology through *Ubuntu.* In M. F. Murove (Ed.). *African ethics: An anthology of comparative and applied ethics* (pp. 308–314). Pietermaritzburg: University of KwaZulu-Natal Press.

Republic of South Africa. (2014). *Twenty year review: South Africa (1994–2004).* Pretoria: Republic of South Africa.

South African History Online. (2015). *Xenophobic violence in democratic South Africa.* Retrieved from http://www.sahistory.org.za/article/xenophobic-violence-democratic-south-africa.

Tangwa, G. (2004). Some African reflections on biomedical and environmental ethics. In K. Wiredu (Ed.), *Companion to African philosophy* (pp. 387–395). Malden, MA: Blackwell.

Wallin, J. J. (2010). *A Deleuzian approach to curriculum: Essays on a pedagogical life.* New York: Palgrave Macmillan.

Waterhouse, M. (2012). Book review [Review of Book A Deleuzian approach to curriculum: Essays on a pedagogical life by J. J Wallin]. *Journal of the Canadian Association for Curriculum Studies, 10*(2), 174–182.

CHAPTER 14

For Us, Today: Understanding Curriculum as Theological Text in the Twenty-First Century

Reta Ugena Whitlock

When I consider the thought of my work in theological curriculum studies advancing worldly, international curriculum studies, I bring to mind Dietrich Bonhoeffer's (2010) prophetic commentary, which I discuss later, concerning a coming "religionless age" (p. 362). In a world, where people were becoming "radically religionless," he pondered, "How do we speak in a 'worldly' way about God?" (p. 364). I wonder whether I can transpose his question. *Can we speak in a "worldly" way about curriculum?* This collection seeks to do that, as the editors outline in their introduction; this chapter accepts their calls. First, *it complicates local understandings of curriculum theorizing* in the present historical moment through a narrative of fundamentalist religion. One need not look far to see a re-centering of narrow, fundamentalist, white-supremacist world views in the USA—a distinct strategy of the Godless tyrants who would use it for political and economic gain. So how might a narrative view of fundamentalist religious thought, such as the one I present in this

R. U. Whitlock (✉)
Kennesaw State University, Kennesaw, GA, USA
e-mail: rwhitlo3@kennesaw.edu

© The Author(s) 2019   227
C. Hébert et al. (eds.), *Internationalizing Curriculum Studies,*
https://doi.org/10.1007/978-3-030-01352-3_14

chapter, have worldly implications? Because it is the collective thinking—and voting—that supports the current despot, allowing him to goad other tyrants (North Korea's Kim Jong-un, for example) and alienate allies who are dedicated toward a common good (the European Union). Thus, fundamentalist Christianity has a worldwide impact.

The editors have a second framework for this volume: *a radical push of curriculum theorizing toward reimagining a better future*, an imagining of *that which is yet to come*. I propose that to speak in a worldly way about curriculum, we engage deeply in the endeavor to speak in a worldly way about God—I seek the mutuality between my question and Bonhoeffer's. Although my narratives on fundamentalism are excellent vehicles for wrongheadedness into context, in themselves they do not facilitate using "the unformed to create form," the editors' final call, from Huebner (1999, p. 227). To believers, God creates matter from void, form from unformed. To give form to imaginings of a world where we treat and entreat one another with love and care—ethically—this chapter considers the theological and the religious. In the curriculum world, this might be akin to rejecting the reduction of either theory or practice apart from the other, for we have witnessed the folly in that. Drawing from Bonhoeffer, the worldliness of curriculum studies lies in the possibility held in our recursive immersion in its powerlessness, in its hardship, or as I see it, the free, responsible actions of radical love. Thus it is to my narrative I turn.

Losing My Religion

I grew up in a fundamentalist church that was pre-Moral Majority, pre-Reagan, pre-Religious Right, pre-Tea Party. Lest one think I look back through the veil of nostalgia for a purer, simpler, kinder fundamentalist Christianity, I do not. When I look backward at the little girl, then young woman who grew up fundamentalist, I can only look from where I am today, and today I see inequality and oppression, valuation of people, and of course, perpetuation of patriarchy. I see ignorance—and this is very hard to say because I am talking about myself and my people. So I will explain that when I say ignorance, I mean lack of knowledge. In this case, lack of knowledge about theological underpinnings of fundamentalist dogma, the denial that there are any such underpinnings, and the delusion that literal reading of scripture is not its own interpretation. But when I look—really look—at the little girl, I see a child who learned

14 FOR US, TODAY: UNDERSTANDING CURRICULUM AS THEOLOGICAL ... 229

to know God in the Sunday school narratives, to fear God in somber sermons, and to love God by drawing as close as she ever could in song. I see a child filled with the spirit, which was her first defiant act.

Growing up fundamentalist, there was a great void where the theology should be. When we see fundamentalism in public institutions, such as government and schools, there still is. This narrative tries to make sense of my autobiographical phenomenological journey to fill that void. The work of theology in the last 500 years has been to eliminate superstition from religion and Christianity—which are two different concepts. So this work moves the conversation beyond superstition—but not beyond the mythopoetic, which, again, is a much different concept. If we as curriculum theorists rail against fundamentalism—which is fundamental partly because it accepts superstition as historical fact, then we will alienate those we really want and need to reach—we will not, perhaps cannot, be heard. We have to talk to the people with whom we disagree, but we must come to common ground. Fundamentalists have denied themselves participation in the great conversation about the divine. I suggest that we have essentially done the same thing.

My granddaddy helped build the church house where I was raised, where my parents and son still attend. My Uncle Earl ran the electrical wiring that has been throughout the old building since 1938. That old church runs as deeply through me still, just as that network of wires thread throughout the structure itself. Although it has received several face-lifts in the attempt to modernize it, much of it is still the same. Over the years, do-it-yourself members have taken on projects like carpeting, painting, and installing updated pews and light fixtures. Ten years ago, they even renovated the old classroom space into a fellowship room— with a *kitchen*—which is maybe the strongest indication of how more than the building has changed. When I was growing up, gyms and kitchens were sure signs of the unscriptural, worldliness of the Baptists, for compared to the Church of Christ, the Baptists were as rowdy as a bunch of Mardi Gras revelers. Whenever I go there, I feel the familiarity of going home.

The building I remember had a sacred austerity about it. It was a stone building, not brick, stone. Brick was expensive in country North Alabama during the depression, whereas stones could be harvested in fields and on riverbanks. Today the façade has been updated with awnings and a new wing, but the stones are still there. Inside, old, dark-stained pine panels lined both the walls and floors. The wooden pews were even darker, and of course they had the obligatory betraying creak. New blond-colored pews—with cushions and matching communion table—replaced those old dark oak ones that had been hand-hewn from tree to building in the 1980s, some 50 years and two generations later. Above our heads were four ceiling fans that hung down from a long-metal pipe called a downrod on which they wobbled precariously; those were the only hope of relief on hot Southern summer Sundays that could get up to a hundred degrees. In front of us was the pulpit, pine stained deep red, and behind that was the baptistery, which had a life-sized pastoral scene painted on the wall behind it. The baptistery made it unnecessary for the congregation to traipse down to the nearby creek to baptize new members as they had done until the 1950s, so someone had painted a stream with a gentle sloping bank shaded by a poplar tree. The baptistery was a site of mystery that we children would slip and get as close to as possible as often as possible.

I learned Bible stories for as far back as I can remember. In Sunday school, curriculum consisted first of flannel boards with cardboard cut-outs of Abraham and Moses, and on Sunday nights one of the joys of my week was getting to sit on the front bench with the other children and have the preacher lead us in Bible songs about the Three Wandering Jews ("wand'ring wand'ring Jew, Jew, Jew"), and the wise man who built his house upon the rock ("The rains came down and the floods came up"). I was in the Lord's Army (yes SIR!). As we got older, our class was in the basement, which was probably my favorite place in the building. In what I am sure broke every building code in the country, the basement smelled of mildew from the moment we opened the door to descend into its belly. I can still smell that odor today, and although I was probably unknowingly breathing in asbestos for years as an adolescent, remembering that smell fills me with a wave of longing. We groped along the walls making our way down two flights of stairs, our way lit by one bare light bulb that hung 10 feet above our heads. The best part about the basement, besides its dankness and gray concrete floors, was its back room. This is where the really old stuff was kept. There were old hymnals and collection baskets, which had been replaced in the 1950s with pewter plates, and old wooden folding chairs like I had never seen. I learned most all the Bible I know in that basement from flash cards and fill in the blank workbooks printed by the one bookstore in the state that printed materials for the Church of Christ, which guards its dogma tenaciously from both the secular and ecumenical.

14 FOR US, TODAY: UNDERSTANDING CURRICULUM AS THEOLOGICAL ...   231

You will notice I have not described the place where the choir and piano stool. That is because of one phrase in the Christian Scriptures we have interpreted to prohibit musical instruments ("as you sing psalms and hymns and spiritual songs among yourselves, singing and making melody to the Lord *in your hearts*," Ephesians 5:19). It was not until I entered seminary that I learned my denomination is called the "non-instrumental" Church of Christ, as opposed, for example, to the heretics who introduced it into the contemporary Church of Christ and the really bad heretics that are unrelated but go under other names like the United Church of Christ. When I was first learning to sing from the hymnal, the song director was an elder who had grown up with Sacred Harp singing or shape note-singing. Today Sacred Harp is considered a piece of Americana, folk culture to be preserved. As a child I was exposed to a hybrid version of it that even then felt foreign as I listened to adults sing doe-re-mi's to the tunes that were familiar. I never did learn how to do it, but our hymnals are still printed with shape notes.

Alan Block has written in his *Symphony in a Minor Key* (2005) about what it feels like to listen to music. He writes about something that I was aware of but had never tried to describe, the importance of music phenomenologically; it made me realize that there are those of us who do not just hear music. We feel it. It elicits in me a visceral response. I have known this from the time I was able to sing in church. There is something about *the minor fall and the major lift* that has drawn—still draws—from me a hallelujah. When my little church friends and I had put away childish things like children's songs on the front pew, we began to learn to sing harmony, first from sitting behind the song director's wife, who sang pitch-perfect alto and who would compliment us on our progress after the service. It is one of my fondest memories. Eventually we sang on the back row as teenagers, between the whispering and doodling in our Bibles.

It was from this vantage point that I remember in 1982, shortly before my wedding, looking around at the congregation as I sang—at my grandparents, up front and to the left, and at my parents two rows in front of me—and thinking, all of this is going to change. One day I will come to this place and these people will not be here, and like Emily in *Our Town,* thought something like, "Oh, earth, you're too wonderful for anybody to realize you. Do any human beings ever realize life while they live it?—every, every minute?" To which the stage manager of my church community might have replied something like, "No. The saints

232   R. U. WHITLOCK

and poets, maybe—they do some" (Act III). The dark years of my life that begin almost at that moment are marked by my having lost music out of it. And the theological turn of my life and work has a distinct musical accompaniment, one that is sacred. You see, there is ever the concept of "was blind but now I see" in Christian fundamentalism, even those of us in recovery from it. But in that moment, I realized life while I lived it.

Paul Tillich (1968) contends that the great old hymns had religious power of the presence of the divine, and for me they certainly did. What I have described as my experience at singing—as *being* music—can only be called a "feeling" in the way Tillich explains Schleiermacher used it in his famous book from 1799, *On Religion, Speeches to Its cultured Despisers* (you have to love the titles of these old books). That is, feeling is the "impact of the universe upon us in the depths of our being which transcends subject and object" (Tillich 1968, p. 392), of intuition of this universe, of divination—of immediate awareness of the divine, of the ground of everything within us. *This* kind of feeling, Schleiermacher later calls "feeling of unconditional dependence" (p. 393). It is one, Tillich tells us, that transcends feeling understood in the psychological, subjective sense, for those feelings have been conditioned. Aesthetic response, to art, poetry, or in my case, music, "takes me into it and strongly awakens emotions," (p. 400) as Tillich so beautifully describes. It is, he says, "the response of our whole being in immediacy" (p. 400). *This* is feeling. It opens up a "dimension in myself" through participation in it (p. 400).

Now here is an interesting connection of narrative and proposition: Tillich (1968) explains that whenever theology makes its way into conversations "anti-theological colleagues" tend to quote "somebody who puts religion into a dark corner of mere subjective feeling" (p. 394). He writes:

> Religion is not dangerous there. They can use their scientific and political words, their ethical and logical analysis, etc., (today he could have used poststructuralist, postmodernist, psychoanalytical, critical, e.g.) without regard to religion... But in the moment in which they are confronted by a theology which interferes much—not from outside but from the inside— with the scientific process, political movements, and moral principles, and which wants to show that within all of them there is an ultimate concern, as I call it, or an unconditional dependence, as Schleiermacher called it, then these people react. (p. 394)

First, I would point out that this is a characteristic, generally, of fundamentalism. Sentimentalism, superstition, and scriptural inerrancy are indeed disservices to fundamentalists religions themselves—it also made them easy marks for the Republican machine in 1980 and kept fundamentalist Christians "in the red," as it were, ever since. It also makes them complicit in the empiric "kingdom of paucity" of the US "national security state" (Brueggemann 2010, p. 29). Fundamentalist exceptionalism is analogous to US exceptionalism, and both concepts are grounded in what Brueggemann calls "nostalgia for the imagined good old days" (p. 44), which Janet Miller reminds curriculum theorists in her 2010 Bergamo keynote address, never was.

Thinking theologically, from a place of theonomy, is my response to what is for me the spiritual emptiness of critical thought (Tillich 1968), an emptiness which is masked by myths of neutrality and objectivity. What is wanted in these difficult times of bullies, inequities, and a violence is an ethics for being-in-the-world-together. For me and my work, it means losing my religion, or shifting the focus and contexts through which I write about curriculum, from religion to thinking theologically about curriculum. And for this, I turn to Dietrich Bonhoeffer.

GOD IN THE WORLD COME OF AGE: BONHOEFFER AND THE RESPONSIBLE ACTION OF LOVE

Bonhoeffer's life's work is both poignant and profound; we know how it ends, and we read his letter that marks the date in time when *he* knew, too (July 21, 1944). His ethics for his time and place lends itself well to my own consideration of Christian ethics for this place and time, or more precisely to my eventual work, Christian sexual ethics, for which I also draw from the field of queer theology. Bonhoeffer and queer theology—strange bedfellows indeed because, granted, there is nothing very queer about Bonhoeffer. There is, however, an awful lot of theological disruptiveness going on in his later writings, composed on scrap paper in his prison cell. Here was a man who—in spite of being privileged, being classically trained by leading German theologians, writing two dissertations, and doing a postdoc—rejected academe in favor of a pastorate. He wanted to preach. He was banned by the Nazis from teaching seminary and later from writing. When Hitler came to power in 1933, Bonhoeffer gave a radio address called *The Younger Generation's*

Altered View of the Concept of Fuhrer that was cut off mid-broadcast; he was three days shy of his 27th birthday. I suppose what fascinates me about him, and what entices me to turn to him as I seek to understand radical love and its place in the world today, lies in his portrayal of God's suffering and powerlessness, his insistence that humans—to be human—must take responsibility for the world—and to do *that*—we must manage our lives without God. "Before God, and with God, we live without God" (Bonhoeffer 2010, p. 479). That is Cheng's (2011) disruptive, source of radical love. That's queer enough for me.

Now, discussing an early twentieth century German theologian—even one as relevant to the present moment as Dietrich Bonhoeffer—will sound a good deal like an old, Enlightenment progress narrative; he had, after all, read an awful lot of old, Enlightenment philosophers. Therefore I shall conclude with a return to queer theology in an attempted *currere* move of synthetical moment. Wish me luck.

During the last year of his life, Bonhoeffer conceived of a new theology, one of "God's solidarity with the world" (Bethge 2000, p. 854), which was organized under the overarching question, "Who is Christ for us, today?" Although this work was never set down in anything other than letters to his student and friend and lifelong biographer Eberhard Bethge, what remains are two phrases that help us as theorists gain entry into curriculum as theological text. They are "the world come of age" and "nonreligious interpretation," known more commonly in non-German scholarship as, "religionless Christianity" (Bonhoeffer 2010, pp. 586–587). I should say that whether we are examining his *Letters and Papers from Prison* or his magnum opus, *Ethics*, we must understand that Bonhoeffer's approach is one of Christology, the "presupposition of the presence of Christ" (Bethge, 2000, p. 864). So, while Tillich (1968) sought to suppress the supranatural in his conceptualization of God as the ground of our being and faith as our ultimate concern, Bonhoeffer considers a worldly reality in which Christ is present.

In 1944, Bonhoeffer wrote to Bethge, "We are approaching a completely religionless age" (2010, p. 362), in which people were fast becoming "radically religionless." "How do we speak in a 'worldly' way about God?" (2010, p. 364). Bonhoeffer (2010) rejected what he called the "positivism of revelation" of Karl Barth—an all-too-simplistic doctrine that demands we accept articles of faith—Virgin Birth, resurrection, salvation, for example—unconditionally as true (p. 364).

In the world, we grapple; we are, therefore, worldly. "Our lives must be worldly," Bonhoeffer (2010) says, "so we can share precisely so in God's suffering. A Christian for whom Christ is in the world can then, be fully human (p. 480). The starting point for what he would call his "worldly interpretation" is a God who "gains ground and power in the world by being powerless" (p. 480)—by our participation in a godless world. Religion, on the other hand, is our attempt to transfigure a godless world—religion is our attempt to justify the self. It is by embracing worldliness that we are "delivered from false religious obligations and inhibitions," and further, it is by embracing worldliness that we are become human. "If one wants to speak of God nonreligiously, then one must speak in such a way that the godlessness of the world is not covered up in any way, but rather precisely to uncover it" (p. 482). "This-worldliness," an extension of his thought, means "living fully in the midst of life's tasks, questions, successes and failures, experiences, and perplexities ... And this is how one becomes a human being, a Christian" (p. 486). We experience the powerlessness and suffering of God in the world. How then, do we speak in a worldly way about God? For this, we turn to *Ethics*, more specifically, to Bonhoeffer's ethic of free, responsible action.

In 1943, Bonhoeffer wrote, "I sometimes feel as if my life were more or less over, and as if all I had to do now were to finish my *Ethics*" (2010, p. 222). *Ethics* is a series of often rough, often unfinished manuscripts written from 1940 until his execution in 1945. It was incomplete; it had no table of contents, but it was the first collection published posthumously, situating its significance to his theology. It was *Ethics* he was working on during the years in which he became more deeply involved in the conspiracy to overthrow Hitler; it was *Ethics* he was working on as he traveled under false pretenses through Europe meeting with church officials in the hopes of gaining support for German resistance to the totalitarian regime. And when he was taken away by the Gestapo in 1943 to the first of three prisons, a handwritten section of *Ethics* was on his desk.

Ethics was, in part, written to consider the question, what is the duty of Christian people in tyrannical times? In response, Bonhoeffer explored the concept of free responsible action to reckon with the world's worldliness and God's rule over it. "Responsible action," he wrote, "is nourished not by an ideology but by reality, which is why one can only act within the boundaries of that reality" (2005, p. 225). "Those who act on the basis of ideology refuse on principle to ask the question about the

236   R. U. WHITLOCK

consequence of their action." They are justified by their idea, whereas, "those who act responsibly place their action into the hands of God and live by God's grace and judgment" (p. 226). What is wanted is responsibility based on "vicarious representative action," where "a person is literally required to act on behalf of others" (p. 257). A parent, for example, or a teacher. We stand in the place for another; we cannot escape the responsibility because to my students, for example, I am a teacher.

Here Bonhoeffer (2005) makes another theological observation about being human: Selfless people, that is, those who devote their lives completely to another, live responsibly. Thus, "only selfless people truly live" (p. 259). While the subtext in *Ethics* is, in hindsight almost overwhelming to the text—Bonhoeffer did not reconcile himself quickly to becoming a conspirator. He knew the implications and likely consequences. However, by returning each building block—love, freedom, responsibility, conscience—to the God who became human in Christ—Bonhoeffer rejected a "revelation of positivism," as he referred to Barth's "take it or leave it," other-worldly God in favor of godless world of human participation. He could participate in the overthrow of the government and assassination of the tyrant because his conscience was love incarnate. *This* is radical responsibility: the higher ethos of the personal, the revelation: *love*.

A year ago, before the political primaries, before the parties' conventions, I began reading a book called, *The Coming of the Third Reich*, by Richard Evans (2005), the first of a trilogy in which he attempts to answer the persistent question that scholars and non-scholars alike have asked for almost a century: How could Hitler and the Nazis happen in the modern world? His thesis is clear—the conditions existed in German-speaking countries that facilitated the rise of fascism. Antisemitism had been growing in polite conversation, politics, and academic discourses since the nineteenth century. Economic disparity, which was exacerbated by punitive war reparations, fueled street violence that proved fertile ground for organized brownshirts. Big business interests—of German industries that still thrive and are recognizable to us today, Krupps, Thyssen—bankrolled the charismatic Bavarian whom they believed would best protect those interests. The German populace was deeply divided among the Center Party, Socialists, Communists, and the rising National Socialist German Workers Party—abbreviated as Nazi. It seemed, Evans tells us, that in those conditions the perfect storm brewed to escort in the Third Reich, which would, as Adolf Hitler promised, Make Germany Great Again. I do not have to explicitly state the similarities here between 1930s Germany and 2016 USA.

14 FOR US, TODAY: UNDERSTANDING CURRICULUM AS THEOLOGICAL ...   237

Whether or not the reader believes Donald Trump to be a tyrant or a fascist—or just a regular guy who says what he thinks, we cannot ignore the same storm brewing. The bank bailouts of 2008/09, too big to fail banks and businesses, and the now three-way political polarization of the USA—Bernie Sanders and the radical economic liberals, Hillary Clinton's status quo centrists, and Donald Trump's disenfranchised lower class whites—these are not dissimilar to conditions in Weimar Germany in the 1920s. Further, extreme nationalism—whether it is Aryan supremacy or White American exceptionalism—sets apart one people from all others and thus severs the need to care for—to *feel* for— one another ethically. Finally, when the daily news cycle vacillates among murdered police officers, murdered Black men, active shooters in random public places, and self-declared political terrorists, we desensitize ourselves in a move that paves the way for the law and order candidate, just as it did in 1932. "I alone can fix this," (Trump convention speech) is not that different from the slogan on the famous 1932 poster housed in the National Holocaust Museum—*Hitler: Our Last Hope* (https:// www.ushmm.org/propaganda/archive/poster-our-last-hope/). In this unsettling political climate in which not only the Presidency but also God is up for grabs, it is no wonder that Bonhoeffer speaks to me. His work has the urgency of a man whose days were numbered, an urgency we might shape and direct toward the moral and spiritual crisis in education—and beyond—of today.

While for theology proper I draw from Dietrich Bonhoeffer and Paul Tillich—two theologians whose contextualized and contingent lived experiences led me to their theology, my curriculum of theology comes primarily from Huebner (1999) and Purpel (2004). I turn briefly (here, but more lengthily in a larger work) to queer theologian Marcella Althaus-Reid (2001, 2003), whose queer god and indecent theology might let me queer up "God-talk" enough for some of us to be able to hear it as a language for us, today. I have loosely used as my model for theorizing queer theology curriculum Pinar's analysis of the mystery of Noah's tent and the Curse of Canaan, which I recognize as the first example of this methodology—he wrote it in 2006, almost a decade before I thought of doing it (see Whitlock 2016).

I thought it might be helpful to note here some questions I intentionally leave unaddressed. I do not present a case for the existence of God. Or Jesus Christ. I do not attempt to define God. Or spirituality. Or queer. I am not an apologist for all Christians and Christian behavior throughout all time. Some—much—of it was atrocious, and I do

238 R. U. WHITLOCK

not try to justify it or ask for a pass on their behalf. I do not look for a way to talk about my topic that encompasses multiple belief systems and faith communities. My limited view is a given, so with that disclaimer, I stay pretty close to it. I acknowledge that these issues are central—starting places—for thinking theologically about almost everything. They are important and problematic and deserve to be spoken to—yet they are simply not my questions at this time. I do not ask readers to suspend concerns or biases—or even tolerate such a hotly contested topic. I consider those thoughts and assumptions symptomatic of precisely the necessity for talking about the Divine life and our participation in it (O'Connor 1970). Just because thinking theologically about the world today can be complicated and awkward does not mean we should not do so. As much as I can figure, for most curriculum theorists, schools are not places for talking about God or morality, but neither are they places where the twin idols of standardization and accountability should be worshiped. No wonder we don't take part in meaningful ways in conversations about schools and schooling; we've silenced ourselves out of anything to say. So I thought it might also be helpful to set down a few curriculum points about God:

1. Attempts to prove that God exists makes God small and containable.
2. God is not a superstition. Drawing from Paul Tillich, God is the existential ground of being, and being in relation to the ground of being is humanity's ultimate concern. This is also known as faith.
3. God is not religion.
4. God is not political; people make God political. This is known as religion.
5. God is in schools.
6. Theology preexists the Enlightenment, which came about in the human attempt to answer theological questions. Modernism emerged as a counter movement to the certainty of objectivity and an omnipotent Creator-God. Thus, if the poststructuralist, postmodern project counters both Enlightenment and Modernism, understanding curriculum as theological text might be significant to it.
7. I can use the word transcendent again.
8. God is love, and love in itself is a radical act.

For me, it is no longer enough to talk about place in terms of how it both shapes and is shaped by religious experience. Religion without theology is a vacuous, baseless ritual; and while the narratives have value phenomenologically and autobiographically, they now also beg to be theorized theologically. So, to make the claim that I want to look through a theological lens to discuss curriculum, I have to be able to understand for myself and adequately explain, what is theology? Theology is simply defined as the study of God and God's relation to the universe, whereas religion refers to systems of beliefs and worship practices. Theology is a study by which we come into better understanding of God; religion is what we do with that understanding. Theology is the search; religion is the path. What does it mean, then, to consider curriculum from a theological frame or perspective?

My work until now has been about Southern place from the perspective of my fundamentalist Christian upbringing. Theology was present indirectly, or more precisely, with presumption. There is, no matter how literally fundamental believers like my parents read the Bible, theological grounding in fundamentalist faith. My faith, for example, is in a triune God that affirms that the Son is the homoousios of the Father and that the two have a hypostatic union. Of course, I never knew my beliefs, taught to me in Sunday school and from the pulpit for as far back as I can remember, had a basis in theology. Theology was for Catholics— or at least Methodists. We read the scriptures and we believed these things—without knowing the 2000-year struggles, schisms, and anathema that undergirded them. The fundamentalist parts of my autobiographical narratives about place can still shock, anger, baffle, embarrass, and sadden even me. It is usually the part people ask me to talk more about. And, since my religious upbringing is such a substantial part of my identity, I will continue to talk about these experiences in the context of and to contextualize Southern place. With this work, I begin to move beyond describing practices and feelings—sentimentality—toward making meaning of the divine life and humanity's participation in it. This participation, however, is different from practice in that it refers to our confronting and subsequently engaging with grace.

Although thinking theologically about curriculum is not a new concept, a closer look suggests that when we talk about religion and education, we primarily do so outside of theological contexts. Interdisciplinary theological works proliferate in the academy in the humanities, for example, since pondering the concept of God is not a far stretch in the pondering of other massive questions of existence and meaning. Religion is easy to see: It is provocative and controversial; it is readily historicized and theorized; it has social and cultural implications. It is a topic that may be approached from multiple disciplines and perspectives. Religion is in the news. It is, in short, part of our daily lives and public consciousness. Theology, on the other hand, is talk about God, doctrine, dogma, involving topics that can make non-theological academics nervous. Imagining what understanding curriculum as theological text might look like in a twenty-first century world puts us in conversation with those possibilities posed by MacDonald, Huebner, and Pinar over the last four decades. Existence and meaning lend dimensions to discussions of curriculum as interpreting lived experience.

In 1998, David Purpel boldly proclaimed that there was a moral and spiritual crisis in education and argued that attempts at educational reform (recall this was three years prior to No Child Left Behind and George W. Bush) that failed to attend to this crisis would be empty and ineffective. Since then, I contend that the moral and spiritual crisis has become more pronounced as accountability culture has proliferated in such initiatives as No Child Left Behind, Race to the Top, edTPA, The National Council for Accreditation of Teacher Education, and the Council of the Accreditation of Educator Preparation. We may be, as Peter Taubman (2009) has suggested, beyond our ability to "say no" anymore. These measures are symptomatic of crisis—but not the kind of crisis legislators and educational policy makers would have a deluded public believe. The crisis is indeed a moral and spiritual one, and for that, we must speak a different language; we must employ and develop language alive with spirit and inviting of humanity. The purpose of this work is to think theologically in order to discover a fresh, timely curriculum language—not merely to address moral and spiritual crises, although, again, they do exist and are urgent.

Using theological language runs the risk of making no one happy: It is too rational for postmodernists, too a-social for liberals, and too inclusive for conservatives. In fact, I have found that it is easier in this field to come out as a communist, a socialist, a Marxist, a lesbian, or a feminist (or some combination of these) than it is to come out as a fundamentalist-raised Christian. This says something, I think, about the prejudice in the field. It explains why so few scholars have spoken to spirituality, morality, and religion when we speak of curriculum—although more and more are increasingly doing so. When we resist or reject outright

14 FOR US, TODAY: UNDERSTANDING CURRICULUM AS THEOLOGICAL ... 241

this language—the language of God—we deny ourselves access to language that those of the conservative Right use so effectively for political ends. Theological language is, of course, political. We are quite willing to offer uncritical critiques of fundamentalist appropriations of Christian thought, yet in so doing we close ourselves to ways of thinking that have influenced Western thought for two millennia.

TRUTH SPEAKS TO POWER

What might radical responsibility of love look like in our world today? I wondered whether we might, in this age, have a theologian to turn to who might point the way to the worldliness of God—as opposed to those preachers I grew up hearing who only condemned me for my worldliness. Then I found Walter Brueggemann. In *Truth Speaks to Power* (2013) he uses examples of prophets and holy people from the Hebrew Scriptures who confronted the ancient kings who had broken the "covenantal triad of steadfast love, justice, and righteousness" (p. 76; cf. CG, pp. 60–64). I suggest that a *currere* of radical love seeks to speak truth to power in order to realize its transformative promise. Brueggemann points out that justice to the poor and knowledge of God are not connected—they are equated! This in itself, to our way of thinking, would make love radical. So, it is not merely the case that the moral and spiritual life is not intentionally lived in school spaces; morality, spirituality, and faith have been intentionally relegated to the private sphere. The time has come, Brueggemann (2013) suggests, for truth to speak to power, for power "must now acknowledge truth" (p. 35). Maps of power are complex, not reducible to simplistic assumptions that are "impervious to the transformative potential of the social when it is enacted in the public domain" (p. 36). It is the surge of the spirit, the moral endeavor, the lure of the transcendent, the ground of being that generate disruptions that, Brueggemann argues, "entrenched power cannot negate and social possibility that entrenched power cannot halt" (p. 107).

Brueggemann (2013) points out that destabilized social power holds "revolutionary potential and revelatory purposes" (p. 37). Revelation is another idea that makes academics so uncomfortable we do not even try to deconstruct nor unpack its meanings. Suppressing the revelatory possibilities—those possibilities that stem from the work of radical love—and coopting revelation to its own end are projects of power.

242   R. U. WHITLOCK

Sex education, science and history curricula, textbook content, are examples. The interface, Brueggeman (2013) tells us, "of *revolutionary* and *revelatory* awaits fresh performance" (p. 37). If we are to understand curriculum as queer theological text, we might understand it as radical, revolutionary, and revelatory, rejecting of normative, normalizing systems of power.

By their own admission, the working class Republican base—who are voting overwhelmingly for Trump—are venting their anger and frustration. This presents a difficulty to campaign for values and morality when the Trump discourse is fear and violence (he threatens to sue and beat people up). This unique situation—in which the twenty-first century US parallels pre-Nazi Germany—has thrown into upheaval the political monopoly the GOP held on God. This presents us now with a unique opportunity. As Jim Wallis (2006) argued in *God's Politics: Why the Right Gets It Wrong and the Left Doesn't Get It*, "It is indeed time to take back our faith" (p. 4). We do this by finding our collective prophetic voice, one that links personal ethics with social justice. Wallis makes his argument to religious voting Americans; I make mine as a curriculum theorist.

Conclusion

Marcella Althaus-Reid (2003) proposes to us queer theology that goes beyond revelation in a world of human sexuality, for the revelation that occurs in intimate acts has been silenced and marginalized in the hegemonic theological project. This is no positivistic revelation. The divinity of the Queer God depends on the sexual "turbulence of our intimate relationships" (p. 38); this is a revelation in which God loses God's self and we become human. She offers an epistemology of debauchery (libertinaje), by which we might continue the task of Indecenting, that is, of doing a materialist, concrete theology which has departed from idealist grounds of understanding in a scandalous way. In a biblical sense, a theology which aims to scandalize, that is, to be a stone on the road to force theologians to stop, fall down, while pausing in their pain and thinking during the cause. "Before God, and with God, recall, we live without God" (Bonhoeffer 2010, p. 479). We stand before a dissolute, licentious God of horror, who needs to be emptied again and again through our flawed, persistent humanity, in order to go on existing (Althaus-Reid 2003).

14 FOR US, TODAY: UNDERSTANDING CURRICULUM AS THEOLOGICAL ...   243

A *currere* of radical love, then, may be akin to the "radical negation of the way of closeted knowing found in the tradition of the church and theology" (Althaus-Reid 2003, p. 171), through which Althaus-Reid suggests we come to know the Queer, stranger-God who is our lover. Not only are we worldly and thus made fully human through the pain and suffering of God, but also in God's pleasure. Pleasure is no less intense and no less important, for it requires as deliberate and contemplative emptying. Passion, as we know, means suffering, and it is indistinguishable from desire. One empties oneself at the precise moment before orgasm, before the highest sexual pleasure, passion, only to be satiated in the emptiness of desire.

In this essay, I cannot help but feel as though I have muddied some waters, which, I suppose, was my plan all along. With a nod to Jefferson's famous quote, I tremble for my country in this violent, corporatized political climate. The most pedestrian student of history can see parallels between the social, cultural, economic, and political winds of the USA today and 1930s Germany. God, who had been perverted in a fundamentalist conservative discourse on morals and values, is hardly even a pretense anymore. *God Is On Our* side has morphed into *Make America Great Again*, which Trump supporters—older, disproportionately male, less educated, lower SES—understand as an assurance of maintaining white supremacy. Not all, certainly, but a lot of them. God is no more on the side of white people than God is an Alabama football fan (you'd be surprised).

Theology—thousands of years of study and tradition—shows us that God does not have a side. The very existence and presence of God is "being-there-with-and-for-others" (Bonhoeffer 2010, p. 369) and in that, there are no sides to separate. Ethics of this worldliness—of caring responsibility for those in *this world*—is how we know God, how we are present with God. This is what Bonhoeffer concluded in his cell as he worked against time to shape a way for Christians to be in this world after Hitler. God, the queer one who suffers with us, is already, always present. There is no being human apart from the powerless, emptied, suffering God. Within the free responsible action of helping one another become as fully human as we can be—Bonhoeffer's ethics—lies the possibilities of theological curriculum study. This theological curriculum framework presents God as a lived curriculum, as radical love, as *currere*.

REFERENCES

Althaus-Reid, M. (2001). *Indecent theology: Theological perversions in sex, gender, and politics*. New York: Routledge.

Althaus-Reid, M. (2003). *The queer god*. New York: Routledge.

Bethge, E. (2000). *Dietrich Bonhoeffer: A biography*. Minneapolis, MN: Fortress Press.

Block, A. (2005). *Talmud, curriculum, and the practical: Joseph Schwab and the rabbis*. New York: Peter Lang.

Bonhoeffer, D. (2005). *Ethics: Vol. 6 of Dietrich Bonhoeffer Works* (C. Green, Ed.). Minneapolis, MN: Fortress Press.

Bonhoeffer, D. (2010). *Letters and papers from prison: Vol. 8 of Dietrich Bonhoeffer Works* (C. Gremmels & J. DeGruchy, Eds.). Minneapolis, MN: Fortress Press.

Brueggemann, W. (2010). *Journey to the common good*. Louisville, KY: Westminster John Knox Press.

Brueggemann, W. (2013). *Truth speaks to power: The countercultural nature of scripture*. Louisville: Westminster John Knox.

Cheng, P. (2011). *Radical love: An introduction to queer theology*. New York: Seabury Books.

Evans, R. (2005). *The history of the third reich*. New York: Penguin Books.

Hillis, V. (1999). *The lure of the transcendent: Collected Essays by Dwayne E. Huebner*. Mahwah, NJ: Lawrence Erlbaum Associates.

O'Connor, F. (1970). *Mystery and manners: Occasional prose*. New York: Farrar, Straus, and Giroux.

Purpel, D., & McLaurin, W., Jr. (2004). *Reflections on the moral & spiritual crisis in education*. New York: Peter Lang.

Taubman, P. (2009). *Teaching by numbers: Deconstructing the discourse of standards and accountability in education*. New York: Routledge.

Tillich, P. (1968). *A history of Christian thought: From its Judaic and Hellenistic origins to existentialism* (C. E. Braaten, Ed.). New York: Simon & Schuster.

Wallis, J. (2006). *God's politics: Why the right gets it wrong and the left doesn't get it*. San Francisco: Harper.

Whitlock, R. U. (2016). The practice of radical love: Understanding curriculum as queer theological text. In M. A. Doll (Ed.), *The reconceptualization of curriculum studies: A Festschrift in honor of William F. Pinar* (pp. 179–186). New York: Routledge.

INDEX

A
Academic mobility, 60, 61
Affect, 157–163, 165, 168–170
Affective encounters, 162, 165
Affective turn, 158
Affect theories, 158–160, 168
Applied linguistics, 75
Assessment document, 70, 73
Assumptions, 83, 93
Autobiographical text, 177, 178, 180–182, 184–186, 188
Autobiographic narrative, 177, 180, 193
Autobiography, 142, 146, 150, 185
Autonomy, 152, 154

B
Bonhoeffer, D., 227, 228, 233–237, 243
Border, 108–112, 114–118, 120, 121
Brazil, 55, 62, 65

C
Canadian Language Benchmarks, 69, 73
Choice, 108, 109, 113, 118–121
Christian ethics, 233
Classroom, 125, 126, 129, 133–135, 157, 162–164, 167
Community, 36, 42, 43, 45
Complicated conversations, 17, 18, 54, 62, 65, 80, 139, 153, 207, 210
Concurrent education program, 127
Contemporaneity, 18, 19, 21
Cosmopolitanism, 91
Counter-hegemonic discourses, 55
Crises, 126, 132, 133
Crossing borders, 110
Cultural border, 110, 120, 121
Culture, 36, 47, 152, 153, 167
currere, 178, 188, 212–216, 219–223, 234, 241, 243
Curricular issues, 101

© The Editor(s) (if applicable) and The Author(s) 2019
C. Hébert et al. (eds.), *Internationalizing Curriculum Studies*,
https://doi.org/10.1007/978-3-030-01352-3

246 INDEX

Curricular vision, 188, 193, 197
Curriculum, 35–48, 54–56, 58–65, 70,
73, 74, 76–80, 83–99, 101, 102,
108–110, 112, 115, 117–121,
139–141, 149–152, 154, 158–161,
168–170, 177–179, 182, 186–188,
193, 194, 196–198, 201, 204,
207, 211–214, 223, 227–230, 233,
234, 237–240, 242, 243
Curriculum construction, 80
Curriculum conversation, 229, 238,
240
Curriculum development, 70, 75–77,
85, 86, 88–90, 99, 187
Curriculum paradigms, 17
Curriculum process, 77
Curriculum project, 36
Curriculum researchers, 65
Curriculum scholarship, 16–18, 22, 25
Curriculum studies, 15–24, 26–29,
54, 58, 62, 83–86, 89, 125, 126,
135, 193, 194, 197, 201, 204,
207, 212–214, 223
Curriculum theory, 16–18, 20, 23, 24,
28, 35–37, 39–41, 43–47, 55, 60,
61, 63, 65, 89, 90, 93, 94, 101,
108, 120, 126, 127, 134, 135,
158, 160, 193, 194, 228
Curriculum's moribundity, 16, 23, 27

D
Dadaab Refugee Camp, 109–112,
118, 120
Daily practice, 193, 196, 197, 202, 204
Discursive balkanization, 17, 18, 22, 24
Divine life, 238, 239

E
Education, 70, 71, 78, 80, 107–112,
114, 116, 118–120, 125–128,
133, 135, 140–144, 151–154,

157, 193–197, 200–204,
208–212, 215, 221–223
Educational market, 54
Educational mobility, 55, 60, 64, 65
Educational policy, 163
Educational transfer, 55–60
Educators, 83–85, 93, 94, 96, 98–102
Emancipatory practices, 28, 44
Emergency education, 108, 109, 120
Epistemological, 148
Ethics, 233–236, 242, 243
Experience, 177–188

F
Feminist theology, 240
Flexibility, 94, 95
Fundamentalism, 228, 229, 232, 233

G
Globalization, 53, 54, 57, 61–63

H
Hidden curriculum, 70, 76, 77
Historical roots, 36
Holistic process, 139
Hope, 169, 170
Human-human-nature, 222
Human learning, 139, 142
Human suffering, 36

I
Identity, 139–142, 144–148, 150–154
Identity negotiations, 141, 142, 148
Identity positioning, 139, 142, 153
Indecent theology, 237
Indigeneity, 207
Injustice, 36, 47, 48
Inner life, 125, 134
Intellectual traditions, 194, 197

Intercultural competence, 64, 65
Interdisciplinary learning, 128
International Influences, 17
Internationalization, 54, 55, 58, 60–65, 86, 91, 139, 154, 197, 201, 207, 223
International wisdom traditions, 194, 195

K
Kenya, 107, 109, 111–114
kwerekwere, 208

L
Learning, 139, 142, 146, 148–150, 153, 154
Loss, 109, 110, 118

M
Manifesto, 35, 36, 44, 65, 110
Marginalized communities, 121
Meaning, 178, 181–186
Methodological diffusion, 18, 25
Mobility, 55, 60, 61
Morality, 216, 217

N
Narrative framework, 179
Narrative negotiations, 152, 154
National boundaries, 207, 223
Negotiations, 139, 142, 151
Nonviolence, 193–199, 201–205
Nonviolent engagement, 194, 197
Nonviolent relationships, 194, 199, 200, 202

O
Ontological, 146, 148

Ontopower, 158
Openness, 94, 101
Oppression, 36, 46, 48
Orientation, 36

P
Phenomenography, 84, 94, 98, 101
Physical borders, 110
Pinar's 1978 declaration, 16
Postcolonialism, 207
Post-structuralism, 194, 207, 213
Potentia, 221, 223
Psychoanalysis, 126, 135, 194, 196–199

Q
Qualitative, 84, 90, 182
Queer theology, 233, 234, 237, 242

R
Reconceptualist movement, 36
Reconceptualist paradigm, 17
Reconstructing meaning, 181
Recovering, 181
Reflection, 84, 85, 91, 93, 94, 99–101
Reflective thinking, 92, 94, 99–101
Refugee, 107–115, 118–120
Religion, 227, 229, 232, 233, 235, 238–240
Religionless age, 227, 234

S
School, 128–133, 140–145, 149–154, 160, 162–168, 170
Schwab's 1969 claim, 23
Second language, 70, 71, 75–78
Second Language Education (SLE), 70

248 INDEX

Self, 126, 128, 134, 182, 183, 185, 186, 194, 195, 197, 200, 202–204
Self-reflection, 91, 184
Self-study, 177, 180, 181, 185–188
Social borders, 120, 121
Social reconstruction, 36
Socio-environmental equity, 126, 127, 129, 133
Socio-political contexts, 17
South-Africa, 207, 208, 210–212
Stories of experience, 181, 183, 187
Student learning, 94–96, 101, 187
Subjectivity, 36, 38, 126, 128

T
Teacher autonomy, 63, 152
Teacher education, 125–127, 133, 135
Teachers, 73, 76, 77, 80, 88, 89, 95–98, 100–102, 125–134, 180

Temporality, 109, 118
Tensions, 15, 18, 28
Theological curriculum, 227, 243
Theological text, 234, 238, 240, 242
Theology, 229, 232, 234, 235, 237, 239, 242, 243
Thinking-feeling, 158, 161, 167, 169
Thinking-movement, 161
Transfer, 55, 56, 58–61, 65
Transformation, 84, 92, 101
Truth speaks to power, 241

U
Ubuntu, 207, 216–223
Ubuntu-currere, 221–223

W
Wonder, 159, 162, 168
Working from within, 197, 200

Printed in the United States
By Bookmasters